Programed Ear Training   **VOLUME III: CHORDS,**
Part I

Programed Ear Training
Volume III: CHORDS, PART 1

Leo Horacek and Gerald Lefkoff
West Virginia University

Under the General Editorship of
Guy Alan Bockmon
University of Tennessee

HARCOURT, BRACE & WORLD, INC.

New York   Chicago   San Francisco   Atlanta

ISBN: 0-15-572017-1

Library of Congress Catalog Number: 70-110129

Printed in the United States of America

Preface to the Instructor

PROGRAMED EAR TRAINING is designed to develop the hearing and notational skills required in the freshman and sophomore music theory courses. It consists of four programed workbooks and accompanying tape recordings that provide a complete course of study in melodic and harmonic dictation, sightsinging, and aural harmonic analysis. The four volumes are:

I. INTERVALS
II. MELODY AND RHYTHM
III. CHORDS, Part I
IV. CHORDS, Part II

The flexibility of the program makes it suitable for use in any kind of theory program. The volumes may be used singly or as a group, alone or in combination with other text materials. Except for Volume IV, which depends on Volume III, they need not be taken sequentially; experience has shown, in fact, that for some students it is more profitable to work in several volumes concurrently.

Because the course is programed, the student works entirely on his own, at his own pace. Multiple copies of each written lesson are provided, so that he can repeat lessons as often as necessary to improve his skills. As he reaches recommended levels of proficiency, he takes tests, which are provided separately to the instructor and administered under his direction. A guide to the administration and grading of the program is provided in the Instructor's Manual.

PROGRAMED EAR TRAINING was developed at West Virginia University over a seven-year period during which it was in continuous use and was constantly being revised. It has also been used at more than a dozen other colleges and universities across the country; thus it has been thoroughly tested on large and varying groups of students.

The authors would like to express appreciation to Dr. Guy Bockmon, University of Tennessee, for his careful reading of all the materials and his most helpful recommendations; to Dr. Richard E. Duncan, Dean of the Creative Arts Center, West Virginia University, who suggested and supported the project in which these books were developed; to Dr. Frank Lorince, Chairman of the Theory Department, West Virginia University, for his valuable advice and assistance; to the teachers who have used the books and offered suggestions and criticism, and finally to the many students who have worked patiently or otherwise through the program and whose reactions were always useful.

L. H.
G. L.

Contents

INTRODUCTION

This is the third of four volumes designed to help you to improve your hearing and notational skills through the techniques of programed instruction.

Volume III is devoted to skills involving the most common types of chords and their use in progressions that stay in one key. For each lesson in the program, there is a tape recording that provides all the audio material you will need to complete the lesson.

Programed instruction differs from usual instruction in two ways: first, most of the work can be done with little or no help from a teacher; and second, you can progress at your own rate. Where the material is difficult for you, you can move slowly. Where you find it easy, you can move rapidly, saving time and work. A faculty advisor will probably direct and guide your work, but the responsibility for making progress is yours. Through your test scores and your scores for each of the lessons, you will always know how well you are progressing.

The basic idea of programed instruction is as follows. The material is broken into small units called *frames*. In each frame, a problem is presented and you will be asked to make a response. Immediately after this response, the correct answer is provided so that you will know whether or not your response was correct. Through many confirmations of correct responses and correction of incorrect responses, complicated and difficult skills and concepts can be learned with ease. With the programed instruction procedures in this book, you will find that you can spend as little or as much time in any one area as you need.

For each lesson a goal has been set for you, to show you whether you are ready to move on to the next lesson. If you complete a lesson with no more than the number of errors indicated in the goal, move on to the next lesson. Otherwise you are to repeat the lesson. For this purpose five copies of every worksheet that requires a written response are provided. If after five tries you have not brought the number of errors down to the limit set in the goal, move on to the next lesson anyway.

When you have done an entire series in this fashion, ask your instructor to give you the test on the series. You will take the tests on your own but they will be graded by your instructor. The score you receive on each test is a *weighted score,* which means that your raw score is multiplied by a factor to compensate for the varying length, difficulty, and importance of the series.

The evaluation of your work will depend on the total of all your test scores rather than on an average of these scores. Therefore, every test you take, even if the score is low, can help raise your grade. If you return to a series for more work in that area, you may retake the test and count the highest grade you make on that test. To help you know how well you are doing, three *achievement levels* are provided for each test.

The *first level* represents a very high degree of learning. Generally, when you have achieved this level you should not plan to return to the material in the series but should spend your time on other material.

The *second level* represents a moderate achievement. The material in the series can be considered to be reasonably well learned, but if time permits or you wish to raise your grade, it would be practical to return to that series for further work.

The *third level* represents a rather low but nevertheless significant amount of learning. You should at some time return to the series for further work.

Normally it is most advantageous to move on from one series to the next regardless of the test scores, and then at certain points in the course, go back and do further work on any series on which your test score was lower than you would like. The most profitable pattern of moving on and working back varies from student to student, and it will be best to seek the advice of your instructor when you are undecided.

The *test record sheet* that appears at the end of this volume indicates for each test the three achievement levels and the maximum possible score and provides a convenient place to keep a record of your scores.

The skills developed through this course of study are extremely valuable in almost any musical activity. Not only are they important in performing music, but they can also help you to understand music you hear, to arrange and write music, and to discuss and learn more about music.

With the method of study used in these volumes, you will find that you can work to develop such skills in a manner best suited to your particular needs and abilities. You can move slowly where you find difficulties, change to a different phase of the course if your progress has slowed down, and work at maximum speed where your competencies are strongest. This modern approach to music theory can enable you to learn these important skills in the most efficient manner possible.

Major and minor triads and dominant seventh chords in root position

This series involves three types of chord: the *major triad,* the *minor triad,* and the *dominant seventh chord,* all in root position. The lessons are of four kinds: chord dictation, chord identification, figured bass dictation, and chord identification in a key. The instructions for these lessons appear with each lesson. When you have done this series, take test C1, which includes sections on each of the four kinds of lesson.

In the basic form of the triad, there is an interval of a third between the lowest tone and the next tone, and an interval of a fifth between the lowest tone and the upper tone. The lowest tone is called the root of the triad, the next tone is called the third, and the upper tone is called the fifth.

The tones of a triad may be arranged in many ways. In the following example the triad C E G is set in various ways: some of the tones are doubled (for example, there are several C's), the tones are spaced in various ways, and various tones are in the bass.

A triad is said to be in *root position* when the root of the chord appears as the lowest note.

In the *major triad* in root position, the third is a major third above the root and the fifth is a perfect fifth above the root.

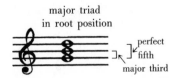

In the *minor triad* in root position, the third is a minor third above the root and the fifth is a perfect fifth above the root.

3

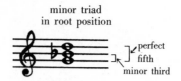

minor triad
in root position

perfect
fifth
minor third

In its basic form, a seventh chord consists of a triad plus a tone at an interval of a seventh above the root, referred to as the *seventh* of the chord.

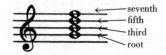

—seventh
—fifth
—third
—root

In the *dominant seventh chord* in root position, the third is a major third above the root, the fifth is a perfect fifth above the root, and the seventh is a minor seventh above the root.

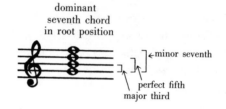

dominant
seventh chord
in root position

←minor seventh
perfect fifth
major third

Lesson **C1-1a**

This is a lesson in *chord dictation*. The following instructions apply to all lessons of this type in this volume.

The purpose of chord dictation is to develop your ability to write chords that you hear. A printed worksheet and tape recording are provided for each lesson. The frames on the worksheet are separated by bar lines. At the beginning of each frame, you will find a note that corresponds to the lowest tone of the chord that you will hear. The complete chord is shown at the end of the frame. To do each frame, start by shielding the chord at the end of the frame. When you have heard the chord on the tape, write the upper notes of the chord above the printed note. Then slide the shield to the right and compare your response with the printed answer. Circle each frame in which your response is incorrect. You may stop the tape occasionally if you need more time, but before going on to the next lesson you should be able to complete the lesson without stopping. Your goal is to complete the lesson with no more than seven errors. When you have done so, go on to the next lesson. If you have made more than seven errors, repeat the lesson until you reach the goal or until you have done the lesson five times, at which point you should go on to the next lesson regardless of your score.

Use tape C1-1 for this lesson. This tape is used for lessons C1-1a and C1-1b. Whenever a tape is used for two lessons, the worksheets for those lessons are distinguished by the letters a and b. These letters do not appear on the label for the tape.

C1–1A
(Copy 1)

Chord dictation

*Shield the answer. Listen to the chord and notate the upper tones above the given note; then uncover
the answer and compare your response. Circle incorrect responses. Goal: No more than seven errors.*

6

C1-1A
(Copy 2)

Chord dictation

Shield the answer. Listen to the chord and notate the upper tones above the given note; then uncover the answer and compare your response. Circle incorrect responses. Goal: No more than seven errors.

7

C1-1A
(Copy 3)

Chord dictation

Shield the answer. Listen to the chord and notate the upper tones above the given note; then uncover the answer and compare your response. Circle incorrect responses. Goal: No more than seven errors.

C1-1A
(Copy 4)

Chord dictation

Shield the answer. Listen to the chord and notate the upper tones above the given note; then uncover the answer and compare your response. Circle incorrect responses. Goal: No more than seven errors.

C1-1A
(Copy 5)

Chord dictation

Shield the answer. Listen to the chord and notate the upper tones above the given note; then uncover the answer and compare your response. Circle incorrect responses. Goal: No more than seven errors.

Lesson **C1-1b**

This lesson involves *figured bass symbols,* which are used to identify chord types. Figured bass symbols specify the intervals between the *bass* and each of the other pitches in the chord by means of Arabic numerals and some qualifying signs, as in the following example.

The symbol for a major or perfect interval is an Arabic numeral alone: the symbol ³, for example, specifies a major third; ⁵ specifies a perfect fifth; and ⁷ specifies a major seventh.

The symbol for a minor interval is an Arabic numeral preceded by a minus sign: the symbol ⁻³, for example, specifies a minor third, and ⁻⁶ specifies a minor sixth.

Pitches more than an octave above the bass are described as though they were in the octave above the bass. When two or more pitches with the same letter-name appear in a chord, that pitch is said to be *doubled.* Doubled tones are indicated only once in the figured bass symbols.

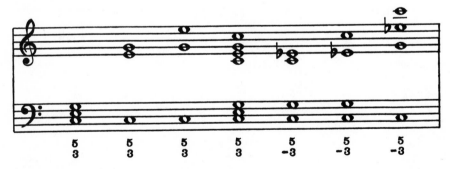

Figured bass symbols for the most common chord types are usually abbreviated. In this volume, abbreviated figured bass symbols will always be used. Lesson C1-1a covers only two types of chords: the major triad in root position and the minor triad in root position. The complete figured bass symbol for the major triad is $\frac{5}{3}$, since the upper tones of the chord are at intervals of a perfect fifth and a major third above the bass. The abbreviated form of this symbol is a blank, that is, no symbol at all. Thus when there is no figured bass symbol under a chord, the chord is a major triad in root position.

The complete figured bass symbol for the minor triad in root position is $\frac{5}{-3}$, since the upper tones of the chord are at intervals of a perfect fifth and a minor third above the bass. The abbreviated form of this symbol is a minus sign (⁻).

There is a traditional system of figured bass symbols that you may expect to encounter in your study of music. In this system, the figured bass symbol indicates the number of scale steps between the bass and the upper tones without indicating the exact size of the interval. For example, in the old system, the symbol $\frac{5}{3}$ indicates that there is some kind of fifth and some kind of third above the bass. This symbol identifies a triad in root position but does not indicate the type of triad. The specific size of each interval in this case depends on the location of the chord in the key. The system used in this book differs from the older system in that additional symbols are used to indicate the exact interval of each tone above the bass.

Lesson C1–1b is a lesson in *chord identification*. The following instructions apply to all lessons of this type in this volume.

The purpose of these lessons is to develop your ability to identify types of chords that you hear and to associate them with their figured bass symbols. A printed worksheet and a tape recording are provided for each lesson. Each frame contains a blank for your response, followed by the correct answer. To do each frame, start by shielding the answer. When you have heard the chord, write the figured bass symbol for it in the blank; then slide the shield to the right and check your response. Circle each frame in which your response is incorrect. You may stop the tape occasionally if you need more time, but before going on to the next lesson you should be able to complete the lesson without stopping. Your goal is to complete each lesson with no more than seven errors. When you have done so, go on to the next lesson. If you have made more than seven errors, repeat the lesson until you reach the goal or until you have done the lesson five times, at which point you should go on to the next lesson regardless of your score.

C1–1b
(Copy 1)

Chord identification

Shield the answer. Listen to the chord and place the figured bass symbol in the blank; then uncover the answer and compare your response. The answer may be a blank (that is, no symbol) for the major triad in root position or a minus sign (⁻) for the minor triad in root position. Circle incorrect responses. Goal: No more than seven errors.

1 ____ ____ ⁻ ____ ____ ____ ⁻ ____ ⁻ ____ ____ ⁻
2 ____ ____ ⁻ ____ ⁻ ____ ____ ____ ____ ____ ⁻
3 ____ ⁻ ____ ____ ____ ____ ⁻ ____ ____
4 ____ ____ ⁻ ____ ⁻ ____ ____ ⁻ ____ ____
5 ____ ____ ⁻ ____ ⁻ ____ ⁻ ____ ____ ____
6 ____ ⁻ ____ ____ ____ ____ ____ ⁻ ____ ⁻
7 ____ ____ ____ ____ ⁻ ____ ____ ____
8 ____ ____ ⁻ ____ ⁻ ____ ____ ____ ⁻ ____
9 ____ ____ ____ ____ ____ ____ ⁻ ____ ⁻
10 ____ ____ ⁻ ____ ⁻ ____ ____ ____ ⁻ ____

C1–1b
(Copy 2)

Chord identification

Shield the answer. Listen to the chord and place the figured bass symbol in the blank; then uncover the answer and compare your response. The answer may be a blank (that is, no symbol) for the major triad in root position or a minus sign (⁻) for the minor triad in root position. Circle incorrect responses. Goal: No more than seven errors.

1 ____ ____ ⁻ ____ ____ ____ ⁻ ____ ⁻ ____ ____ ⁻
2 ____ ____ ⁻ ____ ⁻ ____ ____ ____ ____ ____ ⁻
3 ____ ⁻ ____ ____ ____ ⁻ ____ ____ ____
4 ____ ____ ⁻ ____ ____ ____ ⁻ ____ ____
5 ____ ____ ⁻ ____ ⁻ ____ ⁻ ____ ____ ____
6 ____ ⁻ ____ ____ ⁻ ____ ____ ____ ⁻ ____ ⁻
7 ____ ____ ____ ⁻ ____ ____ ____ ____
8 ____ ____ ⁻ ____ ____ ____ ____ ____
9 ____ ____ ⁻ ____ ⁻ ____ ⁻ ____ ____ ⁻
10 ____ ____ ⁻ ____ ⁻ ____ ____ ____ ⁻ ____

C1–1b
(Copy 3)

Chord identification

Shield the answer. Listen to the chord and place the figured bass symbol in the blank; then uncover the answer and compare your response. The answer may be a blank (that is, no symbol) for the major triad in root position or a minus sign (–) for the minor triad in root position. Circle incorrect responses. Goal: No more than seven errors.

1 ____   ____   ___[–]   ____   ___[–]   ___[–]   ____   ___[–]

2 ____   ____   ____   ___[–]   ____   ____   ____   ___[–]

3 ____   __[–]_   ____   ___[–]   ____   ___[–]   ____   ____

4 ____   ____   ____   ___[–]   ____   ____   ____   ____

5 ____   ____   ____   ____   ____   ____   ____   ____

6 ____   __[–]_   ____   ____   ____   ____   ____   ___[–]

7 ____   ____   ___[–]   ___[–]   ____   ____   ____

8 ____   ____   ____   ___[–]   ____   ____   ____

9 ____   ____   ____   ____   ____   ___[–]   ____   ___[–]

10 ____   ____   __[–]_   ___[–]   ____   ____   __[–]_

C1–1b
(Copy 4)

Chord identification

Shield the answer. Listen to the chord and place the figured bass symbol in the blank; then uncover the answer and compare your response. The answer may be a blank (that is, no symbol) for the major triad in root position or a minus sign (–) for the minor triad in root position. Circle incorrect responses. Goal: No more than seven errors.

1 ____   ____   __[–]_   ____   __[–]_   __[–]_   ____   ___[–]

2 ____   ____   __[–]_   __[–]_   ____   ____   ____   ___[–]

3 ____   __[–]_   ____   ____   ____   ____   ____   ____

4 ____   ____   __[–]_   ____   ____   ____   ____   ____

5 ____   ____   __[–]_   ____   __[–]_   ____   ____   ____

6 ____   __[–]_   __[–]_   __[–]_   ____   ____   ___[–]   ___[–]

7 ____   ____   ____   __[–]_   ____   ____   ____

8 ____   ____   __[–]_   __[–]_   ____   ____   __[–]_

9 ____   ____   __[–]_   __[–]_   ____   __[–]_   ____   ___[–]

10 ____   ____   __[–]_   __[–]_   ____   ____   __[–]_

C1-1b
(Copy 5)

Chord identification

Shield the answer. Listen to the chord and place the figured bass symbol in the blank; then uncover the answer and compare your response. The answer may be a blank (that is, no symbol) for the major triad in root position or a minus sign (−) for the minor triad in root position. Circle incorrect responses. Goal: No more than seven errors.

1 ____   ____ - ____   ____ - ____ - ____   ____ -

2 ____   ____ - ____ - ____   ____   ____   ____ -

3 ____ - ____   ____   ____   ____ - ____   ____

4 ____   ____ - ____ - ____   ____ - ____   ____

5 ____   ____ - ____ - ____ - ____   ____   ____

6 ____ - ____   ____ - ____   ____   ____ - ____ -

7 ____   ____   ____ - ____ - ____   ____   ____

8 ____   ____ - ____ - ____   ____   ____ - ____

9 ____   ____ - ____ - ____   ____ - ____   ____ -

10 ____   ____ - ____ - ____   ____   ____ - ____

C1-2a

(Copy 1)

Chord dictation

Shield the answer. Listen to the chord and notate the upper tones above the given note; then uncover the answer and compare your response. Circle incorrect responses. Goal: No more than seven errors.

16

C1-2a

Chord dictation

Shield the answer. Listen to the chord and notate the upper tones above the given note; then uncover the answer and compare your response. Circle incorrect responses. Goal: No more than seven errors.

17

C1-2a
(Copy 3)

Chord dictation

Shield the answer. Listen to the chord and notate the upper tones above the given note; then uncover the answer and compare your response. Circle incorrect responses. Goal: No more than seven errors.

C1-2a
(Copy 4)

Chord dictation

Shield the answer. Listen to the chord and notate the upper tones above the given note; then uncover the answer and compare your response. Circle incorrect responses. Goal: No more than seven errors.

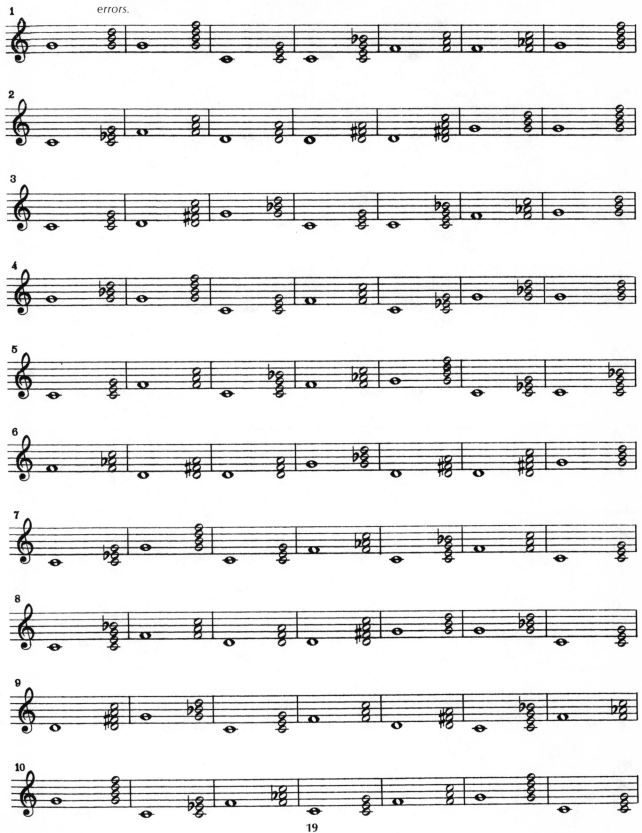

C1-2a

(Copy 5)

Chord dictation

Shield the answer. Listen to the chord and notate the upper tones above the given note; then uncover the answer and compare your response. Circle incorrect responses. Goal: No more than seven errors.

Lesson **C1-2b**

In this lesson the figured bass symbol for the dominant seventh chord in root position is introduced. The complete figured bass symbol is $\begin{smallmatrix}-7\\5\\3\end{smallmatrix}$, since the upper tones of the chord are at intervals of a minor seventh, perfect fifth, and a major third above the bass. The abbreviated form of this symbol is $^{-7}$.

C1-2b
(Copy 1)

Chord identification

Shield the answer. Listen to the chord and place the figured bass symbol in the blank; then uncover the answer and compare your response. The only possible answers are the blank, -, and $^{-7}$. Circle incorrect responses. Goal: No more than seven errors.

1. ____   ____ $^{-7}$ ____   ____ $^{-7}$ ____   ____ -   ____ $^{-7}$

2. ____ -   ____   ____ -   ____   ____ $^{-7}$ ____   ____ $^{-7}$

3. ____   ____ $^{-7}$ ____ -   ____   ____ $^{-7}$ ____ -   ____

4. ____ -   ____ $^{-7}$ ____   ____   ____ -   ____ -   ____

5. ____   ____   ____ $^{-7}$ ____ -   ____ $^{-7}$ ____ -   ____ $^{-7}$

6. ____ -   ____   ____ -   ____ -   ____   ____ $^{-7}$ ____

7. ____ -   ____ $^{-7}$ ____   ____ -   ____ $^{-7}$ ____   ____

8. ____ $^{-7}$ ____   ____ -   ____ $^{-7}$ ____   ____ -   ____

9. ____ $^{-7}$ ____ -   ____   ____   ____   ____ $^{-7}$ ____ -

10. ____ $^{-7}$ ____ -   ____ -   ____   ____   ____ $^{-7}$ ____

C1–2b
(Copy 2)

Chord identification

Shield the answer. Listen to the chord and place the figured bass symbol in the blank; then uncover the answer and compare your response. The only possible answers are the blank, ⁻, and ⁻⁷. Circle incorrect responses. Goal: No more than seven errors.

1 _____ _____ -7 _____ _____ -7 _____ _____ - _____ -7

2 _____ - _____ _____ - _____ _____ -7 _____ _____ -7

3 _____ _____ -7 _____ - _____ _____ -7 _____ - _____

4 _____ - _____ -7 _____ _____ _____ - _____ -

5 _____ _____ _____ -7 _____ - _____ -7 _____ - _____ -7

6 _____ - _____ _____ _____ - _____ _____ -7 _____

7 _____ - _____ -7 _____ _____ - _____ -7 _____

8 _____ -7 _____ _____ - _____ -7 _____ _____ -

9 _____ -7 _____ - _____ _____ _____ _____ -7 _____ -

10 _____ -7 _____ - _____ - _____ _____ -7 _____

C1–2b
(Copy 3)

Chord identification

Shield the answer. Listen to the chord and place the figured bass symbol in the blank; then uncover the answer and compare your response. The only possible answers are the blank, ⁻, and ⁻⁷. Circle incorrect responses. Goal: No more than seven errors.

1 _____ _____ -7 _____ _____ -7 _____ _____ - _____ -7

2 _____ - _____ _____ - _____ _____ -7 _____ _____ -7

3 _____ _____ -7 _____ - _____ _____ -7 _____ - _____

4 _____ - _____ -7 _____ _____ _____ - _____ -

5 _____ _____ _____ -7 _____ - _____ -7 _____ - _____ -7

6 _____ - _____ _____ _____ - _____ _____ -7 _____

7 _____ - _____ -7 _____ _____ - _____ -7 _____

8 _____ -7 _____ _____ - _____ -7 _____ _____ -

9 _____ -7 _____ - _____ _____ _____ _____ -7 _____ -

10 _____ -7 _____ - _____ - _____ _____ -7 _____

22

C1-2b

Chord identification

Shield the answer. Listen to the chord and place the figured bass symbol in the blank; then uncover the answer and compare your response. The only possible answers are the blank, ⁻, and ⁻⁷. Circle incorrect responses. Goal: No more than seven errors.

1 ____ ____ -7 ____ ____ -7 ____ ____ - ____ -7
2 ____ - ____ ____ - ____ ____ -7 ____ ____ -7
3 ____ ____ -7 ____ - ____ ____ -7 ____ - ____
4 ____ - ____ -7 ____ ____ ____ ____ - ____ -
5 ____ ____ ____ -7 ____ - ____ -7 ____ - ____ -7
6 ____ ____ - ____ - ____ - ____ ____ -7 ____
7 ____ - ____ -7 ____ ____ - ____ -7 ____ ____
8 ____ -7 ____ ____ ____ - ____ -7 ____ ____ -
9 ____ -7 ____ - ____ ____ ____ ____ -7 ____ -
10 ____ -7 ____ - ____ - ____ ____ ____ -7 ____

C1-2b

Chord identification

Shield the answer. Listen to the chord and place the figured bass symbol in the blank; then uncover the answer and compare your response. The only possible answers are the blank, ⁻, and ⁻⁷. Circle incorrect responses. Goal: No more than seven errors.

1 ____ ____ -7 ____ ____ -7 ____ ____ - ____ -7
2 ____ - ____ - ____ ____ - ____ -7 ____ ____ -7
3 ____ ____ -7 ____ - ____ ____ -7 ____ - ____
4 ____ - ____ -7 ____ ____ ____ - ____ - ____
5 ____ ____ ____ -7 ____ - ____ -7 ____ - ____ -7
6 ____ - ____ ____ - ____ - ____ ____ -7 ____
7 ____ - ____ -7 ____ ____ - ____ -7 ____ ____
8 ____ -7 ____ ____ ____ - ____ -7 ____ ____ -
9 ____ -7 ____ - ____ ____ ____ ____ -7 ____ -
10 ____ -7 ____ - ____ - ____ ____ ____ -7 ____

C1–3

Chord identification

Shield the answer. Listen to the chord and place the figured bass symbol in the blank; then uncover the answer and compare your response. The only possible answers are the blank, ⁻, and ⁻⁷. Circle incorrect responses. Goal: No more than seven errors.

1 ____ ⁻ ____ ____ ⁻ ____ ____ ⁻ ____ ____ ⁻

2 ____ ____ ⁻⁷ ____ ____ ____ ⁻ ____ ⁻⁷ ____ ⁻⁷

3 ____ ⁻ ____ ⁻ ____ ____ ____ ⁻⁷ ____ ⁻ ____

4 ____ ____ ⁻⁷ ____ ⁻ ____ ⁻ ____ ____ ⁻⁷ ____

5 ____ ⁻ ____ ____ ⁻⁷ ____ ⁻⁷ ____ ____ ⁻ ____ ⁻ ____ ⁻

6 ____ ____ ____ ⁻⁷ ____ ⁻⁷ ____ ____ ____

7 ____ ⁻ ____ ⁻ ____ ⁻ ____ ⁻ ____ ____ ⁻⁷ ____ ⁻

8 ____ ____ ____ ⁻⁷ ____ ____ ⁻⁷ ____ ⁻ ____

9 ____ ⁻ ____ ⁻ ____ ____ ⁻⁷ ____ ____ ____ ⁻⁷

10 ____ ⁻⁷ ____ ____ ⁻⁷ ____ ⁻ ____ ____ ⁻⁷ ____ ⁻

C1–3

Chord identification

Shield the answer. Listen to the chord and place the figured bass symbol in the blank; then uncover the answer and compare your response. The only possible answers are the blank, ⁻, and ⁻⁷. Circle incorrect responses. Goal: No more than seven errors.

1 ____ ⁻ ____ ____ ⁻ ____ ____ ⁻ ____ ____ ⁻

2 ____ ____ ⁻⁷ ____ ____ ____ ⁻ ____ ⁻⁷ ____ ⁻⁷

3 ____ ⁻ ____ ⁻ ____ ____ ____ ⁻⁷ ____ ⁻ ____

4 ____ ____ ⁻⁷ ____ ⁻ ____ ⁻ ____ ____ ⁻⁷ ____

5 ____ ⁻ ____ ____ ⁻⁷ ____ ⁻⁷ ____ ____ ⁻ ____ ⁻

6 ____ ____ ____ ⁻⁷ ____ ⁻⁷ ____ ⁻ ____ ____

7 ____ ⁻ ____ ⁻ ____ ⁻ ____ ⁻ ____ ____ ⁻⁷ ____ ⁻

8 ____ ____ ____ ⁻⁷ ____ ____ ⁻⁷ ____ ⁻ ____

9 ____ ⁻ ____ ⁻ ____ ____ ⁻⁷ ____ ____ ____ ⁻⁷

10 ____ ⁻⁷ ____ ____ ⁻⁷ ____ ⁻ ____ ____ ⁻⁷ ____ ⁻

C1-3

Chord identification

Shield the answer. Listen to the chord and place the figured bass symbol in the blank; then uncover the answer and compare your response. The only possible answers are the blank, ⁻, and ⁻⁷. Circle incorrect responses. Goal: No more than seven errors.

1 ____ -   ____   ____ -   ____   ____ -   ____   ____ -

2 ____   ____ -7   ____   ____   ____ -   ____ -7   ____ -7

3 ____ -   ____ -   ____   ____   ____ -7   ____ -   ____

4 ____   ____ -7   ____ -   ____ -   ____   ____ -7   ____

5 ____ -   ____   ____ -7   ____ -7   ____ -   ____ -   ____ -

6 ____   ____   ____ -7   ____ -7   ____ -   ____   ____

7 ____ -   ____ -   ____ -   ____ -   ____   ____ -7   ____ -

8 ____   ____   ____ -7   ____   ____ -7   ____ -   ____

9 ____ -   ____ -   ____   ____ -7   ____   ____   ____ -7

10 ____ -7   ____   ____ -7   ____ -   ____   ____ -7   ____ -

C1-3

Chord identification

Shield the answer. Listen to the chord and place the figured bass symbol in the blank; then uncover the answer and compare your response. The only possible answers are the blank, ⁻, and ⁻⁷. Circle incorrect responses. Goal: No more than seven errors.

1 ____ -   ____   ____ -   ____   ____ -   ____   ____ -

2 ____   ____ -7   ____   ____   ____ -   ____ -7   ____ -7

3 ____ -   ____ -   ____   ____   ____ -7   ____ -   ____

4 ____   ____ -7   ____ -   ____ -   ____   ____ -7   ____

5 ____ -   ____   ____ -7   ____ -7   ____ -   ____ -   ____ -

6 ____   ____   ____ -7   ____ -7   ____ -   ____   ____

7 ____ -   ____ -   ____ -   ____ -   ____   ____ -7   ____ -

8 ____   ____   ____ -7   ____   ____ -7   ____ -   ____

9 ____ -   ____ -   ____   ____ -7   ____   ____   ____ -7

10 ____ -7   ____   ____ -7   ____ -   ____   ____ -7   ____ -

25

C1-3

Chord identification

Shield the answer. Listen to the chord and place the figured bass symbol in the blank; then uncover the answer and compare your response. The only possible answers are the blank, -, and -7. Circle incorrect responses. Goal: No more than seven errors.

1 ____ - ____ ____ ____ - ____ ____ - ____ ____ -

2 ____ ____ -7 ____ ____ ____ - ____ -7 ____ -7

3 ____ - ____ - ____ ____ ____ -7 ____ - ____

4 ____ ____ -7 ____ - ____ - ____ ____ -7 ____

5 ____ - ____ ____ -7 ____ -7 ____ - ____ - ____ -

6 ____ ____ ____ -7 ____ -7 ____ - ____ ____

7 ____ - ____ - ____ - ____ - ____ ____ -7 ____ -

8 ____ ____ ____ -7 ____ ____ -7 ____ - ____

9 ____ - ____ - ____ ____ -7 ____ ____ ____ -7

10 ____ -7 ____ ____ -7 ____ - ____ ____ -7 ____ -

Lesson C1-4a

This is a lesson in *figured bass dictation*. The following instructions apply to all lessons of this type in this volume.

The purpose of figured bass dictation is to develop your ability to determine the bass note of a chord and its chord type. A printed worksheet and a tape recording are provided for each lesson. The frames on the worksheet are separated by bar lines. The first chord on the tape, whose bass note and figured bass symbol are given in the first frame of the worksheet, serves as a starting reference and requires no response. To do each subsequent frame, start by shielding the answer at the end of the frame. When you have heard the chord, write the bass note on the staff and the figured bass symbol below the staff. Then slide the shield to the right and compare your response to the printed answer. Circle each frame in which your response is incorrect. You may stop the tape occasionally if you need more time, but before going on to the next lesson you should be able to complete the lesson without stopping. If you stop the tape, keep the pause short, because each chord is a frame of reference for the following chord. Your goal is to complete each lesson with no more than seven errors. When you have done so, go on to the next lesson. If you have made more than seven errors repeat the lesson until you reach the goal or until you have done the lesson five times, at which point you should go on to the next lesson regardless of your score.

The only figured bass symbols that occur in lesson C1-4a are the blank for the major triad in root position and $^{-7}$ for the dominant seventh chord in root position.

C1-4a

Figured bass dictation

Shield the answer. Listen to the chord and write the bass note and the figured bass symbol; then uncover the answer and compare your response. Circle incorrect responses. Goal: No more than seven errors. The first frame requires no response.

C1-4a
(Copy 2)

Figured bass dictation

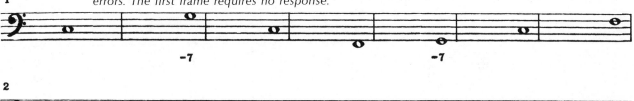

Shield the answer. Listen to the chord and write the bass note and the figured bass symbol; then uncover the answer and compare your response. Circle incorrect responses. Goal: No more than seven errors. The first frame requires no response.

1

2

3

4

5

6

7

8

9

10

C1-4a

Figured bass dictation

Shield the answer. Listen to the chord and write the bass note and the figured bass symbol; then uncover the answer and compare your response. Circle incorrect responses. Goal: No more than seven errors. The first frame requires no response.

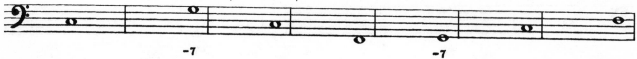

30

C1-4a

Figured bass dictation

Shield the answer. Listen to the chord and write the bass note and the figured bass symbol; then uncover the answer and compare your response. Circle incorrect responses. Goal: No more than seven errors. The first frame requires no response.

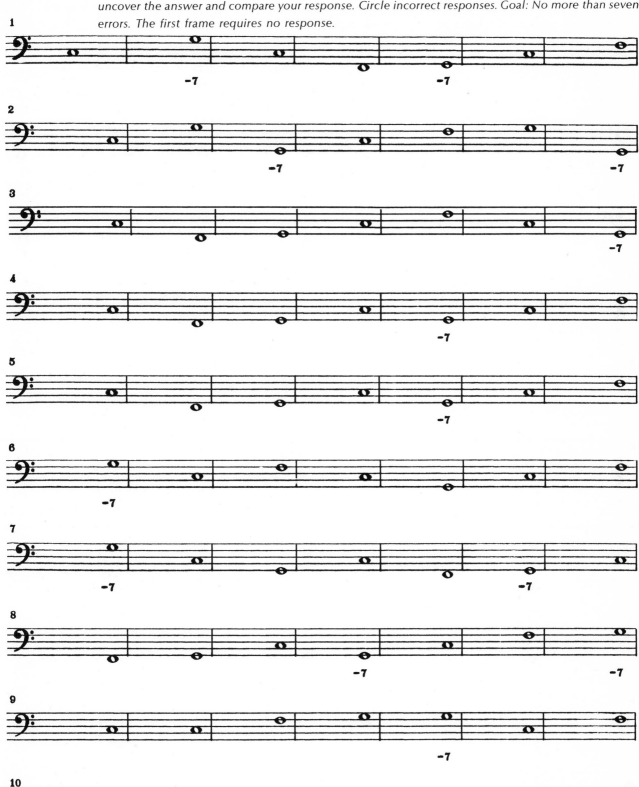

C1-4a

(Copy 5)

Figured bass dictation

Shield the answer. Listen to the chord and write the bass note and the figured bass symbol; then uncover the answer and compare your response. Circle incorrect responses. Goal: No more than seven errors. The first frame requires no response.

32

Lesson C1-4b

This lesson involves locating a chord in a key. A chord's location is found by relating the *root* of the chord to the *tonic* or key center. *Key location symbols* are used to specify the interval formed from the tonic of the key upward to the root of the chord. This interval is indicated by a Roman numeral. (Arabic numerals are reserved for figured bass symbols.) A Roman numeral alone indicates either a major or perfect interval from the tonic up to the root of the chord. Thus the symbol VI stands for a chord with its root a major sixth above the tonic and the symbol V stands for a chord with its root a perfect fifth above the tonic. A Roman numeral preceded by a minus sign indicates a minor interval from the tonic up to the root of the chord. Thus the symbol ⁻VI stands for a chord with its root a minor sixth above the tonic.

Key location symbols are usually accompanied by figured bass symbols. We shall use the term *composite chord symbol* for the combination of the key location symbol and the figured bass symbol. The figured bass portion of the composite chord symbol will always appear to the right of the key location symbol. Thus the symbol IV⁻ stands for a minor triad in root position with its root a perfect fourth above the tonic of the key, and V⁻⁷ stands for a dominant seventh chord in root position with its root a perfect fifth above the tonic. A composite chord symbol that consists of a Roman numeral alone, such as V, should be understood as containing the blank after the Roman numeral that indicates a major triad in root position.

Lesson C1-4b is a lesson in *chord identification in a key*. The following instructions apply to all lessons of this type in this volume.

The purpose of these composite chord symbol identification lessons is to develop your ability to identify the types of chords you hear and determine their location in a key. A printed worksheet and tape recording are provided for each lesson. The first chord on the tape, whose composite chord symbol is given in the first frame of the worksheet, serves as a starting reference and requires no response. Each subsequent frame contains a blank for your response, followed by the correct answer. To do each frame, start by shielding the answer. When you have heard the chord, write the composite chord symbol for it in the blank; then slide the shield to the right and check your response. Circle each frame in which your response is incorrect. You may stop the tape occasionally if you need more time, but before going on to the next lesson you should be able to complete the lesson without stopping. If you stop the tape, keep the pause short, because each chord is a frame of reference for the following chord. Your goal is to complete each lesson with no more than seven errors. When you have done so, go on to the next lesson. If you have more than seven errors, repeat the lesson until you reach the goal or until you have done the lesson five times, at which point you should go on to the next lesson regardless of your score.

Lesson C1–4b is in a major key. The only composite chord symbols that may appear in your answers are I, IV, V, and V^{-7}. In a major key, the triads found on the first, fourth, and fifth degrees are major triads. Thus, when these triads are in root position, the figured bass portion of the composite chord symbol is blank, giving the symbols I, IV, and V.

C1–4b
(Copy 1)

Chord identification in a key

Shield the answer. Listen to the chord and write the composite chord symbol; then uncover the answer and compare your response. Goal: No more than seven errors. The first frame requires no response.

1 I   ___ V^{-7} ___ I   ___ IV   ___ V^{-7} ___ I   ___ IV

2 ___ I   ___ V   ___ V^{-7} ___ I ___ IV   ___ V   ___ V^{-7}

3 ___ I   ___ IV   ___ V   ___ I   ___ IV   ___ I   ___ V^{-7}

4 ___ I   ___ IV   ___ V   ___ I   ___ V^{-7} ___ I ___ IV

5 ___ I   ___ IV   ___ V   ___ I   ___ V^{-7} ___ I ___ IV

6 ___ V^{-7} ___ I   ___ IV   ___ I   ___ V   ___ I   ___ IV

7 ___ V^{-7} ___ I   ___ V   ___ I   ___ IV   ___ V^{-7} ___ I

8 ___ IV   ___ V   ___ I   ___ V^{-7} ___ I ___ IV   ___ V^{-7}

9 ___ I   ___ I   ___ IV   ___ V   ___ V^{-7} ___ I ___ IV

10 ___ IV   ___ V   ___ I   ___ IV   ___ V   ___ V^{-7} ___ I

C1-4b
(Copy 2)

Chord identification in a key

Shield the answer. Listen to the chord and write the composite chord symbol; then uncover the answer and compare your response. Goal: No more than seven errors. The first frame requires no response.

1 I ____ V⁻⁷ ____ I ____ IV ____ V⁻⁷ ____ I ____ IV

2 ____ I ____ V ____ V⁻⁷ ____ I ____ IV ____ V ____ V⁻⁷

3 ____ I ____ IV ____ V ____ I ____ IV ____ I ____ V⁻⁷

4 ____ I ____ IV ____ V ____ I ____ V⁻⁷ ____ I ____ IV

5 ____ I ____ IV ____ V ____ I ____ V⁻⁷ ____ I ____ IV

6 ____ V⁻⁷ ____ I ____ IV ____ I ____ V ____ I ____ IV

7 ____ V⁻⁷ ____ I ____ V ____ I ____ IV ____ V⁻⁷ ____ I

8 ____ IV ____ V ____ I ____ V⁻⁷ ____ I ____ IV ____ V⁻⁷

9 ____ I ____ I ____ IV ____ V ____ V⁻⁷ ____ I ____ IV

10 ____ IV ____ V ____ I ____ IV ____ V ____ V⁻⁷ ____ I

C1-4b
(Copy 3)

Chord identification in a key

Shield the answer. Listen to the chord and write the composite chord symbol; then uncover the answer and compare your response. Goal: No more than seven errors. The first frame requires no response.

1 I ____ V⁻⁷ ____ I ____ IV ____ V⁻⁷ ____ I ____ IV

2 ____ I ____ V ____ V⁻⁷ ____ I ____ IV ____ V ____ V⁻⁷

3 ____ I ____ IV ____ V ____ I ____ IV ____ I ____ V⁻⁷

4 ____ I ____ IV ____ V ____ I ____ V⁻⁷ ____ I ____ IV

5 ____ I ____ IV ____ V ____ I ____ V⁻⁷ ____ I ____ IV

6 ____ V⁻⁷ ____ I ____ IV ____ I ____ V ____ I ____ IV

7 ____ V⁻⁷ ____ I ____ V ____ I ____ IV ____ V⁻⁷ ____ I

8 ____ IV ____ V ____ I ____ V⁻⁷ ____ I ____ IV ____ V⁻⁷

9 ____ I ____ I ____ IV ____ V ____ V⁻⁷ ____ I ____ IV

10 ____ IV ____ V ____ I ____ IV ____ V ____ V⁻⁷ ____ I

C1-4b

(Copy 4)

Chord identification in a key

Shield the answer. Listen to the chord and write the composite chord symbol; then uncover the answer and compare your response. Goal: No more than seven errors. The first frame requires no response.

1   I   ____ V^{-7} ____ I   ____ IV   ____ V^{-7} ____ I   ____ IV

2   ____ I   ____ V   ____ V^{-7} ____ I   ____ IV   ____ V   ____ V^{-7}

3   ____ I   ____ IV   ____ V   ____ I   ____ IV   ____ I   ____ V^{-7}

4   ____ I   ____ IV   ____ V   ____ I   ____ V^{-7} ____ I   ____ IV

5   ____ I   ____ IV   ____ V   ____ I   ____ V^{-7} ____ I   ____ IV

6   ____ V^{-7} ____ I   ____ IV   ____ I   ____ V   ____ I   ____ IV

7   ____ V^{-7} ____ I   ____ V   ____ I   ____ IV   ____ V^{-7} ____ I

8   ____ IV   ____ V   ____ I   ____ V^{-7} ____ I   ____ IV   ____ V^{-7}

9   ____ I   ____ I   ____ IV   ____ V   ____ V^{-7} ____ I   ____ IV

10   ____ IV   ____ V   ____ I   ____ IV   ____ V   ____ V^{-7} ____ I

C1-4b

(Copy 5)

Chord identification in a key

Shield the answer. Listen to the chord and write the composite chord symbol; then uncover the answer and compare your response. Goal: No more than seven errors. The first frame requires no response.

1   I   ____ V^{-7} ____ I   ____ IV   ____ V^{-7} ____ I   ____ IV

2   ____ I   ____ V   ____ V^{-7} ____ I   ____ IV   ____ V   ____ V^{-7}

3   ____ I   ____ IV   ____ V   ____ I   ____ IV   ____ I   ____ V^{-7}

4   ____ I   ____ IV   ____ V   ____ I   ____ V^{-7} ____ I   ____ IV

5   ____ I   ____ IV   ____ V   ____ I   ____ V^{-7} ____ I   ____ IV

6   ____ V^{-7} ____ I   ____ IV   ____ I   ____ V   ____ I   ____ IV

7   ____ V^{-7} ____ I   ____ V   ____ I   ____ IV   ____ V^{-7} ____ I

8   ____ IV   ____ V   ____ I   ____ V^{-7} ____ I   ____ IV   ____ V^{-7}

9   ____ I   ____ I   ____ IV   ____ V   ____ V^{-7} ____ I   ____ IV

10   ____ IV   ____ V   ____ I   ____ IV   ____ V   ____ V^{-7} ____ I

C1-5a
(Copy 1)

Figured bass dictation

Shield the answer. Listen to the chord and write the bass note and the figured bass symbol; then uncover the answer and compare your response. Goal: No more than seven errors. The first frame requires no response.

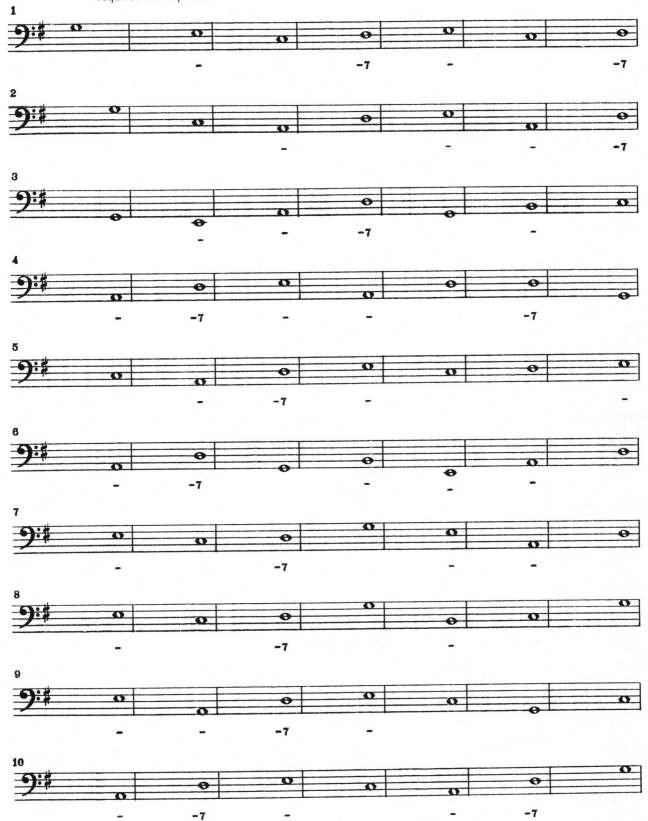

37

C1-5a

(Copy 2)

Figured bass dictation

Shield the answer. Listen to the chord and write the bass note and the figured bass symbol; then uncover the answer and compare your response. Goal: No more than seven errors. The first frame requires no response.

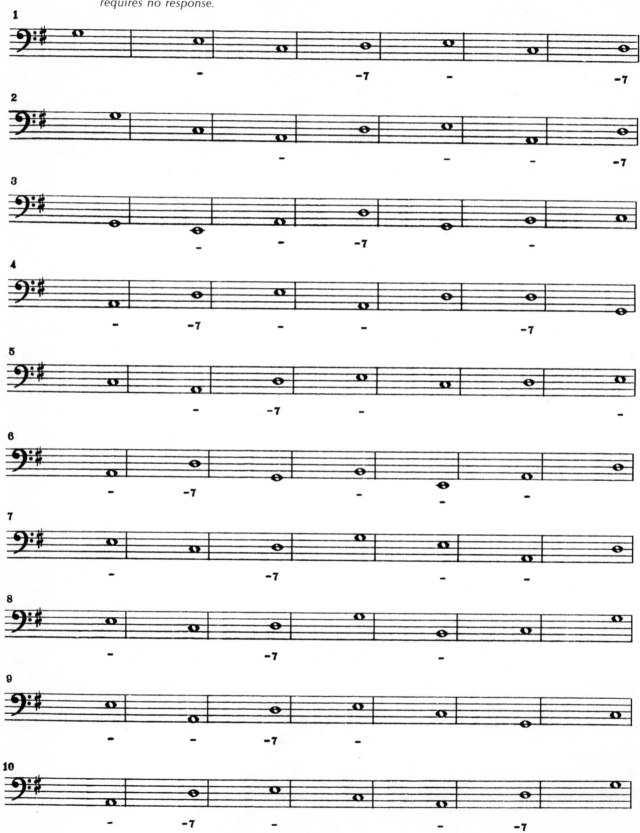

38

C1-5a   Figured bass dictation
(Copy 3)

Shield the answer. Listen to the chord and write the bass note and the figured bass symbol; then uncover the answer and compare your response. Goal: No more than seven errors. The first frame requires no response.

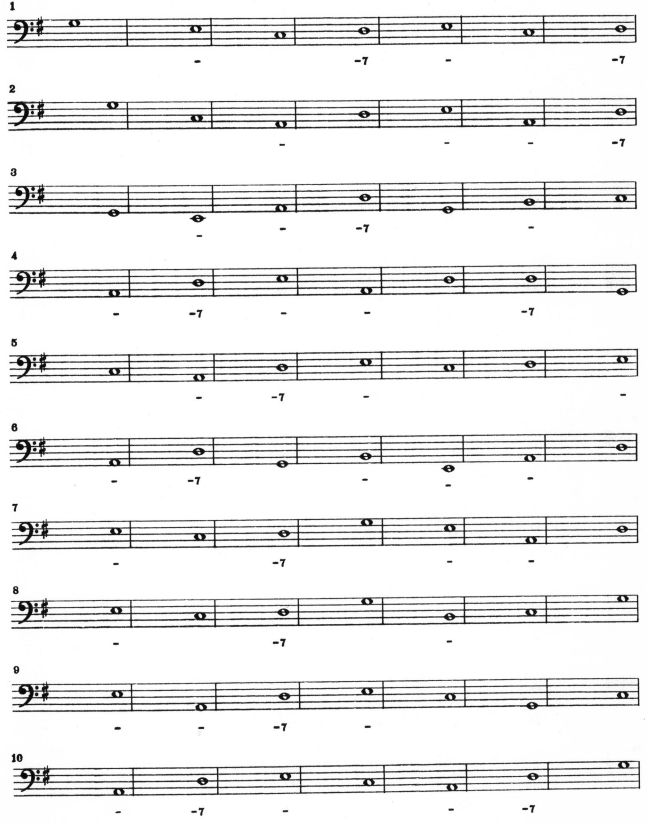

39

C1-5a

Figured bass dictation

Shield the answer. Listen to the chord and write the bass note and the figured bass symbol; then uncover the answer and compare your response. Goal: No more than seven errors. The first frame requires no response.

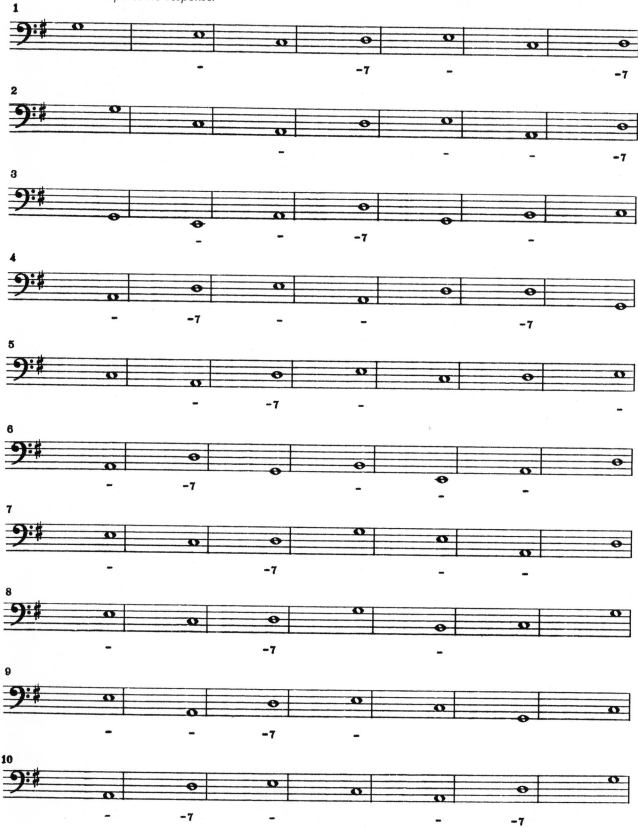

C1-5a Figured bass dictation
(Copy 5)

Shield the answer. Listen to the chord and write the bass note and the figured bass symbol; then uncover the answer and compare your response. Goal: No more than seven errors. The first frame requires no response.

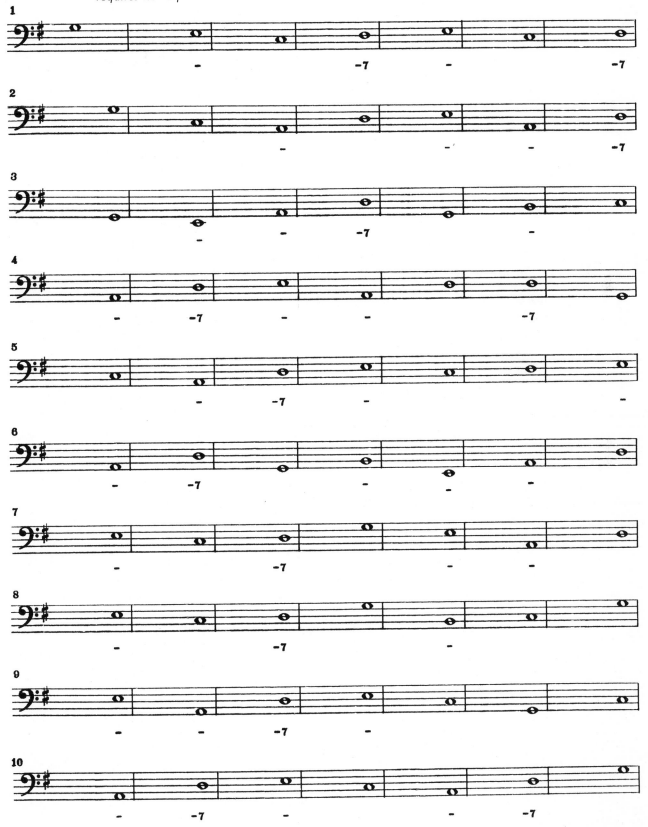

41

Three new composite chord symbols are introduced in this lesson: II⁻, III⁻, and VI⁻. These indicate the minor triads in root position found on the second, third, and sixth degrees of the major key. This lesson also involves the chords I, IV, V and V⁻⁷.

C1-5b
(Copy 1)

Chord identification in a key

Shield the answer. Listen to the chord and write the composite chord symbol; then uncover the answer and compare your response. Circle incorrect responses. Goal: No more than seven errors. The first frame requires no response.

1	I	___ VI⁻	___ IV	___ V⁻⁷	___ VI⁻	___ IV	___ V⁻⁷
2	___ I	___ IV	___ II⁻	___ V	___ VI⁻	___ II⁻	___ V⁻⁷
3	___ I	___ VI⁻	___ II⁻	___ V⁻⁷	___ I	___ III⁻	___ IV
4	___ II⁻	___ V⁻⁷	___ VI⁻	___ II⁻	___ V	___ V⁻⁷	___ I
5	___ IV	___ II⁻	___ V⁻⁷	___ VI⁻	___ IV	___ V	___ VI⁻
6	___ II⁻	___ V⁻⁷	___ I	___ III⁻	___ VI⁻	___ II⁻	___ V
7	___ VI⁻	___ IV	___ V⁻⁷	___ I	___ VI⁻	___ II⁻	___ V
8	___ VI⁻	___ IV	___ V⁻⁷	___ I	___ III⁻	___ IV	___ I
9	___ VI⁻	___ II⁻	___ V⁻⁷	___ VI⁻	___ IV	___ I	___ IV
10	___ II⁻	___ V⁻⁷	___ VI⁻	___ IV	___ II⁻	___ V⁻⁷	___ I

C1–5b
(Copy 2)

Chord identification in a key

Shield the answer. Listen to the chord and write the composite chord symbol; then uncover the answer and compare your response. Circle incorrect responses. Goal: No more than seven errors. The first frame requires no response.

1   I   ____ VI⁻   ____ IV   ____ V⁻⁷   ____ VI⁻   ____ IV   ____ V⁻⁷

$$1 \quad I \qquad \_\_ VI^- \quad \_\_ IV \quad \_\_ V^{-7} \quad \_\_ VI^- \quad \_\_ IV \quad \_\_ V^{-7}$$

$$2 \quad \_\_ I \quad \_\_ IV \quad \_\_ II^- \quad \_\_ V \quad \_\_ VI^- \quad \_\_ II^- \quad \_\_ V^{-7}$$

$$3 \quad \_\_ I \quad \_\_ VI^- \quad \_\_ II^- \quad \_\_ V^{-7} \quad \_\_ I \quad \_\_ III^- \quad \_\_ IV$$

$$4 \quad \_\_ II^- \quad \_\_ V^{-7} \quad \_\_ VI^- \quad \_\_ II^- \quad \_\_ V \quad \_\_ V^{-7} \quad \_\_ I$$

$$5 \quad \_\_ IV \quad \_\_ II^- \quad \_\_ V^{-7} \quad \_\_ VI^- \quad \_\_ IV \quad \_\_ V \quad \_\_ VI^-$$

$$6 \quad \_\_ II^- \quad \_\_ V^{-7} \quad \_\_ I \quad \_\_ III^- \quad \_\_ VI^- \quad \_\_ II^- \quad \_\_ V$$

$$7 \quad \_\_ VI^- \quad \_\_ IV \quad \_\_ V^{-7} \quad \_\_ I \quad \_\_ VI^- \quad \_\_ II^- \quad \_\_ V$$

$$8 \quad \_\_ VI^- \quad \_\_ IV \quad \_\_ V^{-7} \quad \_\_ I \quad \_\_ III^- \quad \_\_ IV \quad \_\_ I$$

$$9 \quad \_\_ VI^- \quad \_\_ II^- \quad \_\_ V^{-7} \quad \_\_ VI^- \quad \_\_ IV \quad \_\_ I \quad \_\_ IV$$

$$10 \quad \_\_ II^- \quad \_\_ V^{-7} \quad \_\_ VI^- \quad \_\_ IV \quad \_\_ II^- \quad \_\_ V^{-7} \quad \_\_ I$$

C1–5b
(Copy 3)

Chord identification in a key

Shield the answer. Listen to the chord and write the composite chord symbol; then uncover the answer and compare your response. Circle incorrect responses. Goal: No more than seven errors. The first frame requires no response.

$$1 \quad I \qquad \_\_ VI^- \quad \_\_ IV \quad \_\_ V^{-7} \quad \_\_ VI^- \quad \_\_ IV \quad \_\_ V^{-7}$$

$$2 \quad \_\_ I \quad \_\_ IV \quad \_\_ II^- \quad \_\_ V \quad \_\_ VI^- \quad \_\_ II^- \quad \_\_ V^{-7}$$

$$3 \quad \_\_ I \quad \_\_ VI^- \quad \_\_ II^- \quad \_\_ V^{-7} \quad \_\_ I \quad \_\_ III^- \quad \_\_ IV$$

$$4 \quad \_\_ II^- \quad \_\_ V^{-7} \quad \_\_ VI^- \quad \_\_ II^- \quad \_\_ V \quad \_\_ V^{-7} \quad \_\_ I$$

$$5 \quad \_\_ IV \quad \_\_ II^- \quad \_\_ V^{-7} \quad \_\_ VI^- \quad \_\_ IV \quad \_\_ V \quad \_\_ VI^-$$

$$6 \quad \_\_ II^- \quad \_\_ V^{-7} \quad \_\_ I \quad \_\_ III^- \quad \_\_ VI^- \quad \_\_ II^- \quad \_\_ V$$

$$7 \quad \_\_ VI^- \quad \_\_ IV \quad \_\_ V^{-7} \quad \_\_ I \quad \_\_ VI^- \quad \_\_ II^- \quad \_\_ V$$

$$8 \quad \_\_ VI^- \quad \_\_ IV \quad \_\_ V^{-7} \quad \_\_ I \quad \_\_ III^- \quad \_\_ IV \quad \_\_ I$$

$$9 \quad \_\_ VI^- \quad \_\_ II^- \quad \_\_ V^{-7} \quad \_\_ VI^- \quad \_\_ IV \quad \_\_ I \quad \_\_ IV$$

$$10 \quad \_\_ II^- \quad \_\_ V^{-7} \quad \_\_ VI^- \quad \_\_ IV \quad \_\_ II^- \quad \_\_ V^{-7} \quad \_\_ I$$

C1–5b
(Copy 4)

Chord identification in a key

Shield the answer. Listen to the chord and write the composite chord symbol; then uncover the answer and compare your response. Circle incorrect responses. Goal: No more than seven errors. The first frame requires no response.

1 I   ____ VI⁻   ____ IV   ____ V⁻⁷   ____ VI⁻   ____ IV   ____ V⁻⁷

2 ____ I   ____ IV   ____ II⁻   ____ V   ____ VI⁻   ____ II⁻   ____ V⁻⁷

3 ____ I   ____ VI⁻   ____ II⁻   ____ V⁻⁷   ____ I   ____ III⁻   ____ IV

4 ____ II⁻   ____ V⁻⁷   ____ VI⁻   ____ II⁻   ____ V   ____ V⁻⁷   ____ I

5 ____ IV   ____ II⁻   ____ V⁻⁷   ____ VI⁻   ____ IV   ____ V   ____ VI⁻

6 ____ II⁻   ____ V⁻⁷   ____ I   ____ III⁻   ____ VI⁻   ____ II⁻   ____ V

7 ____ VI⁻   ____ IV   ____ V⁻⁷   ____ I   ____ VI⁻   ____ II⁻   ____ V

8 ____ VI⁻   ____ IV   ____ V⁻⁷   ____ I   ____ III⁻   ____ IV   ____ I

9 ____ VI⁻   ____ II⁻   ____ V⁻⁷   ____ VI⁻   ____ IV   ____ I   ____ IV

10 ____ II⁻   ____ V⁻⁷   ____ VI⁻   ____ IV   ____ II⁻   ____ V⁻⁷   ____ I

C1–5b
(Copy 5)

Chord identification in a key

Shield the answer. Listen to the chord and write the composite chord symbol; then uncover the answer and compare your response. Circle incorrect responses. Goal: No more than seven errors. The first frame requires no response.

1 I   ____ VI⁻   ____ IV   ____ V⁻⁷   ____ VI⁻   ____ IV   ____ V⁻⁷

2 ____ I   ____ IV   ____ II⁻   ____ V   ____ VI⁻   ____ II⁻   ____ V⁻⁷

3 ____ I   ____ VI⁻   ____ II⁻   ____ V⁻⁷   ____ I   ____ III⁻   ____ IV

4 ____ II⁻   ____ V⁻⁷   ____ VI⁻   ____ II⁻   ____ V   ____ V⁻⁷   ____ I

5 ____ IV   ____ II⁻   ____ V⁻⁷   ____ VI⁻   ____ IV   ____ V   ____ VI⁻

6 ____ II⁻   ____ V⁻⁷   ____ I   ____ III⁻   ____ VI⁻   ____ II⁻   ____ V

7 ____ VI⁻   ____ IV   ____ V⁻⁷   ____ I   ____ VI⁻   ____ II⁻   ____ V

8 ____ VI⁻   ____ IV   ____ V⁻⁷   ____ I   ____ III⁻   ____ IV   ____ I

9 ____ VI⁻   ____ II⁻   ____ V⁻⁷   ____ VI⁻   ____ IV   ____ I   ____ IV

10 ____ II⁻   ____ V⁻⁷   ____ VI⁻   ____ IV   ____ II⁻   ____ V⁻⁷   ____ I

C1-6a

(Copy 1)

Figured bass dictation

Shield the answer. Listen to the chord and write the bass note and the figured bass symbol; then uncover the answer and compare your response. Circle incorrect responses. Goal: No more than seven errors. The first frame requires no response.

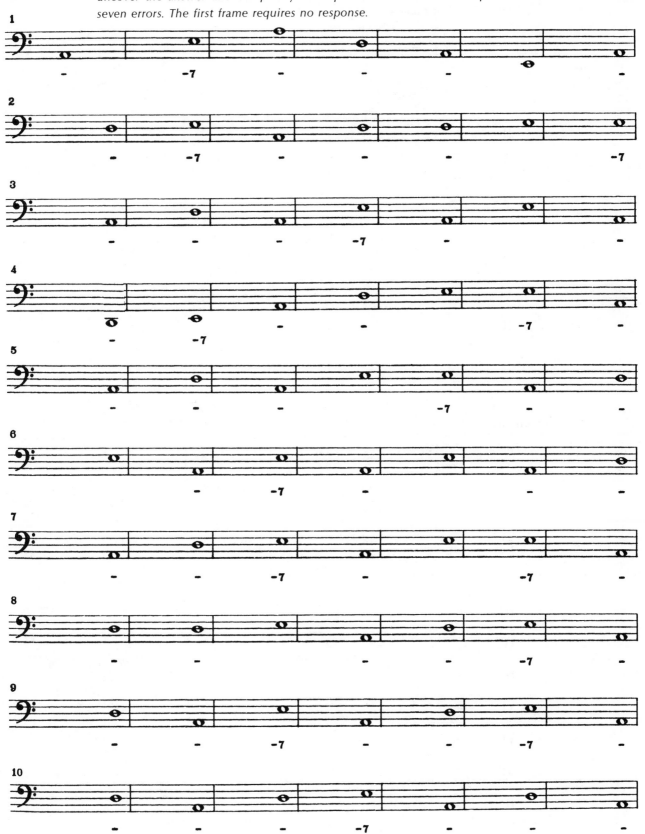

5

C1-6a

Figured bass dictation

Shield the answer. Listen to the chord and write the bass note and the figured bass symbol; then uncover the answer and compare your response. Circle incorrect responses. Goal: No more than seven errors. The first frame requires no response.

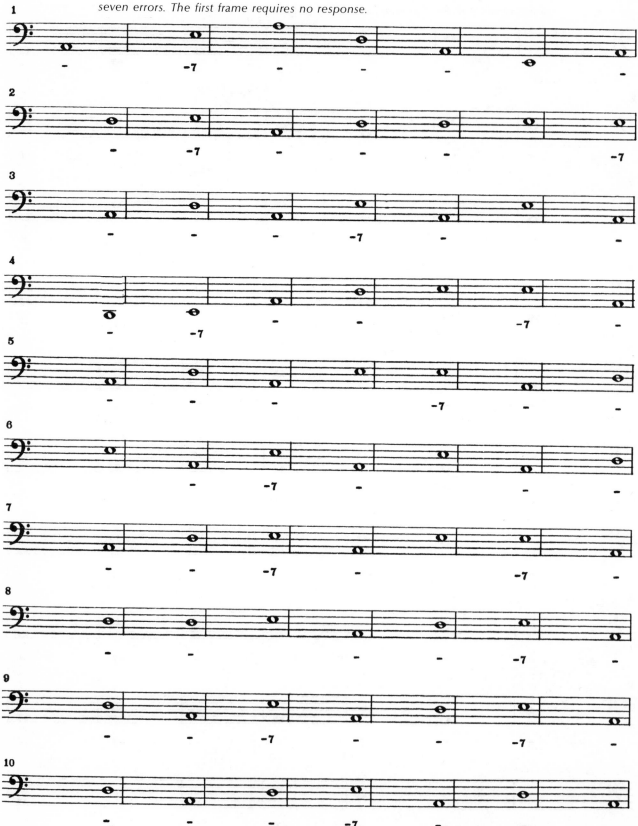

46

C1-6a
(Copy 3)

Figured bass dictation

Shield the answer. Listen to the chord and write the bass note and the figured bass symbol; then uncover the answer and compare your response. Circle incorrect responses. Goal: No more than seven errors. The first frame requires no response.

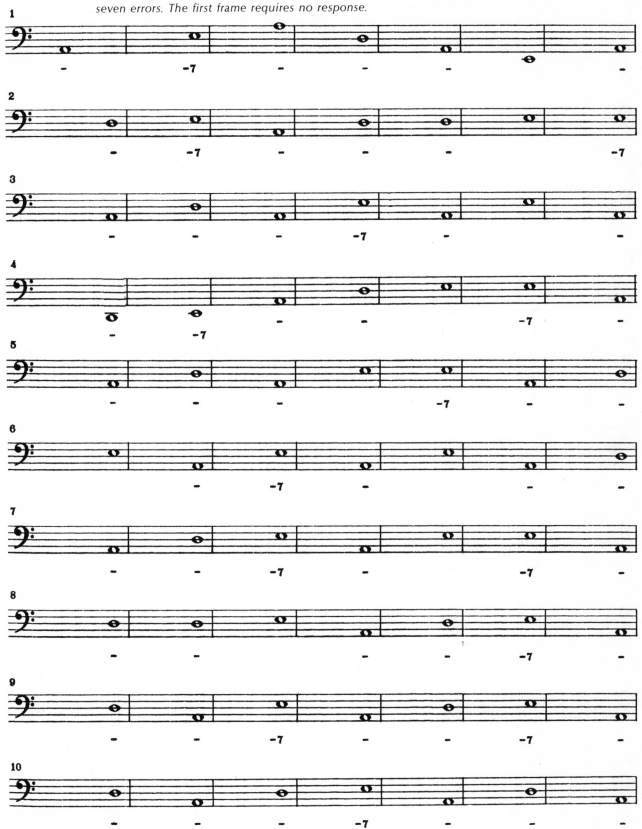

Figured bass dictation

Shield the answer. Listen to the chord and write the bass note and the figured bass symbol; then uncover the answer and compare your response. Circle incorrect responses. Goal: No more than seven errors. The first frame requires no response.

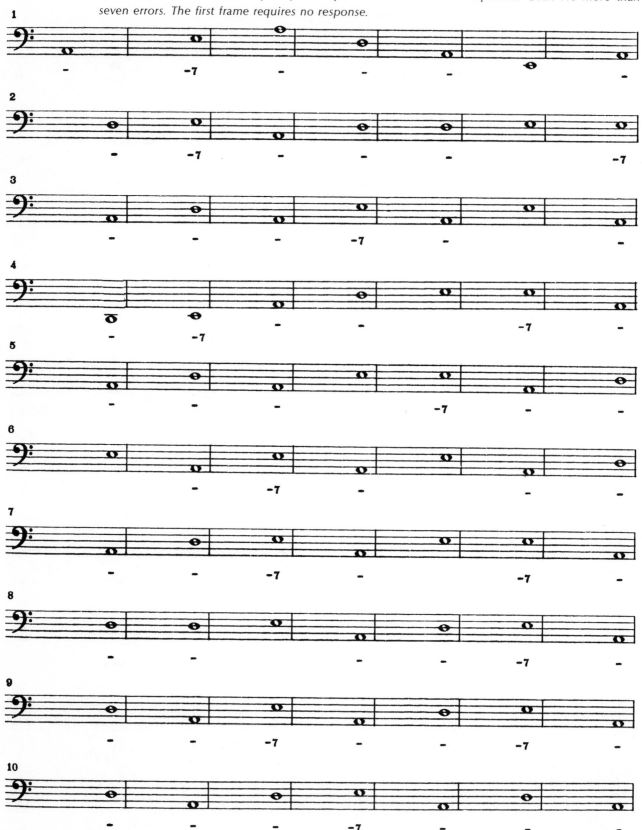

(Copy 5)

Figured bass dictation

Shield the answer. Listen to the chord and write the bass note and the figured bass symbol; then uncover the answer and compare your response. Circle incorrect responses. Goal: No more than seven errors. The first frame requires no response.

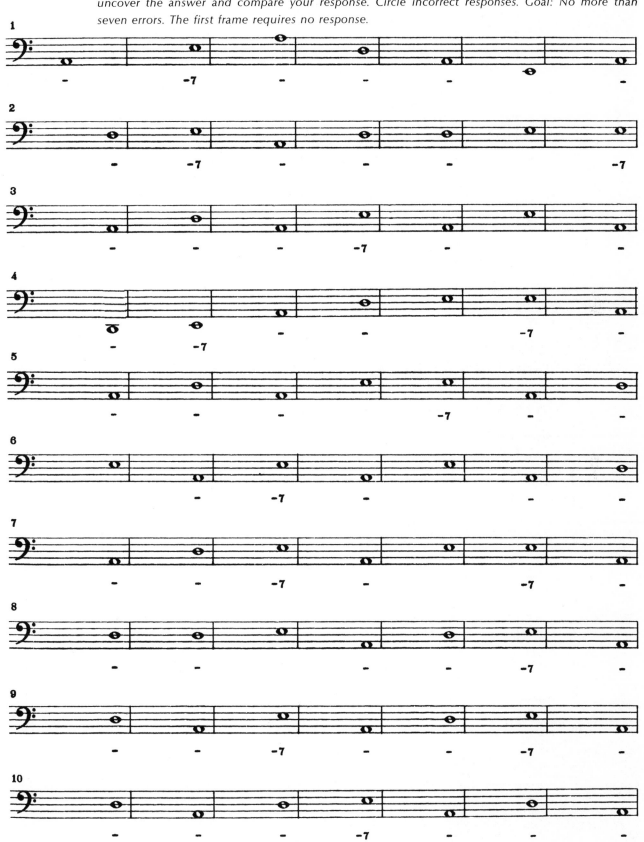

This lesson involves chords in a minor key. The only chord symbols involved are I^-, IV^-, V and V^{-7}. In a minor key, the composite chord symbols for the triads in root position on the first and fourth degree are I^- and IV^-. They include a minus sign for the figured bass portion of the symbol, because they are minor triads. As we have seen, in a major key the triads on these degrees are major. Note that the triad and the seventh chord on the fifth degree of a minor key are the same as in a major key.

C1-6b
(Copy 1)

Chord identification in a key

Shield the answer. Listen to the chord and write the composite chord symbol; then uncover the answer and compare your response. Circle incorrect responses. Goal: No more than seven errors. The first frame requires no response.

#														
1	I^-		___ V^{-7}		___ I^-		___ IV^-		___ I^-		___ V		___ I^-
2	___ IV^-		___ V^{-7}		___ I^-		___ IV^-		___ IV^-		___ V		___ V^{-7}
3	___ I^-		___ IV^-		___ I^-		___ V^{-7}		___ I^-		___ V		___ I^-
4	___ IV^-		___ V^{-7}		___ I^-		___ IV^-		___ V		___ V^{-7}		___ I^-
5	___ I^-		___ IV^-		___ I^-		___ V		___ V^{-7}		___ I^-		___ IV^-
6	___ V		___ I^-		___ V^{-7}		___ I^-		___ V		___ I^-		___ IV^-
7	___ I^-		___ IV^-		___ V^{-7}		___ I^-		___ V		___ V^{-7}		___ I^-
8	___ IV^-		___ IV^-		___ V		___ I^-		___ IV^-		___ V^{-7}		___ I^-
9	___ IV^-		___ I^-		___ V^{-7}		___ I^-		___ IV^-		___ V^{-7}		___ I^-
10	___ IV^-		___ I^-		___ IV^-		___ V^{-7}		___ I^-		___ IV^-		___ I^-

C1–6b

(Copy 2)

Chord identification in a key

Shield the answer. Listen to the chord and write the composite chord symbol; then uncover the answer and compare your response. Circle incorrect responses. Goal: No more than seven errors. The first frame requires no response.

1 I^- ___ V^{-7} ___ I^- ___ IV^- ___ I^- ___ V ___ I^-

2 ___ IV^- ___ V^{-7} ___ I^- ___ IV^- ___ IV^- ___ V ___ V^{-7}

3 ___ I^- ___ IV^- ___ I^- ___ V^{-7} ___ I^- ___ V ___ I^-

4 ___ IV^- ___ V^{-7} ___ I^- ___ IV^- ___ V ___ V^{-7} ___ I^-

5 ___ I^- ___ IV^- ___ I^- ___ V ___ V^{-7} ___ I^- ___ IV^-

6 ___ V ___ I^- ___ V^{-7} ___ I^- ___ V ___ I^- ___ IV^-

7 ___ I^- ___ IV^- ___ V^{-7} ___ I^- ___ V ___ V^{-7} ___ I^-

8 ___ IV^- ___ IV^- ___ V ___ I^- ___ IV^- ___ V^{-7} ___ I^-

9 ___ IV^- ___ I^- ___ V^{-7} ___ I^- ___ IV^- ___ V^{-7} ___ I^-

10 ___ IV^- ___ I^- ___ IV^- ___ V^{-7} ___ I^- ___ IV^- ___ I^-

C1–6b

(Copy 3)

Chord identification in a key

Shield the answer. Listen to the chord and write the composite chord symbol; then uncover the answer and compare your response. Circle incorrect responses. Goal: No more than seven errors. The first frame requires no response.

1 I^- ___ V^{-7} ___ I^- ___ IV^- ___ I^- ___ V ___ I^-

2 ___ IV^- ___ V^{-7} ___ I^- ___ IV^- ___ IV^- ___ V ___ V^{-7}

3 ___ I^- ___ IV^- ___ I^- ___ V^{-7} ___ I^- ___ V ___ I^-

4 ___ IV^- ___ V^{-7} ___ I^- ___ IV^- ___ V ___ V^{-7} ___ I^-

5 ___ I^- ___ IV^- ___ I^- ___ V ___ V^{-7} ___ I^- ___ IV^-

6 ___ V ___ I^- ___ V^{-7} ___ I^- ___ V ___ I^- ___ IV^-

7 ___ I^- ___ IV^- ___ V^{-7} ___ I^- ___ V ___ V^{-7} ___ I^-

8 ___ IV^- ___ IV^- ___ V ___ I^- ___ IV^- ___ V^{-7} ___ I^-

9 ___ IV^- ___ I^- ___ V^{-7} ___ I^- ___ IV^- ___ V^{-7} ___ I^-

10 ___ IV^- ___ I^- ___ IV^- ___ V^{-7} ___ I^- ___ IV^- ___ I^-

C1-6b
(Copy 4)

Chord identification in a key

Shield the answer. Listen to the chord and write the composite chord symbol; then uncover the answer and compare your response. Circle incorrect responses. Goal: No more than seven errors. The first frame requires no response.

1 I^- ___ V^{-7} ___ I^- ___ IV^- ___ I^- ___ V ___ I^-

2 ___ IV^- ___ V^{-7} ___ I^- ___ IV^- ___ IV^- ___ V ___ V^{-7}

3 ___ I^- ___ IV^- ___ I^- ___ V^{-7} ___ I^- ___ V ___ I^-

4 ___ IV^- ___ V^{-7} ___ I^- ___ IV^- ___ V ___ V^{-7} ___ I^-

5 ___ I^- ___ IV^- ___ I^- ___ V ___ V^{-7} ___ I^- ___ IV^-

6 ___ V ___ I^- ___ V^{-7} ___ I^- ___ V ___ I^- ___ IV^-

7 ___ I^- ___ IV^- ___ V^{-7} ___ I^- ___ V ___ V^{-7} ___ I^-

8 ___ IV^- ___ IV^- ___ V ___ I^- ___ IV^- ___ V^{-7} ___ I^-

9 ___ IV^- ___ I^- ___ V^{-7} ___ I^- ___ IV^- ___ V^{-7} ___ I^-

10 ___ IV^- ___ I^- ___ IV^- ___ V^{-7} ___ I^- ___ IV^- ___ I^-

C1-6b
(Copy 5)

Chord identification in a key

Shield the answer. Listen to the chord and write the composite chord symbol; then uncover the answer and compare your response. Circle incorrect responses. Goal: No more than seven errors. The first frame requires no response.

1 I^- ___ V^{-7} ___ I^- ___ IV^- ___ I^- ___ V ___ I^-

2 ___ IV^- ___ V^{-7} ___ I^- ___ IV^- ___ IV^- ___ V ___ V^{-7}

3 ___ I^- ___ IV^- ___ I^- ___ V^{-7} ___ I^- ___ V ___ I^-

4 ___ IV^- ___ V^{-7} ___ I^- ___ IV^- ___ V ___ V^{-7} ___ I^-

5 ___ I^- ___ IV^- ___ I^- ___ V ___ V^{-7} ___ I^- ___ IV^-

6 ___ V ___ I^- ___ V^{-7} ___ I^- ___ V ___ I^- ___ IV^-

7 ___ I^- ___ IV^- ___ V^{-7} ___ I^- ___ V ___ V^{-7} ___ I^-

8 ___ IV^- ___ IV^- ___ V ___ I^- ___ IV^- ___ V^{-7} ___ I^-

9 ___ IV^- ___ I^- ___ V^{-7} ___ I^- ___ IV^- ___ V^{-7} ___ I^-

10 ___ IV^- ___ I^- ___ IV^- ___ V^{-7} ___ I^- ___ IV^- ___ I^-

C1-7a

Figured bass dictation

(Copy 1)

Shield the answer. Listen to the chord and write the bass note and the figured bass symbol; then uncover the answer and compare your response. Circle incorrect responses. Goal: No more than seven errors. The first frame requires no response.

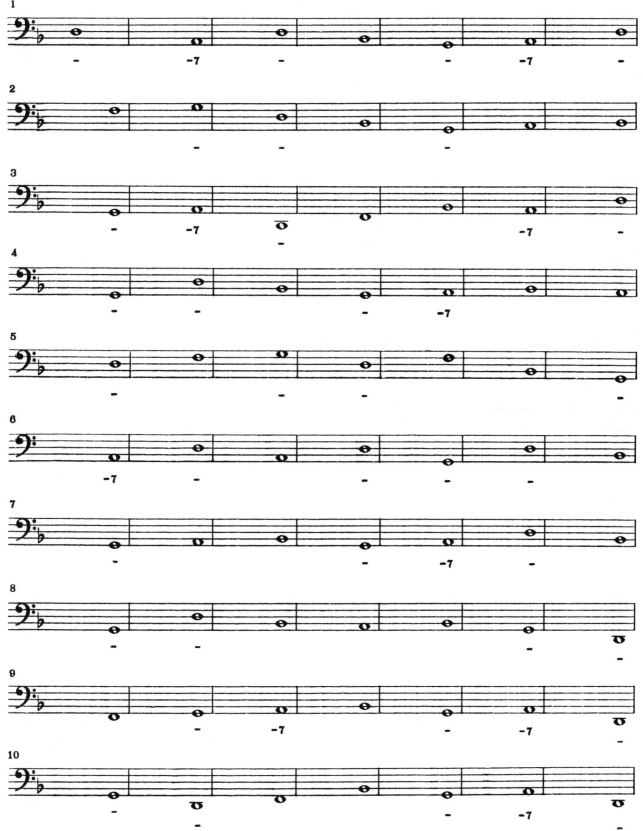

C1-7a

Figured bass dictation

Shield the answer. Listen to the chord and write the bass note and the figured bass symbol; then uncover the answer and compare your response. Circle incorrect responses. Goal: No more than seven errors. The first frame requires no response.

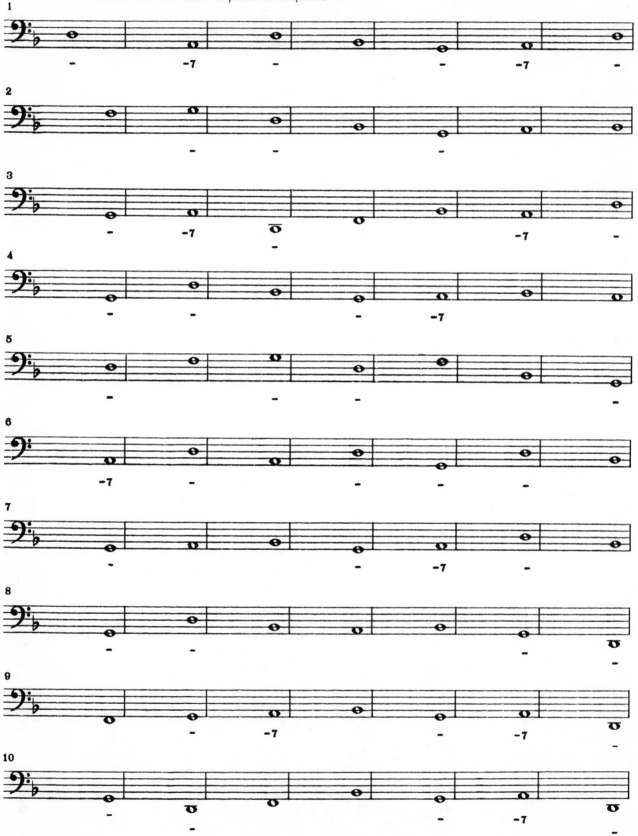

54

C1-7a

(Copy 3)

Figured bass dictation

Shield the answer. Listen to the chord and write the bass note and the figured bass symbol; then uncover the answer and compare your response. Circle incorrect responses. Goal: No more than seven errors. The first frame requires no response.

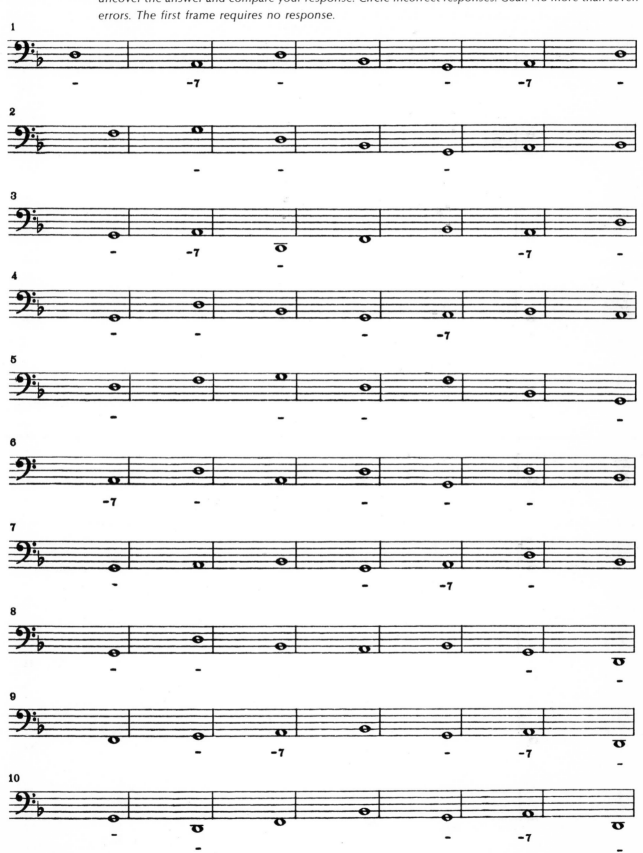

C1-7a

(Copy 4)

Figured bass dictation

Shield the answer. Listen to the chord and write the bass note and the figured bass symbol; then uncover the answer and compare your response. Circle incorrect responses. Goal: No more than seven errors. The first frame requires no response.

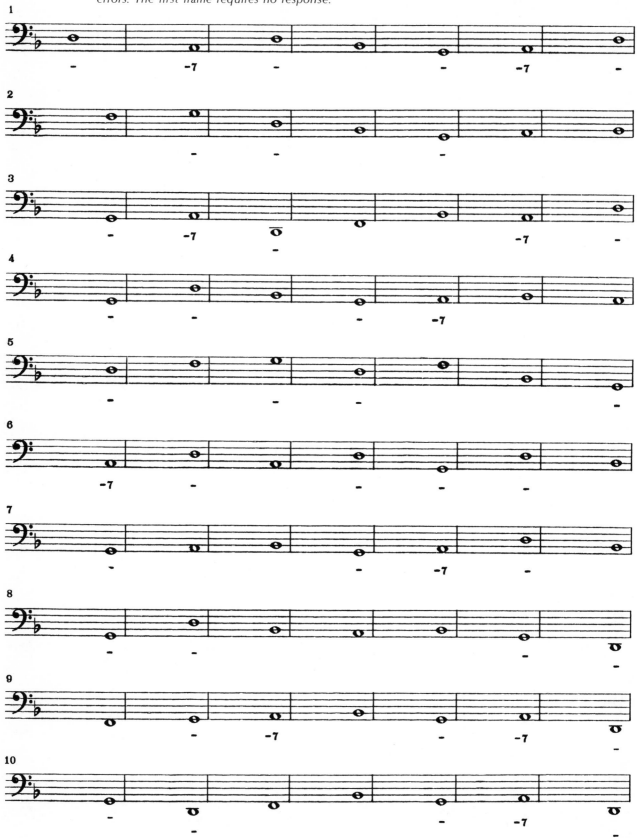

C1-7a
(Copy 5)

Figured bass dictation

Shield the answer. Listen to the chord and write the bass note and the figured bass symbol; then uncover the answer and compare your response. Circle incorrect responses. Goal: No more than seven errors. The first frame requires no response.

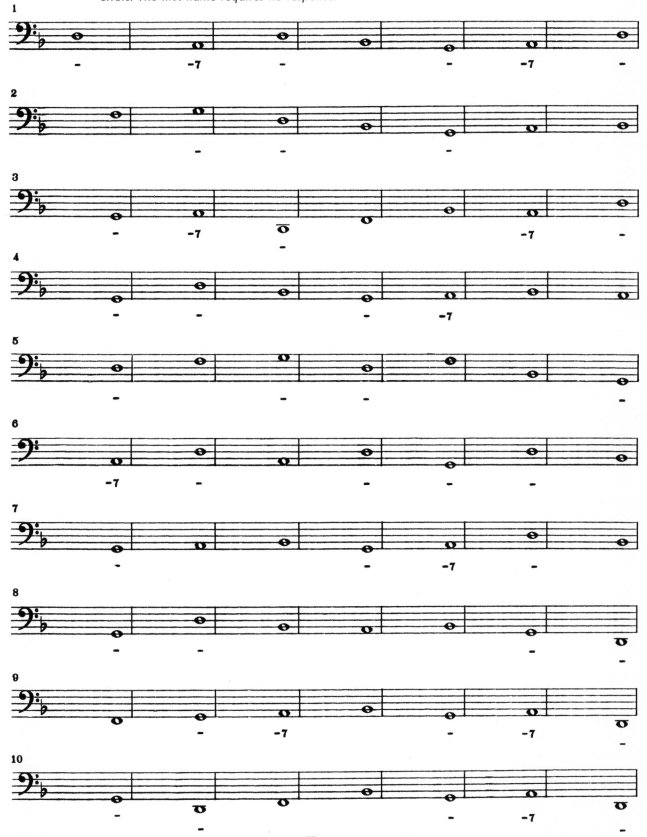

This lesson involves some new key location symbols. Because the Roman numeral is used to indicate the interval between the tonic of the key and the root of the chord, a qualifying sign must be used where this is not a major or perfect interval. In this lesson, the triads found on the third and sixth degrees of the minor key are included. The roots of these chords are at minor intervals above the tonic, and the Roman numerals are therefore preceded by the minus sign. (Note that the minus sign has the same significance as it does in figured bass symbols with Arabic numerals.) Thus the key location symbols for these chords are ⁻III and ⁻VI. Key location symbols that are not preceded by a qualifying sign indicate a major or perfect interval from the tonic upward to the root.

It is important to note the position of the qualifying sign in a composite chord symbol. Where a minus sign *precedes* the Roman numeral, it applies to the key location symbol. Where it *follows* the Roman numeral, it applies to the figured bass symbol. Thus the composite chord symbol ⁻VI contains the key location symbol ⁻VI and the blank figured bass symbol, indicating a major triad in root position with the root a minor sixth above the tonic. The composite chord symbol VI⁻ contains the key location symbol VI and the figured bass symbol of the minus sign (−), indicating a minor triad in root position with the root a major sixth above the tonic.

The triads in root position on the third and sixth degrees of the minor key are major triads, and therefore the figured bass portion of the symbols for them is blank. The roots of these chords are a minor interval above the tonic; therefore a minus sign precedes the Roman numeral in the key location portion of the composite chord symbols. In a minor key, the composite chord symbols for these two chords are ⁻III and ⁻VI. Remember that in a major key the triads on the third and sixth degrees are minor triads and the roots are at major intervals above the tonic, and therefore the composite chord symbols are III⁻ and VI⁻. In a minor key, then, we find the chords ⁻III and ⁻VI, and in a major key we find III⁻ and VI⁻.

There are two forms of the triad on the third degree of a minor key. The reason is that the fifth of this chord is the seventh degree of the key, and in a minor key there are two positions for this seventh degree. One position of the seventh is that called for by the key signature, and the other is raised by an accidental. In this volume, we will use only the form of the ⁻III chord that involves the seventh called for by the key signature. This form of the ⁻III chord is a major triad. The raised seventh results in an augmented triad that will be taken up in Volume IV.

Lesson C1-7b is in a minor key. The only chords involved are I⁻, ⁻III, IV⁻, V, V⁻⁷ and ⁻VI.

C1–7b
(Copy 1)

Chord identification in a key

Shield the answer. Listen to the chord and write the composite chord symbol; then uncover the answer and compare your response. Circle incorrect responses. Goal: No more than seven errors. The first frame requires no response. After you have done this lesson, take Test C1.

1   I^- ____ V^{-7} ____ I^- ____ ^-VI ____ IV^- ____ V^{-7} ____ I^-

2   ____ ^-III ____ IV^- ____ I^- ____ ^-VI ____ IV^- ____ V ____ ^-VI

3   ____ IV^- ____ V^{-7} ____ I^- ____ ^-III ____ ^-VI ____ V^{-7} ____ I^-

4   ____ IV^- ____ I^- ____ ^-VI ____ IV^- ____ V^{-7} ____ ^-VI ____ V

5   ____ I^- ____ ^-III ____ IV^- ____ I^- ____ ^-III ____ ^-VI ____ IV^-

6   ____ V^{-7} ____ I^- ____ V ____ I^- ____ IV^- ____ I^- ____ ^-VI

7   ____ IV^- ____ V ____ ^-VI ____ IV^- ____ V^{-7} ____ I^- ____ ^-VI

8   ____ IV^- ____ I^- ____ ^-VI ____ V ____ ^-VI ____ IV^- ____ I^-

9   ____ ^-III ____ IV^- ____ V^{-7} ____ ^-VI ____ IV^- ____ V^{-7} ____ I^-

10   ____ IV^- ____ I^- ____ ^-III ____ ^-VI ____ IV^- ____ V^{-7} ____ I^-

C1–7b
(Copy 2)

Chord identification in a key

Shield the answer. Listen to the chord and write the composite chord symbol; then uncover the answer and compare your response. Circle incorrect responses. Goal: No more than seven errors. The first frame requires no response. After you have done this lesson, take Test C1.

1   I^- ____ V^{-7} ____ I^- ____ ^-VI ____ IV^- ____ V^{-7} ____ I^-

2   ____ ^-III ____ IV^- ____ I^- ____ ^-VI ____ IV^- ____ V ____ ^-VI

3   ____ IV^- ____ V^{-7} ____ I^- ____ ^-III ____ ^-VI ____ V^{-7} ____ I^-

4   ____ IV^- ____ I^- ____ ^-VI ____ IV^- ____ V^{-7} ____ ^-VI ____ V

5   ____ I^- ____ ^-III ____ IV^- ____ I^- ____ ^-III ____ ^-VI ____ IV^-

6   ____ V^{-7} ____ I^- ____ V ____ I^- ____ IV^- ____ I^- ____ ^-VI

7   ____ IV^- ____ V ____ ^-VI ____ IV^- ____ V^{-7} ____ I^- ____ ^-VI

8   ____ IV^- ____ I^- ____ ^-VI ____ V ____ ^-VI ____ IV^- ____ I^-

9   ____ ^-III ____ IV^- ____ V^{-7} ____ ^-VI ____ IV^- ____ V^{-7} ____ I^-

10   ____ IV^- ____ I^- ____ ^-III ____ ^-VI ____ IV^- ____ V^{-7} ____ I^-

C1-7b
(Copy 3)

Chord identification in a key

Shield the answer. Listen to the chord and write the composite chord symbol; then uncover the answer and compare your response. Circle incorrect responses. Goal: No more than seven errors. The first frame requires no response. After you have done this lesson, take Test C1.

1 I⁻   ___ V⁻⁷ ___ I⁻ ___ ⁻VI ___ IV⁻ ___ V⁻⁷ ___ I⁻

2 ___ ⁻III ___ IV⁻ ___ I⁻ ___ ⁻VI ___ IV⁻ ___ V ___ ⁻VI

3 ___ IV⁻ ___ V⁻⁷ ___ I⁻ ___ ⁻III ___ ⁻VI ___ V⁻⁷ ___ I⁻

4 ___ IV⁻ ___ I⁻ ___ ⁻VI ___ IV⁻ ___ V⁻⁷ ___ ⁻VI ___ V

5 ___ I⁻ ___ ⁻III ___ IV⁻ ___ I⁻ ___ ⁻III ___ ⁻VI ___ IV⁻

6 ___ V⁻⁷ ___ I⁻ ___ V ___ I⁻ ___ IV⁻ ___ I⁻ ___ ⁻VI

7 ___ IV⁻ ___ V ___ ⁻VI ___ IV⁻ ___ V⁻⁷ ___ I⁻ ___ ⁻VI

8 ___ IV⁻ ___ I⁻ ___ ⁻VI ___ V ___ ⁻VI ___ IV⁻ ___ I⁻

9 ___ ⁻III ___ IV⁻ ___ V⁻⁷ ___ ⁻VI ___ IV⁻ ___ V⁻⁷ ___ I⁻

10 ___ IV⁻ ___ I⁻ ___ ⁻III ___ ⁻VI ___ IV⁻ ___ V⁻⁷ ___ I⁻

C1-7b
(Copy 4)

Chord identification in a key

Shield the answer. Listen to the chord and write the composite chord symbol; then uncover the answer and compare your response. Circle incorrect responses. Goal: No more than seven errors. The first frame requires no response. After you have done this lesson, take Test C1.

1 I⁻   ___ V⁻⁷ ___ I⁻ ___ ⁻VI ___ IV⁻ ___ V⁻⁷ ___ I⁻

2 ___ ⁻III ___ IV⁻ ___ I⁻ ___ ⁻VI ___ IV⁻ ___ V ___ ⁻VI

3 ___ IV⁻ ___ V⁻⁷ ___ I⁻ ___ ⁻III ___ ⁻VI ___ V⁻⁷ ___ I⁻

4 ___ IV⁻ ___ I⁻ ___ ⁻VI ___ IV⁻ ___ V⁻⁷ ___ ⁻VI ___ V

5 ___ I⁻ ___ ⁻III ___ IV⁻ ___ I⁻ ___ ⁻III ___ ⁻VI ___ IV⁻

6 ___ V⁻⁷ ___ I⁻ ___ V ___ I⁻ ___ IV⁻ ___ I⁻ ___ ⁻VI

7 ___ IV⁻ ___ V ___ ⁻VI ___ IV⁻ ___ V⁻⁷ ___ I⁻ ___ ⁻VI

8 ___ IV⁻ ___ I⁻ ___ ⁻VI ___ V ___ ⁻VI ___ IV⁻ ___ I⁻

9 ___ ⁻III ___ IV⁻ ___ V⁻⁷ ___ ⁻VI ___ IV⁻ ___ V⁻⁷ ___ I⁻

10 ___ IV⁻ ___ I⁻ ___ ⁻III ___ ⁻VI ___ IV⁻ ___ V⁻⁷ ___ I⁻

C1-7b

(Copy 5)

Chord identification in a key

Shield the answer. Listen to the chord and write the composite chord symbol; then uncover the answer and compare your response. Circle incorrect responses. Goal: No more than seven errors. The first frame requires no response. After you have done this lesson, take Test C1.

1 I⁻ _____ V⁻⁷ _____ I⁻ _____ ⁻VI _____ IV⁻ _____ V⁻⁷ _____ I⁻

2 _____ ⁻III _____ IV⁻ _____ I⁻ _____ ⁻VI _____ IV⁻ _____ V _____ ⁻VI

3 _____ IV⁻ _____ V⁻⁷ _____ I⁻ _____ ⁻III _____ ⁻VI _____ V⁻⁷ _____ I⁻

4 _____ IV⁻ _____ I⁻ _____ ⁻VI _____ IV⁻ _____ V⁻⁷ _____ ⁻VI _____ V

5 _____ I⁻ _____ ⁻III _____ IV⁻ _____ I⁻ _____ ⁻III _____ ⁻VI _____ IV⁻

6 _____ V⁻⁷ _____ I⁻ _____ V _____ I⁻ _____ IV⁻ _____ I⁻ _____ ⁻VI

7 _____ IV⁻ _____ V _____ ⁻VI _____ IV⁻ _____ V⁻⁷ _____ I⁻ _____ ⁻VI

8 _____ IV⁻ _____ I⁻ _____ ⁻VI _____ V _____ ⁻VI _____ IV⁻ _____ I⁻

9 _____ ⁻III _____ IV⁻ _____ V⁻⁷ _____ ⁻VI _____ IV⁻ _____ V⁻⁷ _____ I⁻

10 _____ IV⁻ _____ I⁻ _____ ⁻III _____ ⁻VI _____ IV⁻ _____ V⁻⁷ _____ I⁻

Major Triads in First Inversion   SERIES C2

A triad is said to be in first inversion when the third of the chord appears as the lowest note or bass:

In a major triad in first inversion, the upper tones of the chord are at the intervals of a minor sixth and a minor third above the bass.

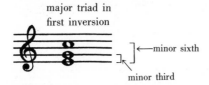

When you have done this series, take Test C2, which includes sections on each of the four kinds of lessons found in this series.

C2-1a Chord dictation

(Copy 1)

Shield the answer. Listen to the chord and notate the upper tones above the given note; then uncover the answer and compare your response. Circle incorrect responses. Goal: No more than seven errors.

C2-1a
(Copy 2)

Chord dictation

Shield the answer. Listen to the chord and notate the upper tones above the given note; then uncover the answer and compare your response. Circle incorrect responses. Goal: No more than seven errors.

C2-1a
(Copy 3)

Chord dictation

Shield the answer. Listen to the chord and notate the upper tones above the given note; then uncover the answer and compare your response. Circle incorrect responses. Goal: No more than seven errors.

66

C2-1a
(Copy 4)

Chord dictation

Shield the answer. Listen to the chord and notate the upper tones above the given note; then uncover the answer and compare your response. Circle incorrect responses. Goal: No more than seven errors.

67

C2-1a

Chord dictation

Shield the answer. Listen to the chord and notate the upper tones above the given note; then uncover the answer and compare your response. Circle incorrect responses. Goal: No more than seven errors.

68

In this lesson the figured bass symbol for the major triad in first inversion is introduced. The intervals between the upper tones and the bass of major triad in first inversion are a minor sixth and a minor third. The complete figured bass symbol is $-^6_3$, and the abbreviated form of the symbol is $^{-6}$. Note that the minus sign in this figured bass symbol refers to the interval above the bass and does not indicate that the triad is minor. Thus, we may have a minus sign in the figured bass symbol for a chord that is not a minor triad.

C2-1b

(Copy 1)

Chord identification

Shield the answer. Listen to the chord and write the figured bass symbol (blank, $^{-6}$, or $^-$); then uncover the answer and compare your response. Circle incorrect responses. Goal: No more than seven errors.

1. ____ $^{-6}$ ____ ____ $^{-6}$ ____ $^{-6}$ ____ $^{-6}$ ____ $^{-6}$ ____

2. ____ $^-$ ____ $^{-6}$ ____ ____ $^{-6}$ ____ ____ $^{-6}$ ____ $^{-6}$

3. ____ ____ $^{-6}$ ____ $^{-6}$ ____ ____ ____ ____ $^-$ ____ $^{-6}$

4. ____ $^{-6}$ ____ ____ $^-$ ____ $^{-6}$ ____ ____ $^{-6}$ ____ $^-$

5. ____ $^{-6}$ ____ $^{-6}$ ____ $^{-6}$ ____ ____ $^{-6}$ ____ ____ $^{-6}$

6. ____ $^{-6}$ ____ ____ $^-$ ____ $^{-6}$ ____ $^{-6}$ ____ ____ $^-$

7. ____ $^{-6}$ ____ $^{-6}$ ____ ____ ____ ____ $^{-6}$ ____ $^{-6}$ ____

8. ____ $^{-6}$ ____ ____ $^{-6}$ ____ $^{-6}$ ____ $^-$ ____ $^{-6}$ ____

9. ____ $^{-6}$ ____ $^{-6}$ ____ ____ ____ $^{-6}$ ____ $^{-6}$ ____

10. ____ $^{-6}$ ____ $^-$ ____ $^{-6}$ ____ $^{-6}$ ____ ____ ____ $^{-6}$

C2–1b

(Copy 2)

Chord identification

Shield the answer. Listen to the chord and write the figured bass symbol (blank, ⁻⁶, or ⁻); then uncover the answer and compare your response. Circle incorrect responses. Goal: No more than seven errors.

1 ____ ⁻⁶   ____   ____ ⁻⁶   ____ ⁻⁶   ____ ⁻⁶   ____ ⁻⁶   ____

2 ____ ⁻   ____ ⁻⁶   ____   ____ ⁻⁶   ____   ____ ⁻⁶   ____ ⁻⁶

3 ____   ____ ⁻⁶   ____ ⁻⁶   ____   ____   ____ ⁻   ____ ⁻⁶

4 ____ ⁻⁶   ____   ____ ⁻   ____ ⁻⁶   ____   ____ ⁻⁶   ____ ⁻

5 ____ ⁻⁶   ____ ⁻⁶   ____ ⁻⁶   ____   ____ ⁻⁶   ____   ____ ⁻⁶

6 ____ ⁻⁶   ____   ____ ⁻   ____ ⁻⁶   ____ ⁻⁶   ____   ____ ⁻

7 ____ ⁻⁶   ____ ⁻⁶   ____   ____   ____ ⁻⁶   ____ ⁻⁶   ____

8 ____ ⁻⁶   ____   ____ ⁻⁶   ____ ⁻⁶   ____ ⁻   ____ ⁻⁶   ____

9 ____ ⁻⁶   ____ ⁻⁶   ____   ____   ____ ⁻⁶   ____ ⁻⁶   ____

10 ____ ⁻⁶   ____ ⁻   ____ ⁻⁶   ____ ⁻⁶   ____   ____   ____ ⁻⁶

C2–1b

(Copy 3)

Chord identification

Shield the answer. Listen to the chord and write the figured bass symbol (blank, ⁻⁶, or ⁻); then uncover the answer and compare your response. Circle incorrect responses. Goal: No more than seven errors.

1 ____ ⁻⁶   ____   ____ ⁻⁶   ____ ⁻⁶   ____ ⁻⁶   ____ ⁻⁶   ____

2 ____ ⁻   ____ ⁻⁶   ____   ____ ⁻⁶   ____   ____ ⁻⁶   ____ ⁻⁶

3 ____   ____ ⁻⁶   ____ ⁻⁶   ____   ____   ____ ⁻   ____ ⁻⁶

4 ____ ⁻⁶   ____   ____ ⁻   ____ ⁻⁶   ____   ____ ⁻⁶   ____ ⁻

5 ____ ⁻⁶   ____ ⁻⁶   ____ ⁻⁶   ____   ____ ⁻⁶   ____   ____ ⁻⁶

6 ____ ⁻⁶   ____   ____ ⁻   ____ ⁻⁶   ____ ⁻⁶   ____   ____ ⁻

7 ____ ⁻⁶   ____ ⁻⁶   ____   ____   ____ ⁻⁶   ____ ⁻⁶   ____

8 ____ ⁻⁶   ____   ____ ⁻⁶   ____ ⁻⁶   ____ ⁻   ____ ⁻⁶   ____

9 ____ ⁻⁶   ____ ⁻⁶   ____   ____   ____ ⁻⁶   ____ ⁻⁶   ____

10 ____ ⁻⁶   ____ ⁻   ____ ⁻⁶   ____ ⁻⁶   ____   ____   ____ ⁻⁶

C2-1b
(Copy 4)

Chord identification

Shield the answer. Listen to the chord and write the figured bass symbol (blank, ⁻⁶, or ⁻); then uncover the answer and compare your response. Circle incorrect responses. Goal: No more than seven errors.

1 ____ ⁻⁶ ____ ____ ⁻⁶ ____ ⁻⁶ ____ ⁻⁶ ____ ⁻⁶ ____

2 ____ ⁻ ____ ⁻⁶ ____ ____ ⁻⁶ ____ ____ ⁻⁶ ____ ⁻⁶

3 ____ ____ ⁻⁶ ____ ⁻⁶ ____ ____ ____ ⁻ ____ ⁻⁶

4 ____ ⁻⁶ ____ ____ ⁻ ____ ⁻⁶ ____ ____ ⁻⁶ ____ ⁻

5 ____ ⁻⁶ ____ ⁻⁶ ____ ⁻⁶ ____ ____ ⁻⁶ ____ ____ ⁻⁶

6 ____ ⁻⁶ ____ ____ ⁻ ____ ⁻⁶ ____ ⁻⁶ ____ ____ ⁻

7 ____ ⁻⁶ ____ ⁻⁶ ____ ____ ____ ⁻⁶ ____ ⁻⁶ ____

8 ____ ⁻⁶ ____ ____ ⁻⁶ ____ ⁻⁶ ____ ⁻ ____ ⁻⁶ ____

9 ____ ⁻⁶ ____ ⁻⁶ ____ ____ ____ ⁻⁶ ____ ⁻⁶ ____

10 ____ ⁻⁶ ____ ⁻ ____ ⁻⁶ ____ ⁻⁶ ____ ____ ____ ⁻⁶

C2-1b
(Copy 5)

Chord identification

Shield the answer. Listen to the chord and write the figured bass symbol (blank, ⁻⁶, or ⁻); then uncover the answer and compare your response. Circle incorrect responses. Goal: No more than seven errors.

1 ____ ⁻⁶ ____ ____ ⁻⁶ ____ ⁻⁶ ____ ⁻⁶ ____ ⁻⁶ ____

2 ____ ⁻ ____ ⁻⁶ ____ ____ ⁻⁶ ____ ____ ⁻⁶ ____ ⁻⁶

3 ____ ____ ⁻⁶ ____ ⁻⁶ ____ ____ ____ ⁻ ____ ⁻⁶

4 ____ ⁻⁶ ____ ____ ⁻ ____ ⁻⁶ ____ ____ ⁻⁶ ____ ⁻

5 ____ ⁻⁶ ____ ⁻⁶ ____ ⁻⁶ ____ ____ ⁻⁶ ____ ____ ⁻⁶

6 ____ ⁻⁶ ____ ____ ⁻ ____ ⁻⁶ ____ ⁻⁶ ____ ____ ⁻

7 ____ ⁻⁶ ____ ⁻⁶ ____ ____ ____ ⁻⁶ ____ ⁻⁶ ____

8 ____ ⁻⁶ ____ ____ ⁻⁶ ____ ⁻⁶ ____ ⁻ ____ ⁻⁶ ____

9 ____ ⁻⁶ ____ ⁻⁶ ____ ____ ____ ⁻⁶ ____ ⁻⁶ ____

10 ____ ⁻⁶ ____ ⁻ ____ ⁻⁶ ____ ⁻⁶ ____ ____ ____ ⁻⁶

C2-2
(Copy 1)

Chord identification

Shield the answer. Listen to the chord and write the figured bass symbol (blank, ⁻⁶, or ⁻); then uncover the answer and compare your response. Circle incorrect responses. Goal: No more than seven errors.

```
1  ____      ____ -6   ____      ____ -6   ____ -6   ____      ____
2  ____ -6   ____      ____ -    ____ -6   ____      ____ -6   ____
3  ____ -6   ____ -6   ____      ____ -    ____      ____      ____ -6
4  ____ -6   ____      ____ -6   ____ -    ____ -6   ____      ____ -6
5  ____      ____ -6   ____      ____      ____ -6   ____ -    ____ -6
6  ____      ____ -    ____      ____ -6   ____ -    ____ -6   ____
7  ____ -6   ____      ____ -6   ____ -6   ____      ____      ____ -
8  ____ -6   ____ -6   ____      ____      ____ -6   ____      ____ -
9  ____ -6   ____      ____ -6   ____ -6   ____      ____ -    ____ -6
10 ____      ____ -6   ____ -6   ____      ____ -    ____ -6   ____
```

C2-2
(Copy 2)

Chord identification

Shield the answer. Listen to the chord and write the figured bass symbol (blank, ⁻⁶, or ⁻); then uncover the answer and compare your response. Circle incorrect responses. Goal: No more than seven errors.

```
1  ____      ____ -6   ____      ____ -6   ____ -6   ____      ____
2  ____ -6   ____      ____ -    ____ -6   ____      ____ -6   ____
3  ____ -6   ____ -6   ____      ____ -    ____      ____      ____ -6
4  ____ -6   ____      ____ -6   ____ -    ____ -6   ____      ____ -6
5  ____      ____ -6   ____      ____      ____ -6   ____ -    ____ -6
6  ____      ____ -    ____      ____ -6   ____ -    ____ -6   ____
7  ____ -6   ____      ____ -6   ____ -6   ____      ____      ____ -
8  ____ -6   ____ -6   ____      ____      ____ -6   ____      ____ -
9  ____ -6   ____      ____ -6   ____ -6   ____      ____ -    ____ -6
10 ____      ____ -6   ____ -6   ____      ____ -    ____ -6   ____
```

C2-2
(Copy 3)

Chord identification

Shield the answer. Listen to the chord and write the figured bass symbol (blank, ⁻⁶, or ⁻); then uncover the answer and compare your response. Circle incorrect responses. Goal: No more than seven errors.

1 ____ ____ -6 ____ ____ -6 ____ -6 ____ ____

2 ____ -6 ____ ____ - ____ -6 ____ ____ -6

3 ____ -6 ____ -6 ____ ____ - ____ ____ ____ -6

4 ____ -6 ____ ____ -6 ____ - ____ -6 ____ ____ -6

5 ____ ____ -6 ____ ____ ____ -6 ____ - ____ -6

6 ____ ____ ____ - ____ ____ -6 ____ - ____ -6

7 ____ -6 ____ ____ ____ -6 ____ -6 ____ ____ -

8 ____ -6 ____ -6 ____ ____ ____ -6 ____ ____ -

9 ____ -6 ____ ____ ____ -6 ____ -6 ____ ____ - ____ -6

10 ____ ____ -6 ____ -6 ____ ____ - ____ -6

C2-2
(Copy 4)

Chord identification

Shield the answer. Listen to the chord and write the figured bass symbol (blank, ⁻⁶, or ⁻); then uncover the answer and compare your response. Circle incorrect responses. Goal: No more than seven errors.

1 ____ ____ -6 ____ ____ -6 ____ -6 ____ ____

2 ____ -6 ____ ____ - ____ -6 ____ ____ -6 ____

3 ____ -6 ____ -6 ____ ____ - ____ ____ ____ -6

4 ____ -6 ____ ____ -6 ____ - ____ -6 ____ ____ -6

5 ____ ____ -6 ____ ____ ____ -6 ____ - ____ -6

6 ____ ____ - ____ ____ -6 ____ - ____ -6

7 ____ -6 ____ ____ -6 ____ -6 ____ ____ -

8 ____ -6 ____ -6 ____ ____ ____ -6 ____ ____ -

9 ____ -6 ____ ____ -6 ____ -6 ____ ____ - ____ -6

10 ____ ____ -6 ____ -6 ____ ____ - ____ -6 ____

C2-2

Chord identification

Shield the answer. Listen to the chord and write the figured bass symbol (blank, ⁻⁶, or ⁻); then uncover the answer and compare your response. Circle incorrect responses. Goal: No more than seven errors.

1 ____   ____ -6   ____   ____ -6   ____ -6   ____   ____

2 ____ -6   ____   ____ -   ____ -6   ____   ____ -6   ____

3 ____ -6   ____ -6   ____   ____ -   ____   ____   ____ -6

4 ____ -6   ____   ____ -6   ____ -   ____ -6   ____   ____ -6

5 ____   ____ -6   ____   ____   ____ -6   ____ -   ____ -6

6 ____   ____   ____ -   ____   ____ -6   ____ -   ____ -6   ____

7 ____ -6   ____   ____ -6   ____ -6   ____   ____ -   ____

8 ____ -6   ____ -6   ____   ____   ____ -6   ____   ____ -

9 ____ -6   ____   ____ -6   ____ -6   ____   ____ -   ____ -6

10 ____   ____ -6   ____ -6   ____   ____   ____ -   ____ -6   ____

C2-3a

(Copy 1)

Figured bass dictation

Shield the answer. Listen to the chord and write the bass note and the figured bass symbol; then uncover the answer and compare your response. Circle incorrect responses. Goal: No more than seven errors. The first frame requires no response.

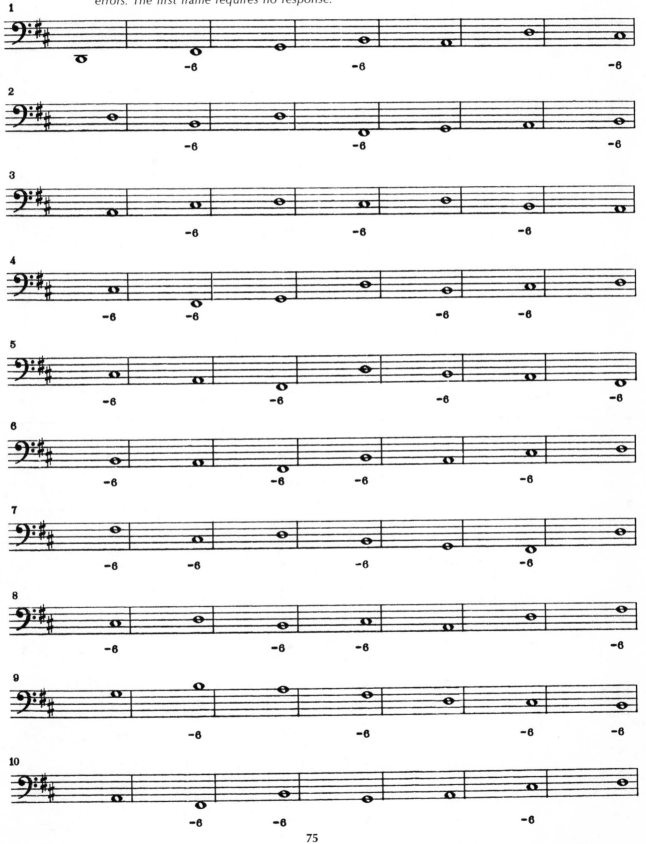

75

Figured bass dictation

Shield the answer. Listen to the chord and write the bass note and the figured bass symbol; then uncover the answer and compare your response. Circle incorrect responses. Goal: No more than seven errors. The first frame requires no response.

C2-3a

(Copy 3)

Figured bass dictation

Shield the answer. Listen to the chord and write the bass note and the figured bass symbol; then uncover the answer and compare your response. Circle incorrect responses. Goal: No more than seven errors. The first frame requires no response.

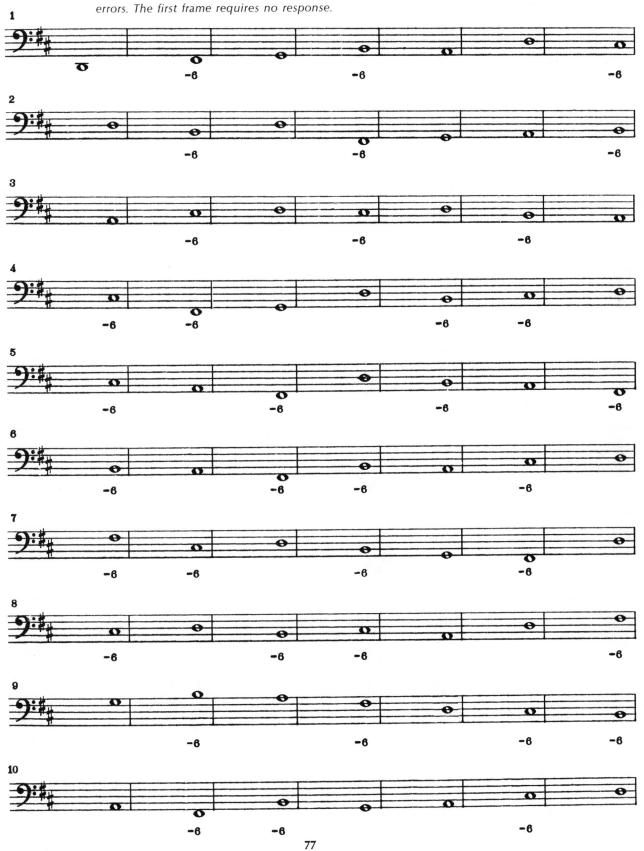

C2-3a

Figured bass dictation

Shield the answer. Listen to the chord and write the bass note and the figured bass symbol; then uncover the answer and compare your response. Circle incorrect responses. Goal: No more than seven errors. The first frame requires no response.

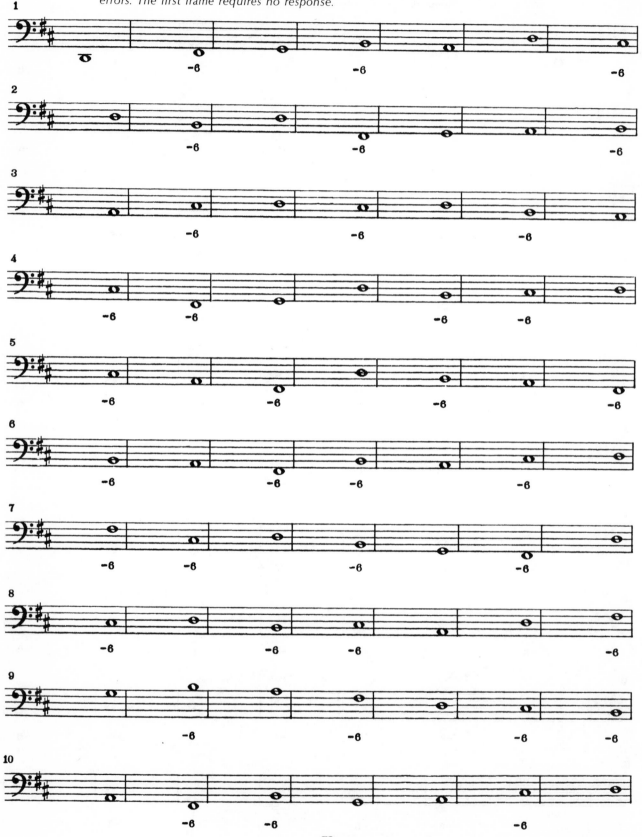

78

C2-3a
(Copy 5)

Figured bass dictation

Shield the answer. Listen to the chord and write the bass note and the figured bass symbol; then uncover the answer and compare your response. Circle incorrect responses. Goal: No more than seven errors. The first frame requires no response.

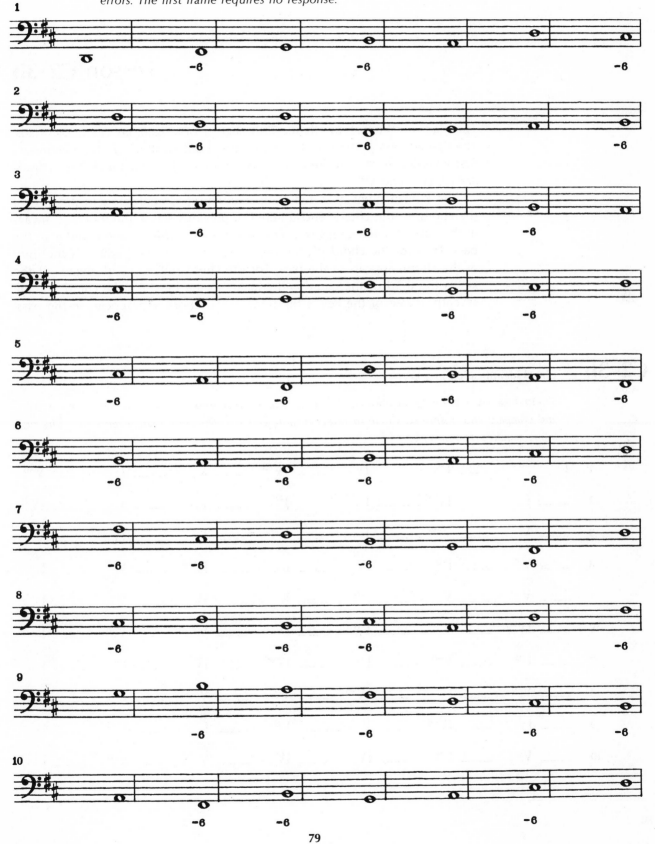

The triads on the first, fourth and fifth degrees of a major key are major triads. The figured bass portion of the composite chord symbols for these chords in first inversion is $^{-6}$, and the composite chord symbols for these three chords are I^{-6}, IV^{-6}, and V^{-6}.

The Roman numeral in the composite chord symbol refers to the *root* of the chord. In the chords encountered in previous series, the root was always in the bass. When a chord is in first inversion, the *third* of the chord is in the bass. Thus for the chord I^{-6}, the third degree of the scale, which is the third of the chord, appears in the bass. For the chord IV^{-6}, the sixth degree of the key is the third of the chord and appears in the bass. For the chord V^{-6}, the seventh degree of the key is the third of the chord and appears in the bass.

C2-3b
(Copy 1)

Chord identification in a key

Shield the answer. Listen to the chord and write the composite chord symbol; then uncover the answer and compare your response. Circle incorrect responses. Goal: No more than seven errors. The first frame requires no response.

1 I ___ I^{-6} ___ IV ___ IV^{-6} ___ V ___ I ___ V^{-6}

2 ___ I ___ IV^{-6} ___ I ___ I^{-6} ___ IV ___ V ___ IV^{-6}

3 ___ V ___ V^{-6} ___ I ___ V^{-6} ___ I ___ IV^{-6} ___ V

4 ___ V^{-6} ___ I^{-6} ___ IV ___ I ___ IV^{-6} ___ V^{-6} ___ I

5 ___ V^{-6} ___ V ___ I^{-6} ___ I ___ IV^{-6} ___ V ___ I^{-6}

6 ___ IV^{-6} ___ V ___ I^{-6} ___ IV^{-6} ___ V ___ V^{-6} ___ I

7 ___ I^{-6} ___ V^{-6} ___ I ___ IV^{-6} ___ IV ___ I^{-6} ___ I

8 ___ V^{-6} ___ I ___ IV^{-6} ___ V^{-6} ___ V ___ I ___ I^{-6}

9 ___ IV ___ IV^{-6} ___ V ___ I^{-6} ___ I ___ V^{-6} ___ IV^{-6}

10 ___ V ___ I^{-6} ___ IV^{-6} ___ IV ___ V ___ V^{-6} ___ I

C2-3b
(Copy 2)

Chord identification in a key

Shield the answer. Listen to the chord and write the composite chord symbol; then uncover the answer and compare your response. Circle incorrect responses. Goal: No more than seven errors. The first frame requires no response.

1 I ____ I^{-6} ____ IV ____ IV^{-6} ____ V ____ I ____ V^{-6}

2 ____ I ____ IV^{-6} ____ I ____ I^{-6} ____ IV ____ V ____ IV^{-6}

3 ____ V ____ V^{-6} ____ I ____ V^{-6} ____ I ____ IV^{-6} ____ V

4 ____ V^{-6} ____ I^{-6} ____ IV ____ I ____ IV^{-6} ____ V^{-6} ____ I

5 ____ V^{-6} ____ V ____ I^{-6} ____ I ____ IV^{-6} ____ V ____ I^{-6}

6 ____ IV^{-6} ____ V ____ I^{-6} ____ IV^{-6} ____ V ____ V^{-6} ____ I

7 ____ I^{-6} ____ V^{-6} ____ I ____ IV^{-6} ____ IV ____ I^{-6} ____ I

8 ____ V^{-6} ____ I ____ IV^{-6} ____ V^{-6} ____ V ____ I ____ I^{-6}

9 ____ IV ____ IV^{-6} ____ V ____ I^{-6} ____ I ____ V^{-6} ____ IV^{-6}

10 ____ V ____ I^{-6} ____ IV^{-6} ____ IV ____ V ____ V^{-6} ____ I

C2-3b
(Copy 3)

Chord identification in a key

Shield the answer. Listen to the chord and write the composite chord symbol; then uncover the answer and compare your response. Circle incorrect responses. Goal: No more than seven errors. The first frame requires no response.

1 I ____ I^{-6} ____ IV ____ IV^{-6} ____ V ____ I ____ V^{-6}

2 ____ I ____ IV^{-6} ____ I ____ I^{-6} ____ IV ____ V ____ IV^{-6}

3 ____ V ____ V^{-6} ____ I ____ V^{-6} ____ I ____ IV^{-6} ____ V

4 ____ V^{-6} ____ I^{-6} ____ IV ____ I ____ IV^{-6} ____ V^{-6} ____ I

5 ____ V^{-6} ____ V ____ I^{-6} ____ I ____ IV^{-6} ____ V ____ I^{-6}

6 ____ IV^{-6} ____ V ____ I^{-6} ____ IV^{-6} ____ V ____ V^{-6} ____ I

7 ____ I^{-6} ____ V^{-6} ____ I ____ IV^{-6} ____ IV ____ I^{-6} ____ I

8 ____ V^{-6} ____ I ____ IV^{-6} ____ V^{-6} ____ V ____ I ____ I^{-6}

9 ____ IV ____ IV^{-6} ____ V ____ I^{-6} ____ I ____ V^{-6} ____ IV^{-6}

10 ____ V ____ I^{-6} ____ IV^{-6} ____ IV ____ V ____ V^{-6} ____ I

C2-3b
(Copy 4)

Chord identification in a key

Shield the answer. Listen to the chord and write the composite chord symbol; then uncover the answer and compare your response. Circle incorrect responses. Goal: No more than seven errors. The first frame requires no response.

1 I   _____ I^{-6} _____ IV   _____ IV^{-6} _____ V   _____ I   _____ V^{-6}

2 _____ I   _____ IV^{-6} _____ I   _____ I^{-6} _____ IV   _____ V   _____ IV^{-6}

3 _____ V   _____ V^{-6} _____ I   _____ V^{-6} _____ I   _____ IV^{-6} _____ V

4 _____ V^{-6} _____ I^{-6} _____ IV   _____ I   _____ IV^{-6} _____ V^{-6} _____ I

5 _____ V^{-6} _____ V   _____ I^{-6} _____ I   _____ IV^{-6} _____ V   _____ I^{-6}

6 _____ IV^{-6} _____ V   _____ I^{-6} _____ IV^{-6} _____ V   _____ V^{-6} _____ I

7 _____ I^{-6} _____ V^{-6} _____ I   _____ IV^{-6} _____ IV   _____ I^{-6} _____ I

8 _____ V^{-6} _____ I   _____ IV^{-6} _____ V^{-6} _____ V   _____ I   _____ I^{-6}

9 _____ IV   _____ IV^{-6} _____ V   _____ I^{-6} _____ I   _____ V^{-6} _____ IV^{-6}

10 _____ V   _____ I^{-6} _____ IV^{-6} _____ IV   _____ V   _____ V^{-6} _____ I

C2-3b
(Copy 5)

Chord identification in a key

Shield the answer. Listen to the chord and write the composite chord symbol; then uncover the answer and compare your response. Circle incorrect responses. Goal: No more than seven errors. The first frame requires no response.

1 I   _____ I^{-6} _____ IV   _____ IV^{-6} _____ V   _____ I   _____ V^{-6}

2 _____ I   _____ IV^{-6} _____ I   _____ I^{-6} _____ IV   _____ V   _____ IV^{-6}

3 _____ V   _____ V^{-6} _____ I   _____ V^{-6} _____ I   _____ IV^{-6} _____ V

4 _____ V^{-6} _____ I^{-6} _____ IV   _____ I   _____ IV^{-6} _____ V^{-6} _____ I

5 _____ V^{-6} _____ V   _____ I^{-6} _____ I   _____ IV^{-6} _____ V   _____ I^{-6}

6 _____ IV^{-6} _____ V   _____ I^{-6} _____ IV^{-6} _____ V   _____ V^{-6} _____ I

7 _____ I^{-6} _____ V^{-6} _____ I   _____ IV^{-6} _____ IV   _____ I^{-6} _____ I

8 _____ V^{-6} _____ I   _____ IV^{-6} _____ V^{-6} _____ V   _____ I   _____ I^{-6}

9 _____ IV   _____ IV^{-6} _____ V   _____ I^{-6} _____ I   _____ V^{-6} _____ IV^{-6}

10 _____ V   _____ I^{-6} _____ IV^{-6} _____ IV   _____ V   _____ V^{-6} _____ I

C2-4a
(Copy 1)

Figured bass dictation

Shield the answer. Listen to the chord and write the bass note and the figured bass symbol; then uncover the answer and compare your response. Circle incorrect responses. Goal: No more than seven errors. The first frame requires no response.

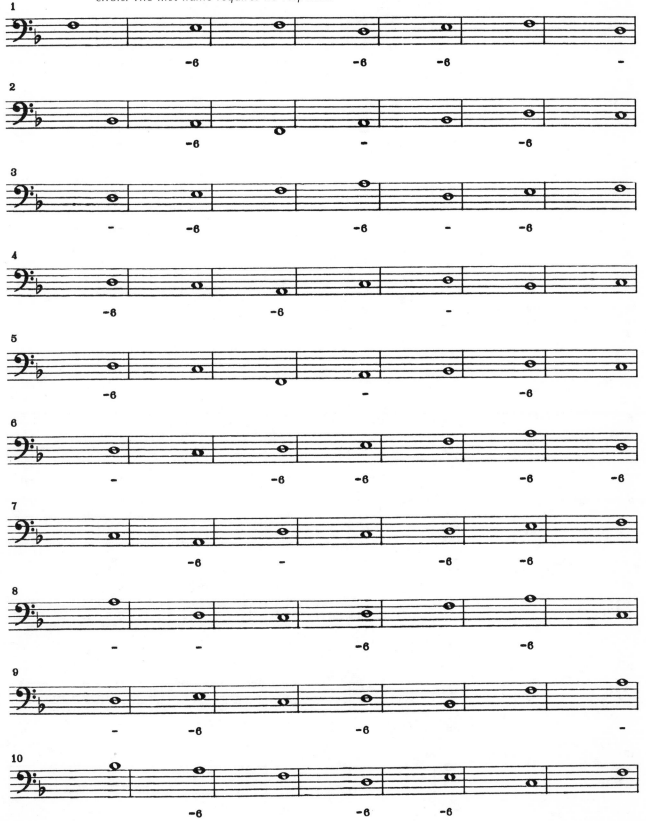

C2-4a

(Copy 2)

Figured bass dictation

Shield the answer. Listen to the chord and write the bass note and the figured bass symbol; then uncover the answer and compare your response. Circle incorrect responses. Goal: No more than seven errors. The first frame requires no response.

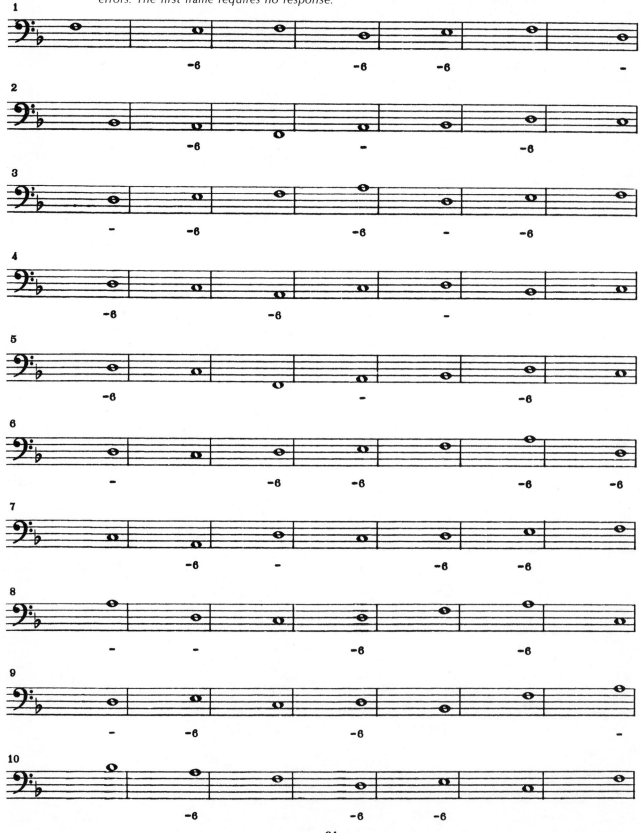

C2-4a

Figured bass dictation

Shield the answer. Listen to the chord and write the bass note and the figured bass symbol; then uncover the answer and compare your response. Circle incorrect responses. Goal: No more than seven errors. The first frame requires no response.

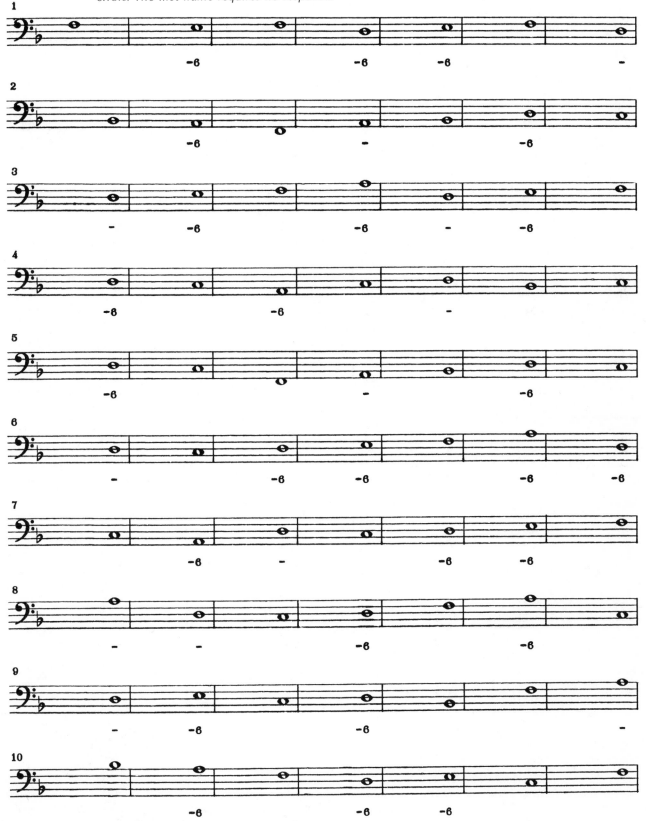

85

C2-4a

Figured bass dictation

Shield the answer. Listen to the chord and write the bass note and the figured bass symbol; then uncover the answer and compare your response. Circle incorrect responses. Goal: No more than seven errors. The first frame requires no response.

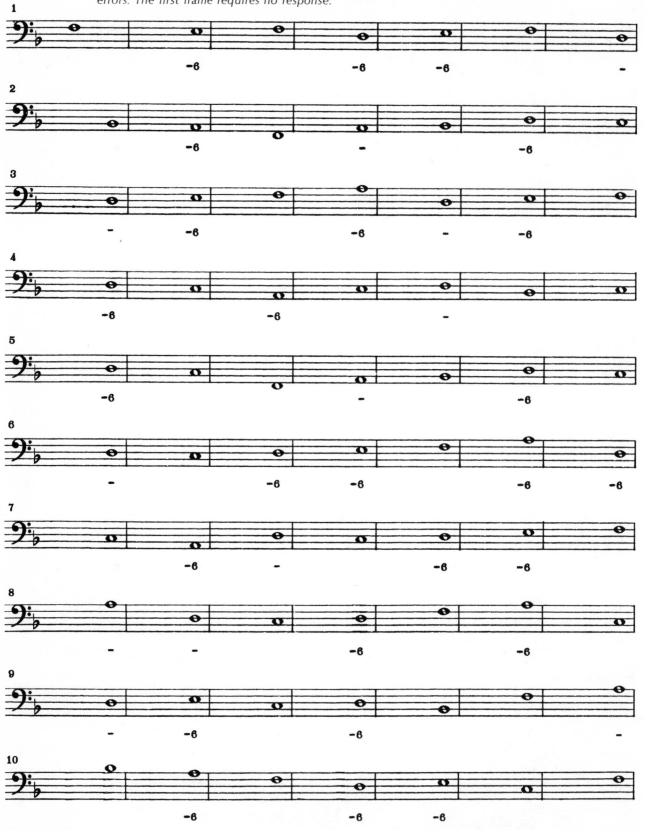

C2-4a
(Copy 5)

Figured bass dictation

Shield the answer. Listen to the chord and write the bass note and the figured bass symbol; then uncover the answer and compare your response. Circle incorrect responses. Goal: No more than seven errors. The first frame requires no response.

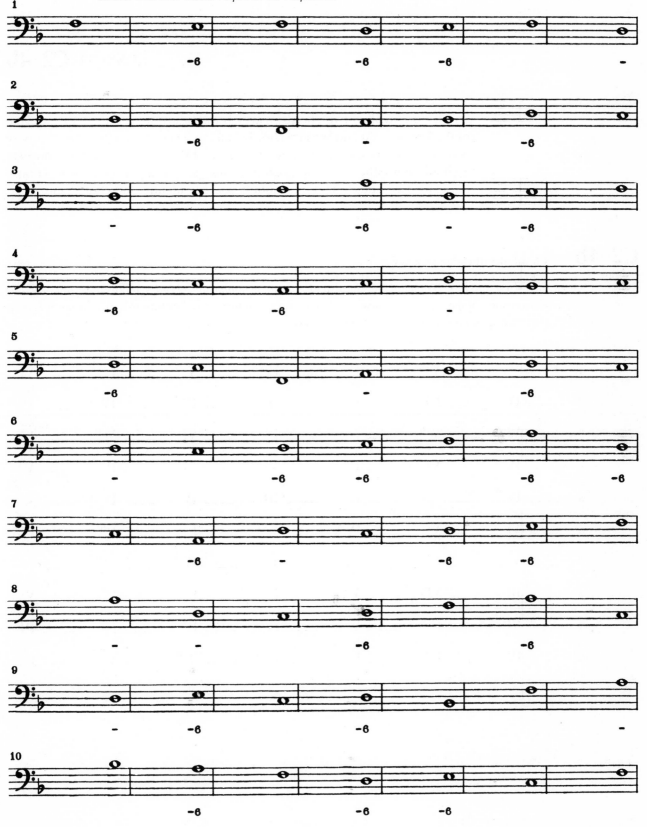

This lesson involves two chords in which the bass note is on the sixth degree of the key—the VI⁻ and the IV⁻⁶ chords—and two chords in which the bass note is on the third degree of the key—the III⁻ and the I⁻⁶ chords. When you hear a chord with either of these degrees in the bass, you will be able to choose the correct composite chord symbol if you can identify the chord type.

C2-4b
(Copy 1)

Chord identification in a key

Shield the answer. Listen to the chord and write the composite chord symbol; then uncover the answer and compare your response. Circle incorrect responses. Goal: No more than seven errors. The first frame requires no response. After you have done this lesson, take Test C2.

1	I	___ V^{-6}	___ I	___ IV^{-6}	___ V^{-6}	___ I	___ VI^-
2	___ IV	___ I^{-6}	___ I	___ III^-	___ IV	___ IV^{-6}	___ V
3	___ VI^-	___ V^{-6}	___ I	___ I^{-6}	___ VI^-	___ V^{-6}	___ I
4	___ IV^{-6}	___ V	___ I^{-6}	___ V	___ VI^-	___ IV	___ V
5	___ IV^{-6}	___ V	___ I	___ III^-	___ IV	___ IV^{-6}	___ V
6	___ VI^-	___ V	___ IV^{-6}	___ V^{-6}	___ I	___ I^{-6}	___ IV^{-6}
7	___ V	___ I^{-6}	___ VI^-	___ V	___ IV^{-6}	___ V^{-6}	___ I
8	___ III^-	___ VI^-	___ V	___ IV^{-6}	___ I	___ I^{-6}	___ V
9	___ VI^-	___ V^{-6}	___ V	___ IV^{-6}	___ IV	___ I	___ III^-
10	___ IV	___ I^{-6}	___ I	___ IV^{-6}	___ V^{-6}	___ V	___ I

C2-4b
(Copy 2)

Chord identification in a key

Shield the answer. Listen to the chord and write the composite chord symbol; then uncover the answer and compare your response. Circle incorrect responses. Goal: No more than seven errors. The first frame requires no response. After you have done this lesson, take Test C2.

1 I ____ V^{-6} ____ I ____ IV^{-6} ____ V^{-6} ____ I ____ VI^{-}

2 ____ IV ____ I^{-6} ____ I ____ III^{-} ____ IV ____ IV^{-6} ____ V

3 ____ VI^{-} ____ V^{-6} ____ I ____ I^{-6} ____ VI^{-} ____ V^{-6} ____ I

4 ____ IV^{-6} ____ V ____ I^{-6} ____ V ____ VI^{-} ____ IV ____ V

5 ____ IV^{-6} ____ V ____ I ____ III^{-} ____ IV ____ IV^{-6} ____ V

6 ____ VI^{-} ____ V ____ IV^{-6} ____ V^{-6} ____ I ____ I^{-6} ____ IV^{-6}

7 ____ V ____ I^{-6} ____ VI^{-} ____ V ____ IV^{-6} ____ V^{-6} ____ I

8 ____ III^{-} ____ VI^{-} ____ V ____ IV^{-6} ____ I ____ I^{-6} ____ V

9 ____ VI^{-} ____ V^{-6} ____ V ____ IV^{-6} ____ IV ____ I ____ III^{-}

10 ____ IV ____ I^{-6} ____ I ____ IV^{-6} ____ V^{-6} ____ V ____ I

C2-4b
(Copy 3)

Chord identification in a key

Shield the answer. Listen to the chord and write the composite chord symbol; then uncover the answer and compare your response. Circle incorrect responses. Goal: No more than seven errors. The first frame requires no response. After you have done this lesson, take Test C2.

1 I ____ V^{-6} ____ I ____ IV^{-6} ____ V^{-6} ____ I ____ VI^{-}

2 ____ IV ____ I^{-6} ____ I ____ III^{-} ____ IV ____ IV^{-6} ____ V

3 ____ VI^{-} ____ V^{-6} ____ I ____ I^{-6} ____ VI^{-} ____ V^{-6} ____ I

4 ____ IV^{-6} ____ V ____ I^{-6} ____ V ____ VI^{-} ____ IV ____ V

5 ____ IV^{-6} ____ V ____ I ____ III^{-} ____ IV ____ IV^{-6} ____ V

6 ____ VI^{-} ____ V ____ IV^{-6} ____ V^{-6} ____ I ____ I^{-6} ____ IV^{-6}

7 ____ V ____ I^{-6} ____ VI^{-} ____ V ____ IV^{-6} ____ V^{-6} ____ I

8 ____ III^{-} ____ VI^{-} ____ V ____ IV^{-6} ____ I ____ I^{-6} ____ V

9 ____ VI^{-} ____ V^{-6} ____ V ____ IV^{-6} ____ IV ____ I ____ III^{-}

10 ____ IV ____ I^{-6} ____ I ____ IV^{-6} ____ V^{-6} ____ V ____ I

C2–4b
(Copy 4)

Chord identification in a key

Shield the answer. Listen to the chord and write the composite chord symbol; then uncover the answer and compare your response. Circle incorrect responses. Goal: No more than seven errors. The first frame requires no response. After you have done this lesson, take Test C2.

1 I   ___ V^{-6} ___ I   ___ IV^{-6} ___ V^{-6} ___ I   ___ VI^-

2 ___ IV ___ I^{-6} ___ I   ___ III^- ___ IV ___ IV^{-6} ___ V

3 ___ VI^- ___ V^{-6} ___ I   ___ I^{-6} ___ VI^- ___ V^{-6} ___ I

4 ___ IV^{-6} ___ V ___ I^{-6} ___ V ___ VI^- ___ IV ___ V

5 ___ IV^{-6} ___ V ___ I   ___ III^- ___ IV ___ IV^{-6} ___ V

6 ___ VI^- ___ V ___ IV^{-6} ___ V^{-6} ___ I   ___ I^{-6} ___ IV^{-6}

7 ___ V ___ I^{-6} ___ VI^- ___ V ___ IV^{-6} ___ V^{-6} ___ I

8 ___ III^- ___ VI^- ___ V ___ IV^{-6} ___ I   ___ I^{-6} ___ V

9 ___ VI^- ___ V^{-6} ___ V ___ IV^{-6} ___ IV ___ I   ___ III^-

10 ___ IV ___ I^{-6} ___ I   ___ IV^{-6} ___ V^{-6} ___ V ___ I

C2–4b
(Copy 5)

Chord identification in a key

Shield the answer. Listen to the chord and write the composite chord symbol; then uncover the answer and compare your response. Circle incorrect responses. Goal: No more than seven errors. The first frame requires no response. After you have done this lesson, take Test C2.

1 I   ___ V^{-6} ___ I   ___ IV^{-6} ___ V^{-6} ___ I   ___ VI^-

2 ___ IV ___ I^{-6} ___ I   ___ III^- ___ IV ___ IV^{-6} ___ V

3 ___ VI^- ___ V^{-6} ___ I   ___ I^{-6} ___ VI^- ___ V^{-6} ___ I

4 ___ IV^{-6} ___ V ___ I^{-6} ___ V ___ VI^- ___ IV ___ V

5 ___ IV^{-6} ___ V ___ I   ___ III^- ___ IV ___ IV^{-6} ___ V

6 ___ VI^- ___ V ___ IV^{-6} ___ V^{-6} ___ I   ___ I^{-6} ___ IV^{-6}

7 ___ V ___ I^{-6} ___ VI^- ___ V ___ IV^{-6} ___ V^{-6} ___ I

8 ___ III^- ___ VI^- ___ V ___ IV^{-6} ___ I   ___ I^{-6} ___ V

9 ___ VI^- ___ V^{-6} ___ V ___ IV^{-6} ___ IV ___ I   ___ III^-

10 ___ IV ___ I^{-6} ___ I   ___ IV^{-6} ___ V^{-6} ___ V ___ I

Minor Triads in First Inversion   SERIES C3

In this series, the minor triad in first inversion is introduced. The upper tones of this chord are at the intervals of a major sixth and a major third above the bass.

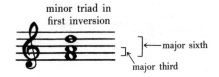

In addition to minor triads in first inversion, this series will involve minor triads in root position and major triads in root position.

When you have done this series, take Test C3 which includes sections on each of the four kinds of lessons found in this series.

C3-1a

(Copy 1)

Chord dictation

Shield the answer. Listen to the chord and notate the upper tones above the given note; then uncover the answer and compare your response. Circle incorrect responses. Goal: No more than seven errors.

C3-1a
(Copy 2)

Chord dictation

Shield the answer. Listen to the chord and notate the upper tones above the given note; then uncover the answer and compare your response. Circle incorrect responses. Goal: No more than seven errors.

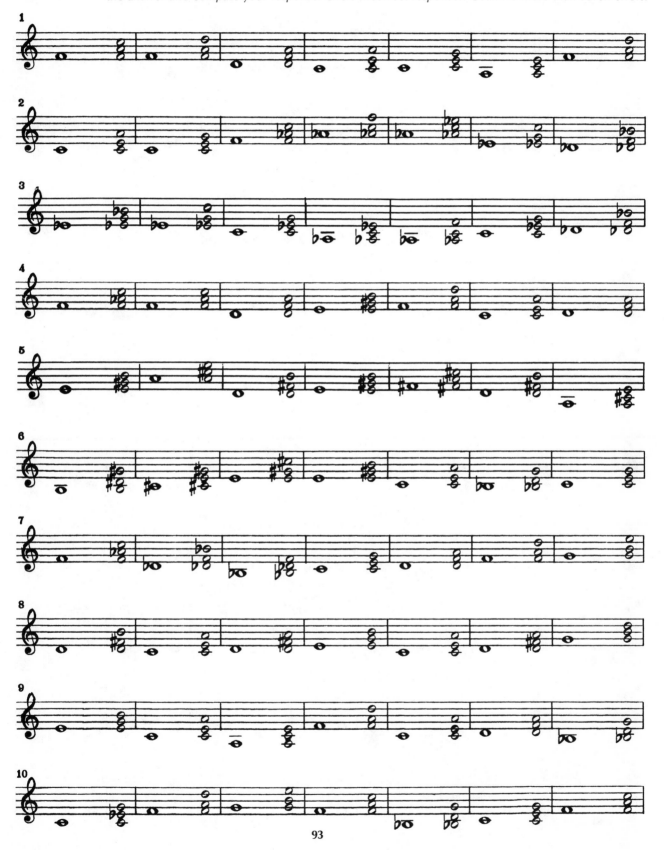

C3-1a
(Copy 3)

Chord dictation

Shield the answer. Listen to the chord and notate the upper tones above the given note; then uncover the answer and compare your response. Circle incorrect responses. Goal: No more than seven errors.

94

C3-1a

(Copy 4)

Chord dictation

Shield the answer. Listen to the chord and notate the upper tones above the given note; then uncover the answer and compare your response. Circle incorrect responses. Goal: No more than seven errors.

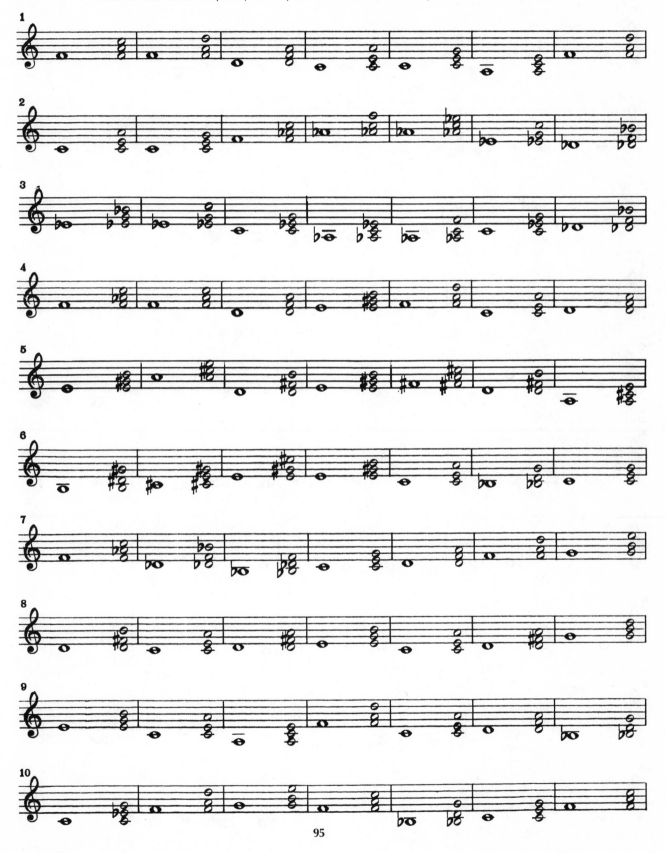

95

C3-1a
(Copy 5)

Chord dictation

Shield the answer. Listen to the chord and notate the upper tones above the given note; then uncover the answer and compare your response. Circle incorrect responses. Goal: No more than seven errors.

96

Lesson **C3-1b**

In the minor triad in first inversion, the intervals between the upper tones and the bass are a major sixth and a major third. The complete figured bass symbol is $^6_3$, and the abbreviated form is ^{6}. Remember that a qualifying minus sign in the figured bass symbol refers to the interval above the bass, and not to the chord type. Thus we may have a figured bass symbol without a minus sign standing for a minor triad. The symbol for the minor triad in first inversion does not contain a minus sign and the symbol for the major triad in first inversion does: thus ^{6} refers to the minor triad in first inversion, and $^{-6}$ refers to the major triad in first inversion.

C3-1b
(Copy 1)

Chord identification

Shield the answer. Listen to the chord and write the figured bass symbol (⁻, ⁶, or blank); then uncover the answer and compare your response. Circle incorrect responses. Goal: No more than seven errors.

#								
1	___	___ 6	___ -	___ 6	___	___ -	___ 6	
2	___ 6	___	___ -	___ 6	___	___ 6	___ 6	
3	___	___ 6	___ -	___	___ 6	___ -	___ 6	
4	___ -	___	___ -	___	___ 6	___ 6	___ -	
5	___	___	___ 6	___	___ -	___ 6	___	
6	___ 6	___ -	___ 6	___	___ 6	___ 6	___	
7	___ -	___ 6	___ -	___	___ -	___ 6	___ 6	
8	___ 6	___ 6	___	___ -	___ 6	___		
9	___ -	___ 6	___ -	___ 6	___ 6	___ -	___ 6	
10	___ -	___ 6	___ 6	___	___ 6	___		

97

C3-1b

Chord identification

Shield the answer. Listen to the chord and write the figured bass symbol (⁻, ⁶, or blank); then uncover the answer and compare your response. Circle incorrect responses. Goal: No more than seven errors.

1   ___   ___⁶   ⁻___   ___⁶   ___   ⁻___   ___⁶

2   ___⁶   ___   ⁻___   ___⁶   ___   ___⁶   ___⁶

3   ___   ___⁶   ⁻___   ___   ___⁶   ⁻___   ___⁶

4   ___   ⁻___   ___   ⁻___   ___   ___⁶   ___⁶   ___⁻

5   ___   ___   ___⁶   ___   ⁻___   ___⁶

6   ___⁶   ⁻___   ___⁶   ___   ___⁶   ___⁶

7   ___⁻   ___⁶   ⁻___   ___   ⁻___   ___⁶   ___⁶

8   ___⁶   ___⁶   ___   ⁻___   ___⁶

9   ___⁻   ___⁶   ⁻___   ___⁶   ___⁶   ⁻___   ___⁶

10   ___⁻   ___⁶   ___⁶   ___   ___⁶   ___   ___

C3-1b

Chord identification

Shield the answer. Listen to the chord and write the figured bass symbol (⁻, ⁶, or blank); then uncover the answer and compare your response. Circle incorrect responses. Goal: No more than seven errors.

1   ___   ___⁶   ⁻___   ___⁶   ___   ⁻___   ___⁶

2   ___⁶   ___   ⁻___   ___⁶   ___   ___⁶   ___⁶

3   ___   ___⁶   ⁻___   ___   ___⁶   ⁻___   ___⁶

4   ___   ⁻___   ___   ⁻___   ___   ___⁶   ___⁶   ___⁻

5   ___   ___   ___⁶   ___   ⁻___   ___⁶

6   ___⁶   ⁻___   ___⁶   ___   ___⁶   ___⁶

7   ___⁻   ___⁶   ⁻___   ___   ⁻___   ___⁶   ___⁶

8   ___⁶   ___⁶   ___   ⁻___   ___⁶

9   ___⁻   ___⁶   ⁻___   ___⁶   ___⁶   ⁻___   ___⁶

10   ___⁻   ___⁶   ___⁶   ___   ___⁶   ___

C3-1b

Chord identification

Shield the answer. Listen to the chord and write the figured bass symbol (⁻, ⁶, or blank); then uncover the answer and compare your response. Circle incorrect responses. Goal: No more than seven errors.

1 ___   ___ 6   ___ -   ___ 6   ___   ___ -   ___ 6

2 ___ 6   ___   ___   - ___   ___ 6   ___   ___ 6   ___ 6

3 ___   ___   6 ___   - ___   ___   ___ 6   - ___   ___ 6

4 ___ -   ___   ___   - ___   ___   ___ 6   ___ 6   ___ -

5 ___   ___   ___   6 ___   ___   ___ -   ___ 6

6 ___ 6   ___   - ___   ___ 6   ___   ___ 6   ___ 6   ___

7 ___ -   ___   6 ___   - ___   ___   ___ -   ___ 6   ___ 6

8 ___ 6   ___ 6   ___   ___ -   ___ 6   ___

9 ___ -   ___   6 ___   - ___   6 ___   ___ 6   ___ -   ___ 6

10 ___ -   ___   6 ___   6 ___   ___   ___ 6   ___   ___

C3-1b

Chord identification

Shield the answer. Listen to the chord and write the figured bass symbol (⁻, ⁶, or blank); then uncover the answer and compare your response. Circle incorrect responses. Goal: No more than seven errors.

1 ___   ___ 6   ___ -   ___ 6   ___   ___   ___ -   ___ 6

2 ___ 6   ___   ___   - ___   ___ 6   ___   ___ 6   ___ 6

3 ___   ___   6 ___   - ___   ___   ___ 6   ___ -   ___ 6

4 ___ -   ___   ___   - ___   ___   ___ 6   ___ 6   ___ -

5 ___   ___   ___   6 ___   ___   ___ -   ___ 6

6 ___ 6   ___   - ___   ___ 6   ___   ___ 6   ___ 6   ___

7 ___ -   ___   6 ___   - ___   ___   ___ -   ___ 6   ___ 6

8 ___ 6   ___ 6   ___   ___ -   ___ 6   ___

9 ___ -   ___   6 ___   - ___   6 ___   ___ 6   ___ -   ___ 6

10 ___ -   ___   6 ___   6 ___   ___   ___ 6   ___   ___

C3-2
(Copy 1)

Chord identification

Shield the answer. Listen to the chord and write the figured bass symbol (⁻, ⁶, or blank); then uncover the answer and compare your response. Circle incorrect responses. Goal: No more than seven errors.

1 ____ ⁻ ____ ⁶ ____ ⁻ ____ ⁶ ____ ____ ____ ⁻ ____

2 ____ ⁶ ____ ____ ⁶ ____ ____ ____ ⁶ ____ ⁶ ____

3 ____ ____ ⁶ ____ ____ ⁶ ____ ⁶ ____ ____ ⁶

4 ____ ⁶ ____ ____ ⁶ ____ ⁻ ____ ⁶ ____ ⁻ ____ ⁶

5 ____ ____ ⁶ ____ ⁻ ____ ____ ____ ⁶ ____ ⁶

6 ____ ⁻ ____ ⁶ ____ ____ ⁻ ____ ⁶ ____ ⁶ ____

7 ____ ____ ____ ⁶ ____ ____ ⁻ ____ ⁶ ____

8 ____ ⁶ ____ ⁻ ____ ⁶ ____ ⁶ ____ ⁻ ____ ____ ⁻

9 ____ ⁶ ____ ⁶ ____ ⁻ ____ ⁶ ____ ⁶ ____ ____

10 ____ ⁻ ____ ⁶ ____ ____ ____ ⁶ ____ ⁶ ____ ____

C3-2
(Copy 2)

Chord identification

Shield the answer. Listen to the chord and write the figured bass symbol (⁻, ⁶, or blank); then uncover the answer and compare your response. Circle incorrect responses. Goal: No more than seven errors.

1 ____ ⁻ ____ ⁶ ____ ⁻ ____ ⁶ ____ ____ ____ ⁻ ____

2 ____ ⁶ ____ ____ ⁶ ____ ____ ____ ⁶ ____ ⁶ ____

3 ____ ____ ⁶ ____ ____ ⁶ ____ ⁶ ____ ____ ⁶

4 ____ ⁶ ____ ____ ⁶ ____ ⁻ ____ ⁶ ____ ⁻ ____ ⁶

5 ____ ____ ⁶ ____ ⁻ ____ ____ ____ ⁶ ____ ⁶

6 ____ ⁻ ____ ⁶ ____ ____ ⁻ ____ ⁶ ____ ⁶ ____

7 ____ ____ ____ ⁶ ____ ____ ⁻ ____ ⁶ ____

8 ____ ⁶ ____ ⁻ ____ ⁶ ____ ⁶ ____ ⁻ ____ ____ ⁻

9 ____ ⁶ ____ ⁶ ____ ⁻ ____ ⁶ ____ ⁶ ____ ____

10 ____ ⁻ ____ ⁶ ____ ____ ____ ⁶ ____ ⁶ ____ ____

C3-2

(Copy 3)

Chord identification

Shield the answer. Listen to the chord and write the figured bass symbol (⁻, ⁶, or blank); then uncover the answer and compare your response. Circle incorrect responses. Goal: No more than seven errors.

1 ___ ⁻ ___ ⁶ ___ ⁻ ___ ⁶ ___ ___ ⁻ ___

2 ___ ⁶ ___ ___ ⁶ ___ ___ ⁶ ___ ⁶ ___

3 ___ ___ ⁶ ___ ___ ⁶ ___ ⁶ ___ ___ ⁶

4 ___ ⁶ ___ ___ ⁶ ___ ⁻ ___ ⁶ ___ ⁻ ___ ⁶

5 ___ ___ ⁶ ___ ⁻ ___ ___ ___ ⁶ ___ ⁶

6 ___ ⁻ ___ ⁶ ___ ___ ⁻ ___ ⁶ ___ ⁶ ___

7 ___ ___ ___ ⁶ ___ ___ ___ ⁻ ___ ⁶ ___

8 ___ ⁶ ___ ⁻ ___ ⁶ ___ ⁶ ___ ⁻ ___ ___ ⁻

9 ___ ⁶ ___ ⁶ ___ ⁻ ___ ⁶ ___ ⁶ ___ ___

10 ___ ⁻ ___ ⁶ ___ ___ ___ ⁶ ___ ⁶ ___ ___

C3-2

(Copy 4)

Chord identification

Shield the answer. Listen to the chord and write the figured bass symbol (⁻, ⁶, or blank); then uncover the answer and compare your response. Circle incorrect responses. Goal: No more than seven errors.

1 ___ ⁻ ___ ⁶ ___ ⁻ ___ ⁶ ___ ___ ⁻ ___

2 ___ ⁶ ___ ___ ⁶ ___ ___ ⁶ ___ ⁶ ___

3 ___ ___ ⁶ ___ ___ ⁶ ___ ⁶ ___ ___ ⁶

4 ___ ⁶ ___ ___ ⁶ ___ ⁻ ___ ⁶ ___ ⁻ ___ ⁶

5 ___ ___ ⁶ ___ ⁻ ___ ___ ___ ⁶ ___ ⁶

6 ___ ⁻ ___ ⁶ ___ ___ ⁻ ___ ⁶ ___ ⁶ ___

7 ___ ___ ___ ⁶ ___ ___ ___ ⁻ ___ ⁶ ___

8 ___ ⁶ ___ ⁻ ___ ⁶ ___ ⁶ ___ ⁻ ___ ___ ⁻

9 ___ ⁶ ___ ⁶ ___ ⁻ ___ ⁶ ___ ⁶ ___ ___

10 ___ ⁻ ___ ⁶ ___ ___ ___ ⁶ ___ ⁶ ___ ___

C3-2
(Copy 5)

Chord identification

Shield the answer. Listen to the chord and write the figured bass symbol (⁻, ⁶, or blank); then uncover the answer and compare your response. Circle incorrect responses. Goal: No more than seven errors.

1 ____ ⁻ ____ ⁶ ____ ⁻ ____ ⁶ ____   ____ ⁻ ____

2 ____ ⁶ ____   ____ ⁶ ____   ____ ⁶ ____ ⁶ ____

3 ____   ____ ⁶ ____   ____ ⁶ ____ ⁶ ____   ____ ⁶

4 ____ ⁶ ____   ____ ⁶ ____ ⁻ ____ ⁶ ____ ⁻ ____ ⁶

5 ____   ____ ⁶ ____ ⁻ ____   ____   ____ ⁶ ____ ⁶

6 ____ ⁻ ____ ⁶ ____   ____ ⁻ ____ ⁶ ____ ⁶ ____

7 ____   ____   ____ ⁶ ____   ____ ⁻ ____ ⁶ ____

8 ____ ⁶ ____ ⁻ ____ ⁶ ____ ⁶ ____ ⁻ ____   ____ ⁻

9 ____ ⁶ ____ ⁶ ____ ⁻ ____ ⁶ ____ ⁶ ____   ____

10 ____ ⁻ ____ ⁶ ____   ____ ⁶ ____ ⁶ ____   ____

102

C3-3a
(Copy 1)

Figured bass dictation

Shield the answer. Listen to the chord and write the bass note and the figured bass symbol; then uncover the answer and compare your response. Circle incorrect responses. Goal: No more than seven errors. The first frame requires no response.

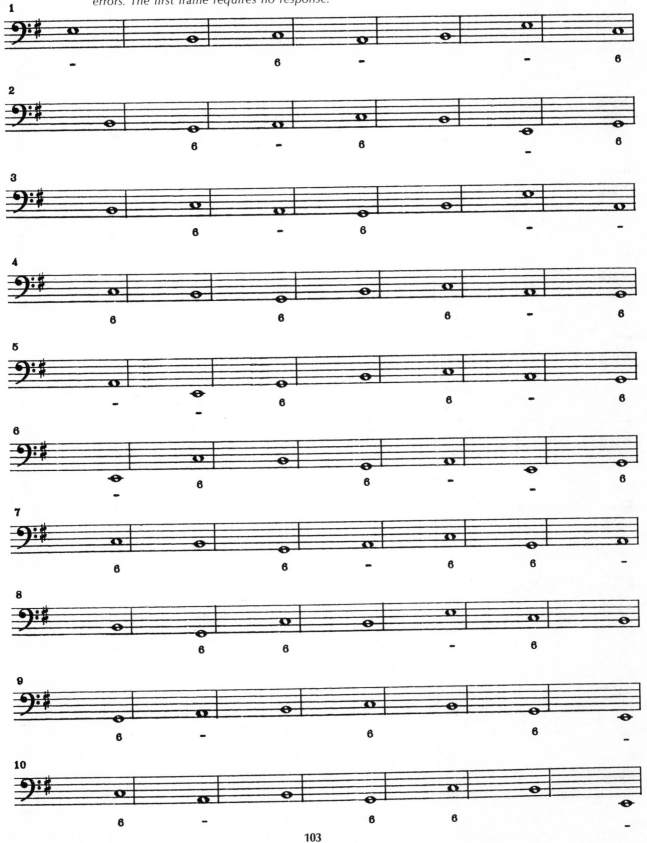

C3-3a
(Copy 2)

Figured bass dictation

Shield the answer. Listen to the chord and write the bass note and the figured bass symbol; then uncover the answer and compare your response. Circle incorrect responses. Goal: No more than seven errors. The first frame requires no response.

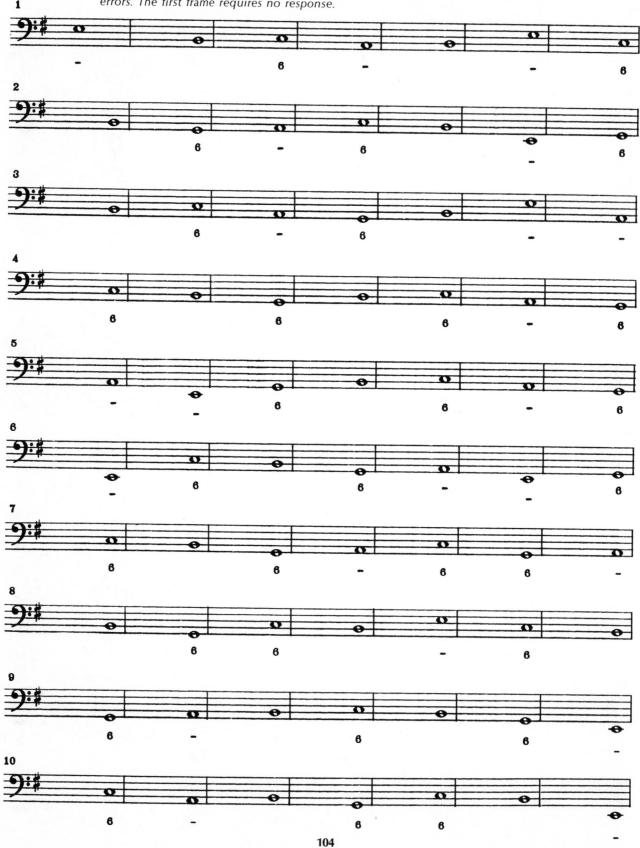

04

C3-3a
(Copy 3)

Figured bass dictation

Shield the answer. Listen to the chord and write the bass note and the figured bass symbol; then uncover the answer and compare your response. Circle incorrect responses. Goal: No more than seven errors. The first frame requires no response.

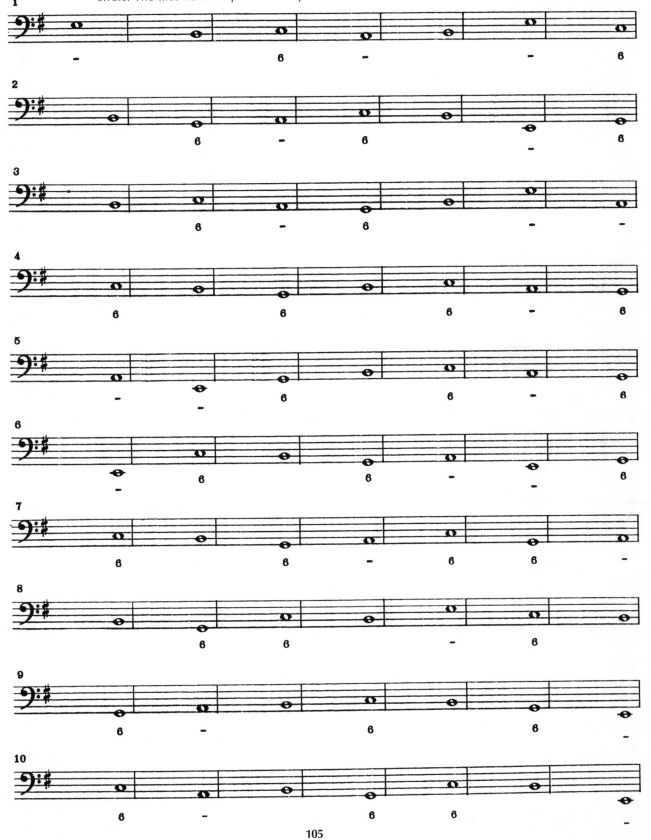

C3-3a

Figured bass dictation

Shield the answer. Listen to the chord and write the bass note and the figured bass symbol; then uncover the answer and compare your response. Circle incorrect responses. Goal: No more than seven errors. The first frame requires no response.

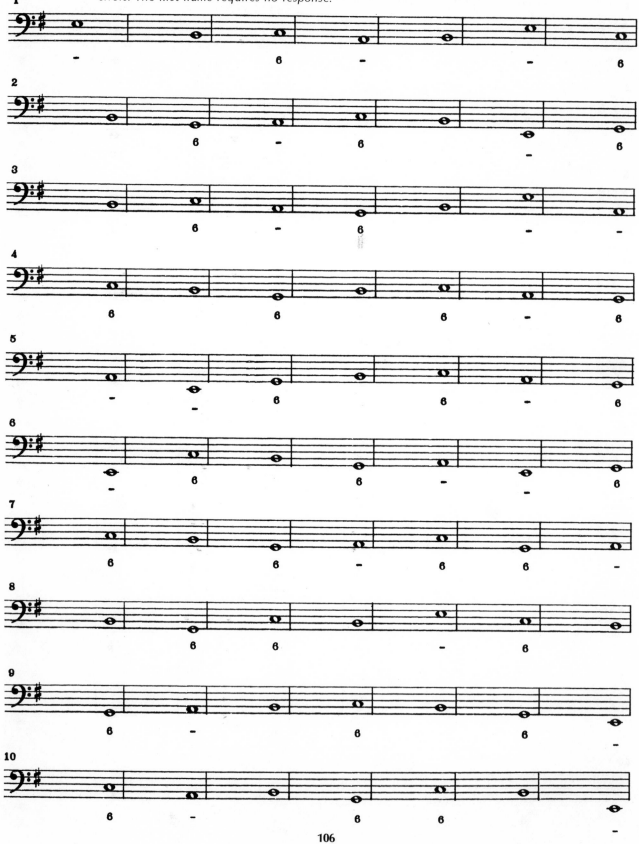

C3-3a
(Copy 5)

Figured bass dictation

Shield the answer. Listen to the chord and write the bass note and the figured bass symbol; then uncover the answer and compare your response. Circle incorrect responses. Goal: No more than seven errors. The first frame requires no response.

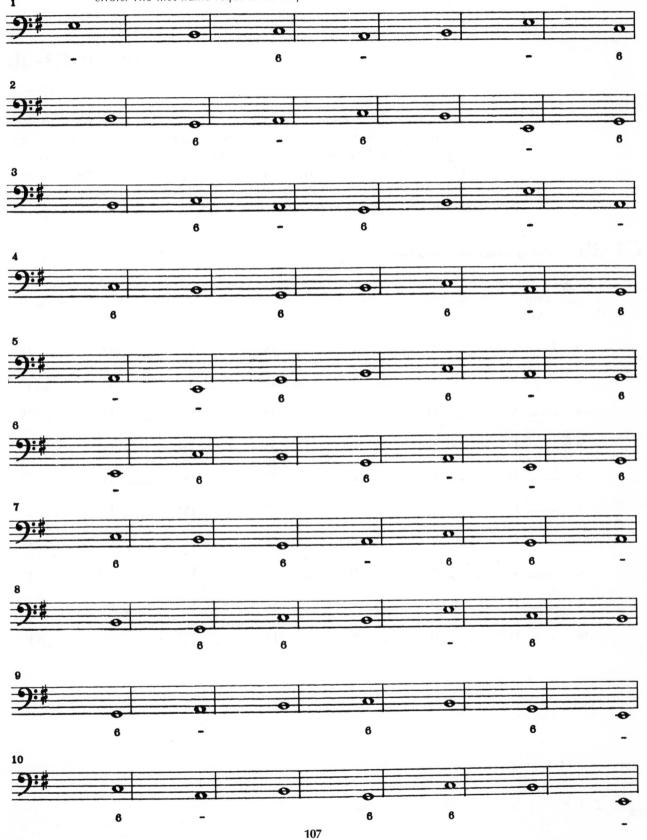

Lesson **C3–3b**

The triads on the first and fourth degrees of a minor key are minor triads. The figured bass portion of the composite chord symbols for these chords in first inversion is ^{6}, and the composite chord symbols for these two chords are I^6 and IV^6. Remember that in a major key these are major triads and the composite chord symbols are I^{-6} and IV^{-6}. Hence we find the chords I^6 and IV^6 in a minor key; in a major key we find I^{-6} and IV^{-6}.

C3–3b
(Copy 1)

Chord identification in a key

Shield the answer. Listen to the chord and write the composite chord symbol; then uncover the answer and compare your response. Circle incorrect responses. Goal: No more than seven errors. The first frame requires no response.

1	I^-	___ V	___ IV^6	___ IV^-	___ V	___ I^-	___ IV^6
2	___ V	___ I^6	___ IV^-	___ IV^6	___ V	___ I^-	___ I^6
3	___ V	___ IV^6	___ IV^-	___ I^6	___ V	___ I^-	___ IV^-
4	___ IV^6	___ V	___ I^6	___ V	___ IV^6	___ IV^-	___ I^6
5	___ IV^-	___ I^-	___ I^6	___ V	___ IV^6	___ IV^-	___ I^6
6	___ I^-	___ IV^6	___ V	___ I^6	___ IV^-	___ I^-	___ I^6
7	___ IV^6	___ V	___ I^6	___ IV^-	___ IV^6	___ I^6	___ IV^-
8	___ V	___ I^6	___ IV^6	___ V	___ I^-	___ IV^6	___ V
9	___ I^6	___ IV^-	___ V	___ IV^6	___ V	___ I^6	___ I^-
10	___ IV^6	___ IV^-	___ V	___ I^6	___ IV^6	___ V	___ I^-

C3-3b
(Copy 2)

Chord identification in a key

Shield the answer. Listen to the chord and write the composite chord symbol; then uncover the answer and compare your response. Circle incorrect responses. Goal: No more than seven errors. The first frame requires no response.

1   I⁻   ___ V   ___ IV⁶   ___ IV⁻   ___ V   ___ I⁻   ___ IV⁶

2   ___ V   ___ I⁶   ___ IV⁻   ___ IV⁶   ___ V   ___ I⁻   ___ I⁶

3   ___ V   ___ IV⁶   ___ IV⁻   ___ I⁶   ___ V   ___ I⁻   ___ IV⁻

4   ___ IV⁶   ___ V   ___ I⁶   ___ V   ___ IV⁶   ___ IV⁻   ___ I⁶

5   ___ IV⁻   ___ I⁻   ___ I⁶   ___ V   ___ IV⁶   ___ IV⁻   ___ I⁶

6   ___ I⁻   ___ IV⁶   ___ V   ___ I⁶   ___ IV⁻   ___ I⁻   ___ I⁶

7   ___ IV⁶   ___ V   ___ I⁶   ___ IV⁻   ___ IV⁶   ___ I⁶   ___ IV⁻

8   ___ V   ___ I⁶   ___ IV⁶   ___ V   ___ I⁻   ___ IV⁶   ___ V

9   ___ I⁶   ___ IV⁻   ___ V   ___ IV⁶   ___ V   ___ I⁶   ___ I⁻

10   ___ IV⁶   ___ IV⁻   ___ V   ___ I⁶   ___ IV⁶   ___ V   ___ I⁻

C3-3b
(Copy 3)

Chord identification in a key

Shield the answer. Listen to the chord and write the composite chord symbol; then uncover the answer and compare your response. Circle incorrect responses. Goal: No more than seven errors. The first frame requires no response.

1   I⁻   ___ V   ___ IV⁶   ___ IV⁻   ___ V   ___ I⁻   ___ IV⁶

2   ___ V   ___ I⁶   ___ IV⁻   ___ IV⁶   ___ V   ___ I⁻   ___ I⁶

3   ___ V   ___ IV⁶   ___ IV⁻   ___ I⁶   ___ V   ___ I⁻   ___ IV⁻

4   ___ IV⁶   ___ V   ___ I⁶   ___ V   ___ IV⁶   ___ IV⁻   ___ I⁶

5   ___ IV⁻   ___ I⁻   ___ I⁶   ___ V   ___ IV⁶   ___ IV⁻   ___ I⁶

6   ___ I⁻   ___ IV⁶   ___ V   ___ I⁶   ___ IV⁻   ___ I⁻   ___ I⁶

7   ___ IV⁶   ___ V   ___ I⁶   ___ IV⁻   ___ IV⁶   ___ I⁶   ___ IV⁻

8   ___ V   ___ I⁶   ___ IV⁶   ___ V   ___ I⁻   ___ IV⁶   ___ V

9   ___ I⁶   ___ IV⁻   ___ V   ___ IV⁶   ___ V   ___ I⁶   ___ I⁻

10   ___ IV⁶   ___ IV⁻   ___ V   ___ I⁶   ___ IV⁶   ___ V   ___ I⁻

C3-3b
(Copy 4)

Chord identification in a key

Shield the answer. Listen to the chord and write the composite chord symbol; then uncover the answer and compare your response. Circle incorrect responses. Goal: No more than seven errors. The first frame requires no response.

1 I⁻   ___ V   ___ IV⁶   ___ IV⁻   ___ V   ___ I⁻   ___ IV⁶

2 ___ V   ___ I⁶   ___ IV⁻   ___ IV⁶   ___ V   ___ I⁻   ___ I⁶

3 ___ V   ___ IV⁶   ___ IV⁻   ___ I⁶   ___ V   ___ I⁻   ___ IV⁻

4 ___ IV⁶   ___ V   ___ I⁶   ___ V   ___ IV⁶   ___ IV⁻   ___ I⁶

5 ___ IV⁻   ___ I⁻   ___ I⁶   ___ V   ___ IV⁶   ___ IV⁻   ___ I⁶

6 ___ I⁻   ___ IV⁶   ___ V   ___ I⁶   ___ IV⁻   ___ I⁻   ___ I⁶

7 ___ IV⁶   ___ V   ___ I⁶   ___ IV⁻   ___ IV⁶   ___ I⁶   ___ IV⁻

8 ___ V   ___ I⁶   ___ IV⁶   ___ V   ___ I⁻   ___ IV⁶   ___ V

9 ___ I⁶   ___ IV⁻   ___ V   ___ IV⁶   ___ V   ___ I⁶   ___ I⁻

10 ___ IV⁶   ___ IV⁻   ___ V   ___ I⁶   ___ IV⁶   ___ V   ___ I⁻

C3-3b
(Copy 5)

Chord identification in a key

Shield the answer. Listen to the chord and write the composite chord symbol; then uncover the answer and compare your response. Circle incorrect responses. Goal: No more than seven errors. The first frame requires no response.

1 I⁻   ___ V   ___ IV⁶   ___ IV⁻   ___ V   ___ I⁻   ___ IV⁶

2 ___ V   ___ I⁶   ___ IV⁻   ___ IV⁶   ___ V   ___ I⁻   ___ I⁶

3 ___ V   ___ IV⁶   ___ IV⁻   ___ I⁶   ___ V   ___ I⁻   ___ IV⁻

4 ___ IV⁶   ___ V   ___ I⁶   ___ V   ___ IV⁶   ___ IV⁻   ___ I⁶

5 ___ IV⁻   ___ I⁻   ___ I⁶   ___ V   ___ IV⁶   ___ IV⁻   ___ I⁶

6 ___ I⁻   ___ IV⁶   ___ V   ___ I⁶   ___ IV⁻   ___ I⁻   ___ I⁶

7 ___ IV⁶   ___ V   ___ I⁶   ___ IV⁻   ___ IV⁶   ___ I⁶   ___ IV⁻

8 ___ V   ___ I⁶   ___ IV⁶   ___ V   ___ I⁻   ___ IV⁶   ___ V

9 ___ I⁶   ___ IV⁻   ___ V   ___ IV⁶   ___ V   ___ I⁶   ___ I⁻

10 ___ IV⁶   ___ IV⁻   ___ V   ___ I⁶   ___ IV⁶   ___ V   ___ I⁻

C3-4a
(Copy 1)

Figured bass dictation

Shield the answer. Listen to the chord and write the bass note and the figured bass symbol; then uncover the answer and compare your response. Circle incorrect responses. Goal: No more than seven errors. The first frame requires no response.

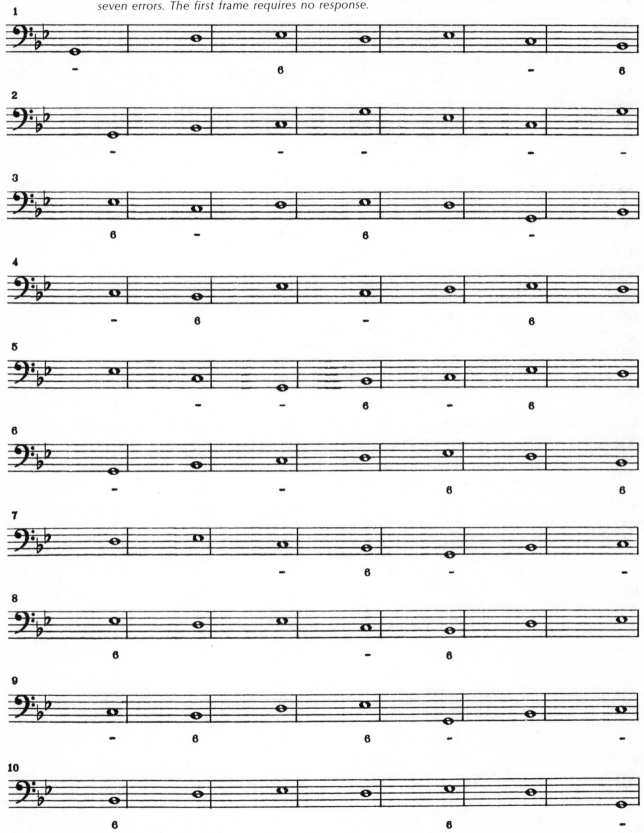

C3-4a
(Copy 2)

Figured bass dictation

Shield the answer. Listen to the chord and write the bass note and the figured bass symbol; then uncover the answer and compare your response. Circle incorrect responses. Goal: No more than seven errors. The first frame requires no response.

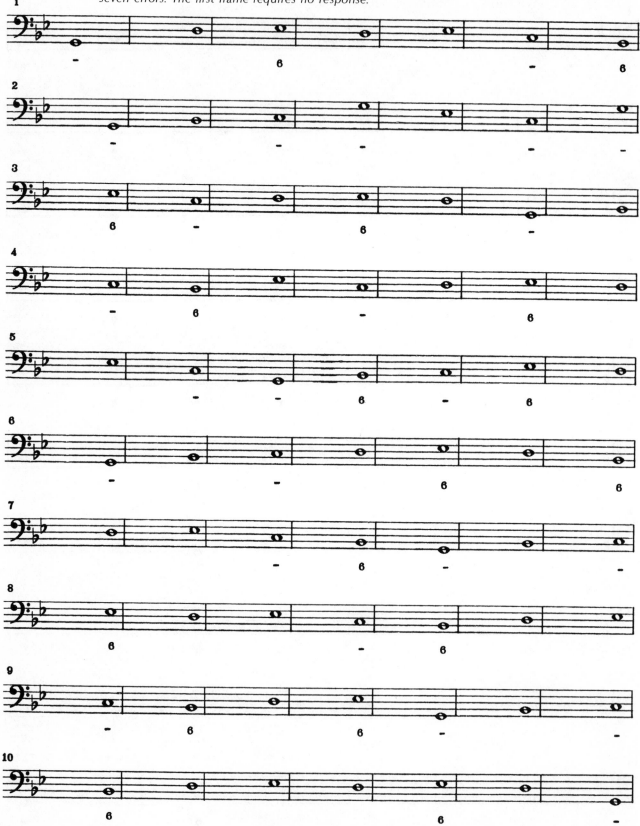

C3-4a

(Copy 3)

Figured bass dictation

Shield the answer. Listen to the chord and write the bass note and the figured bass symbol; then uncover the answer and compare your response. Circle incorrect responses. Goal: No more than seven errors. The first frame requires no response.

113

C3-4a

Figured bass dictation

Shield the answer. Listen to the chord and write the bass note and the figured bass symbol; then uncover the answer and compare your response. Circle incorrect responses. Goal: No more than seven errors. The first frame requires no response.

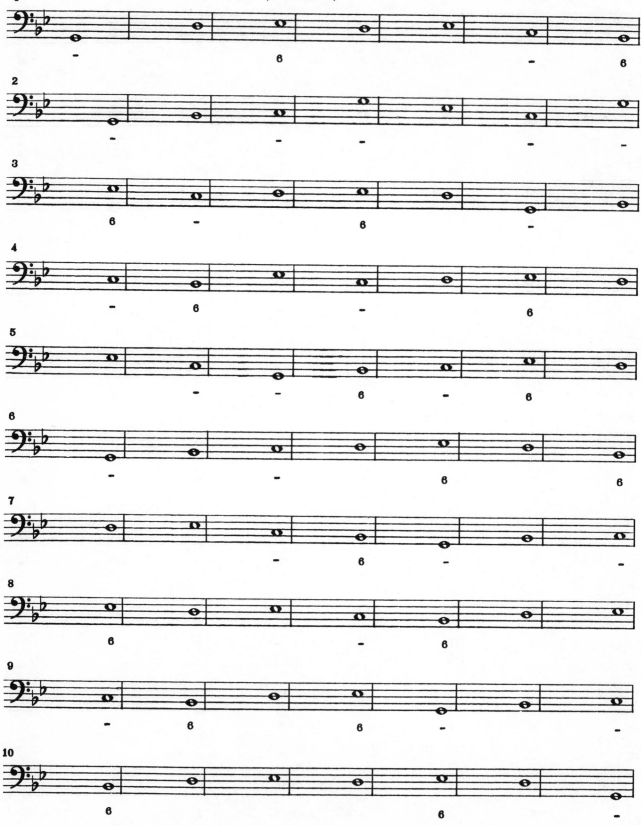

C3-4a

(Copy 5)

Figured bass dictation

Shield the answer. Listen to the chord and write the bass note and the figured bass symbol; then uncover the answer and compare your response. Circle incorrect responses. Goal: No more than seven errors. The first frame requires no response.

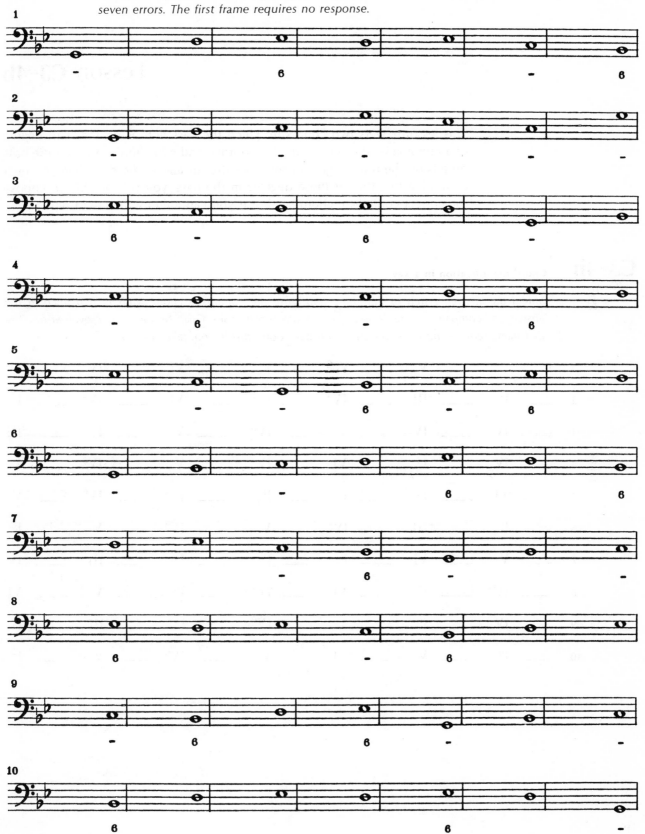

This lesson covers two chords in which the bass note is on the sixth degree of a minor key—the $^-$VI and the IV^6 chords—and two chords in which the bass note is on the third degree of the key—the $^-$III and I^6 chords. When you hear a chord with either of these degrees in the bass, you will be able to choose the correct composite chord symbol if you can identify the chord type.

C3-4b
(Copy 1)

Chord identification in a key

Shield the answer. Listen to the chord and write the composite chord symbol; then uncover the answer and compare your response. Circle incorrect responses. Goal: No more than seven errors. The first frame requires no response. After you have done this lesson, take Test C3.

#							
1	I^-	___ V	___ IV^6	___ V	___ $^-$VI	___ IV^-	___ I^6
2	___ I^-	___ $^-$III	___ IV^-	___ I^-	___ $^-$VI	___ IV^-	___ I^-
3	___ IV^6	___ IV^-	___ V	___ IV^6	___ V	___ I^-	___ $^-$III
4	___ IV^-	___ I^6	___ $^-$VI	___ IV^-	___ V	___ IV^6	___ V
5	___ $^-$VI	___ IV^-	___ I^-	___ I^6	___ IV^-	___ IV^6	___ V
6	___ I^-	___ $^-$III	___ IV^-	___ V	___ IV^6	___ V	___ I^6
7	___ V	___ $^-$VI	___ IV^-	___ I^6	___ I^-	___ $^-$III	___ IV^-
8	___ IV^6	___ V	___ $^-$VI	___ IV^-	___ I^6	___ V	___ $^-$VI
9	___ IV^-	___ I^6	___ V	___ IV^6	___ I^-	___ $^-$III	___ IV
10	___ I^6	___ V	___ $^-$VI	___ V	___ IV^6	___ V	___ I^-

C3-4b
(Copy 2)

Chord identification in a key

Shield the answer. Listen to the chord and write the composite chord symbol; then uncover the answer and compare your response. Circle incorrect responses. Goal: No more than seven errors. The first frame requires no response. After you have done this lesson, take Test C3.

1 I^- _____ V _____ IV^6 _____ V _____ ^-VI _____ IV^- _____ I^6

2 _____ I^- _____ ^-III _____ IV^- _____ I^- _____ ^-VI _____ IV^- _____ I^-

3 _____ IV^6 _____ IV^- _____ V _____ IV^6 _____ V _____ I^- _____ ^-III

4 _____ IV^- _____ I^6 _____ ^-VI _____ IV^- _____ V _____ IV^6 _____ V

5 _____ ^-VI _____ IV^- _____ I^- _____ I^6 _____ IV^- _____ IV^6 _____ V

6 _____ I^- _____ ^-III _____ IV^- _____ V _____ IV^6 _____ V _____ I^6

7 _____ V _____ ^-VI _____ IV^- _____ I^6 _____ I^- _____ ^-III _____ IV^-

8 _____ IV^6 _____ V _____ ^-VI _____ IV^- _____ I^6 _____ V _____ ^-VI

9 _____ IV^- _____ I^6 _____ V _____ IV^6 _____ I^- _____ ^-III _____ IV

10 _____ I^6 _____ V _____ ^-VI _____ V _____ IV^6 _____ V _____ I^-

C3-4b
(Copy 3)

Chord identification in a key

Shield the answer. Listen to the chord and write the composite chord symbol; then uncover the answer and compare your response. Circle incorrect responses. Goal: No more than seven errors. The first frame requires no response. After you have done this lesson, take Test C3.

1 I^- _____ V _____ IV^6 _____ V _____ ^-VI _____ IV^- _____ I^6

2 _____ I^- _____ ^-III _____ IV^- _____ I^- _____ ^-VI _____ IV^- _____ I^-

3 _____ IV^6 _____ IV^- _____ V _____ IV^6 _____ V _____ I^- _____ ^-III

4 _____ IV^- _____ I^6 _____ ^-VI _____ IV^- _____ V _____ IV^6 _____ V

5 _____ ^-VI _____ IV^- _____ I^- _____ I^6 _____ IV^- _____ IV^6 _____ V

6 _____ I^- _____ ^-III _____ IV^- _____ V _____ IV^6 _____ V _____ I^6

7 _____ V _____ ^-VI _____ IV^- _____ I^6 _____ I^- _____ ^-III _____ IV^-

8 _____ IV^6 _____ V _____ ^-VI _____ IV^- _____ I^6 _____ V _____ ^-VI

9 _____ IV^- _____ I^6 _____ V _____ IV^6 _____ I^- _____ ^-III _____ IV

10 _____ I^6 _____ V _____ ^-VI _____ V _____ IV^6 _____ V _____ I^-

C3-4b

(Copy 4)

Chord identification in a key

Shield the answer. Listen to the chord and write the composite chord symbol; then uncover the answer and compare your response. Circle incorrect responses. Goal: No more than seven errors. The first frame requires no response. After you have done this lesson, take Test C3.

1 I⁻   ____ V   ____ IV⁶ ____ V   ____ ⁻VI ____ IV⁻ ____ I⁶

2 ____ I⁻   ____ ⁻III   ____ IV⁻ ____ I⁻   ____ ⁻VI ____ IV⁻ ____ I⁻

3 ____ IV⁶ ____ IV⁻ ____ V   ____ IV⁶ ____ V   ____ I⁻ ____ ⁻III

4 ____ IV⁻ ____ I⁶   ____ ⁻VI ____ IV⁻ ____ V   ____ IV⁶ ____ V

5 ____ ⁻VI ____ IV⁻ ____ I⁻   ____ I⁶   ____ IV⁻ ____ IV⁶ ____ V

6 ____ I⁻   ____ ⁻III ____ IV⁻ ____ V   ____ IV⁶ ____ V   ____ I⁶

7 ____ V   ____ ⁻VI ____ IV⁻ ____ I⁶   ____ I⁻ ____ ⁻III ____ IV⁻

8 ____ IV⁶ ____ V   ____ ⁻VI ____ IV⁻ ____ I⁶   ____ V   ____ ⁻VI

9 ____ IV⁻ ____ I⁶   ____ V   ____ IV⁶ ____ I⁻ ____ ⁻III ____ IV

10 ____ I⁶   ____ V   ____ ⁻VI ____ V   ____ IV⁶ ____ V   ____ I⁻

C3-4b

(Copy 5)

Chord identification in a key

Shield the answer. Listen to the chord and write the composite chord symbol; then uncover the answer and compare your response. Circle incorrect responses. Goal: No more than seven errors. The first frame requires no response. After you have done this lesson, take Test C3.

1 I⁻   ____ V   ____ IV⁶ ____ V   ____ ⁻VI ____ IV⁻ ____ I⁶

2 ____ I⁻   ____ ⁻III   ____ IV⁻ ____ I⁻   ____ ⁻VI ____ IV⁻ ____ I⁻

3 ____ IV⁶ ____ IV⁻ ____ V   ____ IV⁶ ____ V   ____ I⁻ ____ ⁻III

4 ____ IV⁻ ____ I⁶   ____ ⁻VI ____ IV⁻ ____ V   ____ IV⁶ ____ V

5 ____ ⁻VI ____ IV⁻ ____ I⁻   ____ I⁶   ____ IV⁻ ____ IV⁶ ____ V

6 ____ I⁻   ____ ⁻III ____ IV⁻ ____ V   ____ IV⁶ ____ V   ____ I⁶

7 ____ V   ____ ⁻VI ____ IV⁻ ____ I⁶   ____ I⁻ ____ ⁻III ____ IV⁻

8 ____ IV⁶ ____ V   ____ ⁻VI ____ IV⁻ ____ I⁶   ____ V   ____ ⁻VI

9 ____ IV⁻ ____ I⁶   ____ V   ____ IV⁶ ____ I⁻ ____ ⁻III ____ IV

10 ____ I⁶   ____ V   ____ ⁻VI ____ V   ____ IV⁶ ____ V   ____ I⁻

Major and Minor Triads in Root Position and First Inversion

In this series you will be dealing with the triads found in the earlier series, all appearing in the same lessons. When you have done this series, take Test C4, which includes sections on each of the four kinds of lessons found in this series.

C4-1a
(Copy 1)

Chord dictation

Shield the answer. Listen to the chord and notate the upper tones above the given note; then uncover the answer and compare your response. Circle incorrect responses. Goal: No more than seven errors.

120

C4-1a

(Copy 2)

Chord dictation

Shield the answer. Listen to the chord and notate the upper tones above the given note; then uncover the answer and compare your response. Circle incorrect responses. Goal: No more than seven errors.

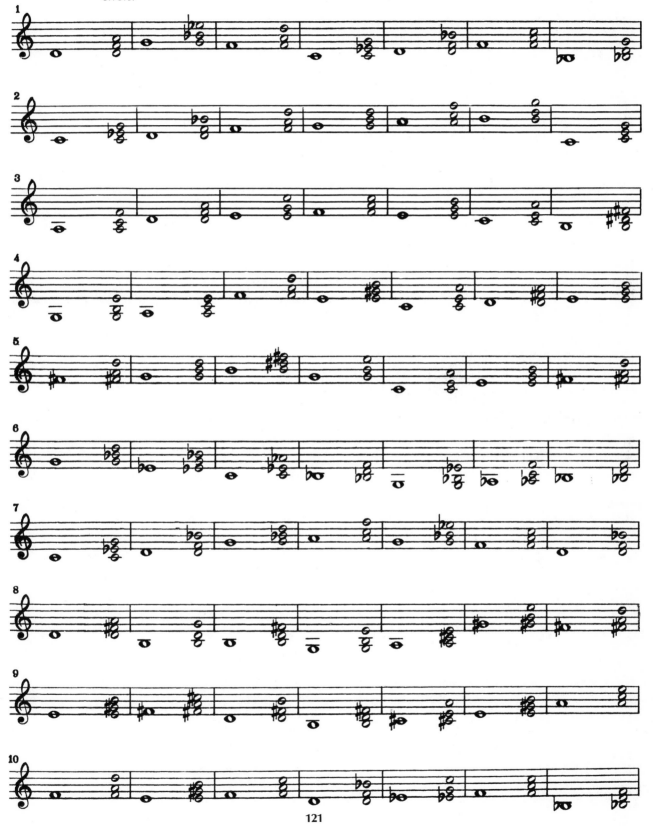

121

C4-1a

(Copy 3)

Chord dictation

Shield the answer. Listen to the chord and notate the upper tones above the given note; then un-cover the answer and compare your response. Circle incorrect responses. Goal: No more than seven errors.

122

C4-1a
(Copy 4)

Chord dictation

Shield the answer. Listen to the chord and notate the upper tones above the given note; then uncover the answer and compare your response. Circle incorrect responses. Goal: No more than seven errors.

123

C4-1a

Chord dictation

Shield the answer. Listen to the chord and notate the upper tones above the given note; then un-cover the answer and compare your response. Circle incorrect responses. Goal: No more than seven errors.

C4-1b
(Copy 1)

Chord identification

Shield the answer. Listen to the chord and write the figured bass symbol (blank, ⁻, ⁻⁶, or ⁶); then uncover the answer and compare your response. Circle incorrect responses. Goal: No more than seven errors.

1 ____ – ____ –6 ____ 6 ____ – ____ –6 ____ ____ 6

2 ____ – ____ –6 ____ 6 ____ ____ –6 ____ –6 ____

3 ____ –6 ____ – ____ –6 ____ ____ – ____ 6 ____

4 ____ 6 ____ – ____ 6 ____ ____ 6 ____ ____ –

5 ____ –6 ____ ____ ____ 6 ____ 6 ____ – ____ –6

6 ____ – ____ ____ –6 ____ ____ –6 ____ 6 ____

7 ____ – ____ –6 ____ – ____ –6 ____ –6 ____ ____ –6

8 ____ ____ –6 ____ – ____ 6 ____ ____ –6 ____ –6

9 ____ ____ – ____ 6 ____ – ____ –6 ____ ____ –

10 ____ 6 ____ ____ ____ –6 ____ 6 ____

C4-1b
(Copy 2)

Chord identification

Shield the answer. Listen to the chord and write the figured bass symbol (blank, ⁻, ⁻⁶, or ⁶); then uncover the answer and compare your response. Circle incorrect responses. Goal: No more than seven errors.

1 ____ – ____ –6 ____ 6 ____ – ____ –6 ____ ____ 6

2 ____ – ____ –6 ____ 6 ____ ____ –6 ____ –6 ____

3 ____ –6 ____ – ____ –6 ____ ____ – ____ 6 ____

4 ____ 6 ____ – ____ 6 ____ ____ 6 ____ ____ –

5 ____ –6 ____ ____ ____ 6 ____ 6 ____ – ____ –6

6 ____ – ____ ____ –6 ____ ____ –6 ____ 6 ____

7 ____ – ____ –6 ____ – ____ –6 ____ –6 ____ ____ –6

8 ____ ____ –6 ____ – ____ 6 ____ ____ –6 ____ –6

9 ____ ____ – ____ 6 ____ – ____ –6 ____ ____ –

10 ____ 6 ____ ____ ____ –6 ____ 6 ____

C4-1b
(Copy 3)

Chord identification

Shield the answer. Listen to the chord and write the figured bass symbol (blank, -, -6, or 6); then uncover the answer and compare your response. Circle incorrect responses. Goal: No more than seven errors.

#						
1	-	-6	6	-	-6	6
2	-	-6	6		-6	-6
3	-6	-	-6		-	6
4	6	-	6		6	-
5	-6			6	6	- / -6
6	-		-6		-6	6
7	-	-6	-	-6	-6	-6
8		-6	-	6		-6 / -6
9			-	6	-	-6 / -
10	6			-6	6	

C4-1b
(Copy 4)

Chord identification

Shield the answer. Listen to the chord and write the figured bass symbol (blank, -, -6, or 6); then uncover the answer and compare your response. Circle incorrect responses. Goal: No more than seven errors.

#						
1	-	-6	6	-	-6	6
2	-	-6	6		-6	-6
3	-6	-	-6		-	6
4	6	-	6		6	-
5	-6			6	6	- / -6
6	-		-6		-6	6
7	-	-6	-	-6	-6	-6
8		-6	-	6		-6 / -6
9			-	6	-	-6 / -
10	6			-6	6	

C4-1b

Chord identification

Shield the answer. Listen to the chord and write the figured bass symbol (blank, -, -6, or 6); then uncover the answer and compare your response. Circle incorrect responses. Goal: No more than seven errors.

#							
1	___ -	___ -6	___ 6	___ -	___ -6	___	___ 6
2	___ -	___ -6	___ 6	___	___ -6	___ -6	___
3	___ -6	___ -	___ -6	___	___ -	___ 6	___
4	___ 6	___ -	___ 6	___	___ 6	___	___ -
5	___ -6	___	___	___ 6	___ 6	___ -	___ -6
6	___ -	___	___ -6	___	___ -6	___ 6	___
7	___ -	___ -6	___ -	___ -6	___ -6	___	___ -6
8	___	___ -6	___ -	___ 6	___	___ -6	___ -6
9	___	___	___ -	___ 6	___ -	___ -6	___	___ -
10	___ 6	___	___	___ -6	___ 6	___	___

C4-2
(Copy 1)

Chord identification

Shield the answer. Listen to the chord and write the figured bass symbol (blank, ⁻, ⁻⁶, or ⁶); then uncover the answer and compare your response. Circle incorrect responses. Goal: No more than seven errors.

1. ___ ___ -6 ___ 6 ___ ___ -6 ___ ___ -6
2. ___ - ___ 6 ___ ___ - ___ -6 ___ ___
3. ___ 6 ___ ___ -6 ___ ___ 6 ___ - ___
4. ___ -6 ___ -6 ___ ___ - ___ - ___ -6 ___ 6
5. ___ - ___ ___ -6 ___ 6 ___ - ___ 6 ___ -
6. ___ 6 ___ ___ 6 ___ ___ -6 ___ - ___ -6
7. ___ ___ -6 ___ ___ 6 ___ - ___ 6 ___ -
8. ___ ___ ___ -6 ___ 6 ___ ___ ___ -6
9. ___ ___ -6 ___ -6 ___ ___ 6 ___ ___ 6
10. ___ - ___ -6 ___ 6 ___ ___ -6 ___ -6 ___

C4-2
(Copy 2)

Chord identification

Shield the answer. Listen to the chord and write the figured bass symbol (blank, ⁻, ⁻⁶, or ⁶); then uncover the answer and compare your response. Circle incorrect responses. Goal: No more than seven errors.

1. ___ ___ -6 ___ 6 ___ ___ -6 ___ ___ -6
2. ___, - ___ 6 ___ ___ - ___ -6 ___ ___
3. ___ 6 ___ ___ -6 ___ ___ 6 ___ - ___
4. ___ -6 ___ -6 ___ ___ - ___ - ___ -6 ___ 6
5. ___ - ___ ___ -6 ___ 6 ___ - ___ 6 ___ -
6. ___ 6 ___ ___ 6 ___ ___ -6 ___ - ___ -6
7. ___ ___ -6 ___ ___ 6 ___ - ___ 6 ___ -
8. ___ ___ ___ -6 ___ 6 ___ ___ ___ -6
9. ___ ___ -6 ___ -6 ___ ___ 6 ___ ___ 6
10. ___ - ___ -6 ___ 6 ___ ___ -6 ___ -6 ___

C4-2
(Copy 3)

Chord identification

Shield the answer. Listen to the chord and write the figured bass symbol (blank, -, -6, or 6); then uncover the answer and compare your response. Circle incorrect responses. Goal: No more than seven errors.

1. ___ ___ -6 ___ 6 ___ ___ -6 ___ ___ -6
2. ___ - ___ 6 ___ ___ - ___ -6 ___ ___
3. ___ 6 ___ ___ -6 ___ ___ 6 ___ - ___
4. ___ -6 ___ -6 ___ ___ - ___ - ___ -6 ___ 6
5. ___ - ___ ___ -6 ___ 6 ___ - ___ 6 ___ -
6. ___ 6 ___ ___ 6 ___ ___ -6 ___ - ___ -6
7. ___ ___ -6 ___ ___ 6 ___ - ___ 6 ___ -
8. ___ ___ ___ -6 ___ 6 ___ ___ ___ -6
9. ___ ___ -6 ___ -6 ___ ___ ___ 6 ___ ___ 6
10. ___ - ___ -6 ___ 6 ___ ___ -6 ___ -6 ___

C4-2
(Copy 4)

Chord identification

Shield the answer. Listen to the chord and write the figured bass symbol (blank, -, -6, or 6); then uncover the answer and compare your response. Circle incorrect responses. Goal: No more than seven errors.

1. ___ ___ -6 ___ 6 ___ ___ -6 ___ ___ -6
2. ___ - ___ 6 ___ ___ - ___ -6 ___ ___
3. ___ 6 ___ ___ -6 ___ ___ 6 ___ - ___
4. ___ -6 ___ -6 ___ ___ - ___ - ___ -6 ___ 6
5. ___ - ___ ___ -6 ___ 6 ___ - ___ 6 ___ -
6. ___ 6 ___ ___ 6 ___ ___ -6 ___ - ___ -6
7. ___ ___ -6 ___ ___ 6 ___ - ___ 6 ___ -
8. ___ ___ ___ -6 ___ 6 ___ ___ ___ -6
9. ___ ___ -6 ___ -6 ___ ___ ___ 6 ___ ___ 6
10. ___ - ___ -6 ___ 6 ___ ___ -6 ___ -6 ___

C4-2

Chord identification

Shield the answer. Listen to the chord and write the figured bass symbol (blank, ⁻, ⁻⁶, or ⁶); then uncover the answer and compare your response. Circle incorrect responses. Goal: No more than seven errors.

1 ____   ____ -6   ____ 6   ____   ____ -6   ____   ____ -6

2 ____ -   ____ 6   ____   ____ -   ____ -6   ____   ____

3 ____ 6   ____   ____ -6   ____   ____ 6   ____ -   ____

4 ____ -6   ____ -6   ____   ____ -   ____ -   ____ -6   ____ 6

5 ____ -   ____   ____ -6   ____ 6   ____ -   ____ 6   ____ -

6 ____ 6   ____   ____ 6   ____   ____ -6   ____ -   ____ -6

7 ____   ____ -6   ____   ____ 6   ____ -   ____ 6   ____ -

8 ____   ____   ____ -6   ____ 6   ____   ____   ____ -6

9 ____   ____ -6   ____ -6   ____   ____ 6   ____   ____ 6

10 ____ -   ____ -6   ____ 6   ____   ____ -6   ____ -6   ____

C4-3a   Figured bass dictation

(Copy 1)

Shield the answer. Listen to the chord and write the bass note and the figured bass symbol; then uncover the answer and compare your response. Circle incorrect responses. Goal: No more than seven errors. The first frame requires no response.

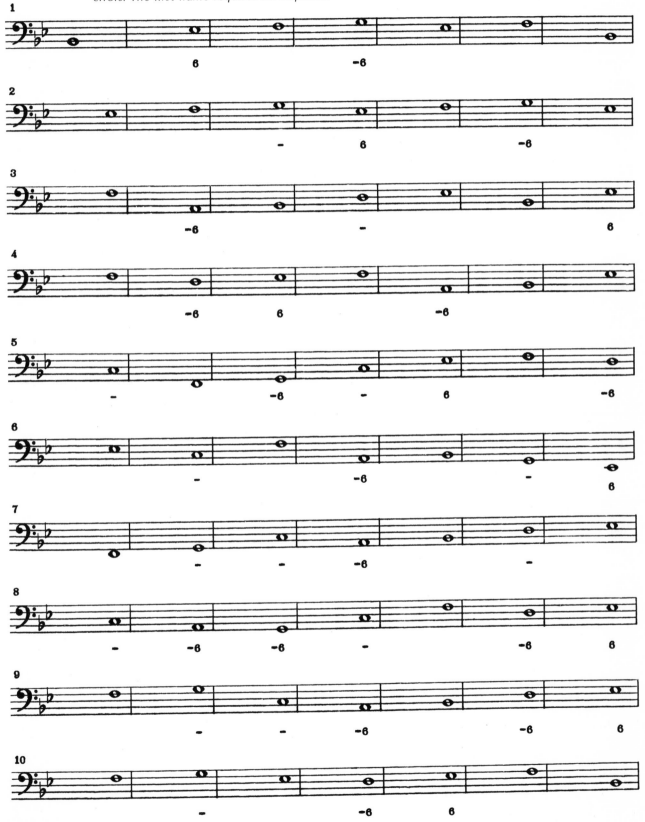

C4-3a Figured bass dictation

(Copy 2)

Shield the answer. Listen to the chord and write the bass note and the figured bass symbol; then uncover the answer and compare your response. Circle incorrect responses. Goal: No more than seven errors. The first frame requires no response.

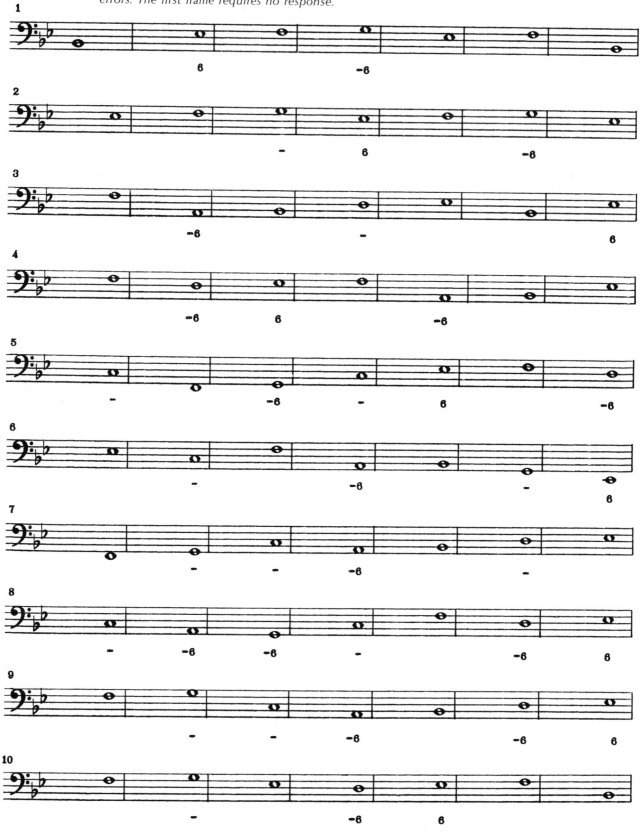

C4-3a
(Copy 3)

Figured bass dictation

Shield the answer. Listen to the chord and write the bass note and the figured bass symbol; then uncover the answer and compare your response. Circle incorrect responses. Goal: No more than seven errors. The first frame requires no response.

133

C4-3a
(Copy 4)

Figured bass dictation

Shield the answer. Listen to the chord and write the bass note and the figured bass symbol; then uncover the answer and compare your response. Circle incorrect responses. Goal: No more than seven errors. The first frame requires no response.

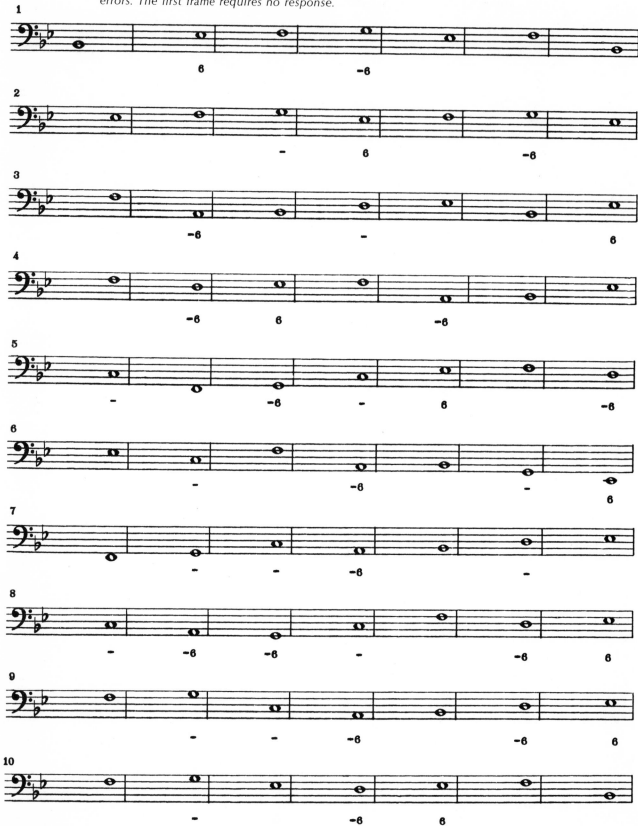

C4-3a
(Copy 5)

Figured bass dictation

Shield the answer. Listen to the chord and write the bass note and the figured bass symbol; then uncover the answer and compare your response. Circle incorrect responses. Goal: No more than seven errors. The first frame requires no response.

This lesson introduces two chords in which the bass note is on the fourth degree of a major key: the IV and II^6 chords. When you hear a chord in which the fourth degree is in the bass, you will be able to choose the correct composite chord symbol if you can identify the chord type. Two similar pairs of chords that appeared together in a previous lesson also occur in this lesson. These are III^- and I^{-6} chords and the VI^- and the IV^{-6} chords.

C4-3b
(Copy 1)

Chord identification in a key

Shield the answer. Listen to the chord and write the composite chord symbol; then uncover the answer and compare your response. Circle incorrect responses. Goal: No more than seven errors. The first frame requires no response. After you have done this lesson, take Test C4.

1	I	___	II^6	___	V	___	IV^{-6}	___	IV	___	V	___	I
2	___	IV	___	V	___	VI^-	___	II^6	___	V	___	IV^{-6}	___ IV
3	___	V	___	V^{-6}	___	I	___	III^-	___	IV	___	I	___ II^6
4	___	V	___	I^{-6}	___	II^6	___	V	___	V^{-6}	___	I	___ IV
5	___	II^-	___	V	___	IV^{-6}	___	II^-	___	II^6	___	V	___ I^{-6}
6	___	IV	___	II^-	___	V	___	V^{-6}	___	I	___	VI^-	___ II^6
7	___	V	___	VI^-	___	II^-	___	V^{-6}	___	I	___	III^-	___ IV
8	___	II^-	___	V^{-6}	___	IV^{-6}	___	II^-	___	V	___	I^{-6}	___ II^6
9	___	V	___	VI^-	___	II^-	___	V^{-6}	___	I	___	I^{-6}	___ II^6
10	___	V	___	VI^-	___	IV	___	I^{-6}	___	II^6	___	V	___ I

C4-3b
(Copy 2)

Chord identification in a key

Shield the answer. Listen to the chord and write the composite chord symbol; then uncover the answer and compare your response. Circle incorrect responses. Goal: No more than seven errors. The first frame requires no response. After you have done this lesson, take Test C4.

1 I   ____ II^6 ____ V   ____ IV^{-6} ____ IV   ____ V   ____ I

2 ____ IV   ____ V   ____ VI^- ____ II^6 ____ V   ____ IV^{-6} ____ IV

3 ____ V   ____ V^{-6} ____ I   ____ III^- ____ IV   ____ I   ____ II^6

4 ____ V   ____ I^{-6} ____ II^6 ____ V   ____ V^{-6} ____ I   ____ IV

5 ____ II^- ____ V   ____ IV^{-6} ____ II^- ____ II^6 ____ V   ____ I^{-6}

6 ____ IV   ____ II^- ____ V   ____ V^{-6} ____ I   ____ VI^- ____ II^6

7 ____ V   ____ VI^- ____ II^- ____ V^{-6} ____ I   ____ III^- ____ IV

8 ____ II^- ____ V^{-6} ____ IV^{-6} ____ II^- ____ V   ____ I^{-6} ____ II^6

9 ____ V   ____ VI^- ____ II^- ____ V^{-6} ____ I   ____ I^{-6} ____ II^6

10 ____ V   ____ VI^- ____ IV   ____ I^{-6} ____ II^6 ____ V   ____ I

C4-3b
(Copy 3)

Chord identification in a key

Shield the answer. Listen to the chord and write the composite chord symbol; then uncover the answer and compare your response. Circle incorrect responses. Goal: No more than seven errors. The first frame requires no response. After you have done this lesson, take Test C4.

1 I   ____ II^6 ____ V   ____ IV^{-6} ____ IV   ____ V   ____ I

2 ____ IV   ____ V   ____ VI^- ____ II^6 ____ V   ____ IV^{-6} ____ IV

3 ____ V   ____ V^{-6} ____ I   ____ III^- ____ IV   ____ I   ____ II^6

4 ____ V   ____ I^{-6} ____ II^6 ____ V   ____ V^{-6} ____ I   ____ IV

5 ____ II^- ____ V   ____ IV^{-6} ____ II^- ____ II^6 ____ V   ____ I^{-6}

6 ____ IV   ____ II^- ____ V   ____ V^{-6} ____ I   ____ VI^- ____ II^6

7 ____ V   ____ VI^- ____ II^- ____ V^{-6} ____ I   ____ III^- ____ IV

8 ____ II^- ____ V^{-6} ____ IV^{-6} ____ II^- ____ V   ____ I^{-6} ____ II^6

9 ____ V   ____ VI^- ____ II^- ____ V^{-6} ____ I   ____ I^{-6} ____ II^6

10 ____ V   ____ VI^- ____ IV   ____ I^{-6} ____ II^6 ____ V   ____ I

C4-3b
(Copy 4)

Chord identification in a key

Shield the answer. Listen to the chord and write the composite chord symbol; then uncover the answer and compare your response. Circle incorrect responses. Goal: No more than seven errors. The first frame requires no response. After you have done this lesson, take Test C4.

1   I   ____ II^6 ____ V   ____ IV^{-6} ____ IV   ____ V   ____ I

2   ____ IV   ____ V   ____ VI^- ____ II^6 ____ V   ____ IV^{-6} ____ IV

3   ____ V   ____ V^{-6} ____ I   ____ III^- ____ IV   ____ I   ____ II^6

4   ____ V   ____ I^{-6} ____ II^6 ____ V   ____ V^{-6} ____ I   ____ IV

5   ____ II^- ____ V   ____ IV^{-6} ____ II^- ____ II^6 ____ V   ____ I^{-6}

6   ____ IV   ____ II^- ____ V   ____ V^{-6} ____ I   ____ VI^- ____ II^6

7   ____ V   ____ VI^- ____ II^- ____ V^{-6} ____ I   ____ III^- ____ IV

8   ____ II^- ____ V^{-6} ____ IV^{-6} ____ II^- ____ V   ____ I^{-6} ____ II^6

9   ____ V   ____ VI^- ____ II^- ____ V^{-6} ____ I   ____ I^{-6} ____ II^6

10   ____ V   ____ VI^- ____ IV   ____ I^{-6} ____ II^6 ____ V   ____ I

C4-3b
(Copy 5)

Chord identification in a key

Shield the answer. Listen to the chord and write the composite chord symbol; then uncover the answer and compare your response. Circle incorrect responses. Goal: No more than seven errors. The first frame requires no response. After you have done this lesson, take Test C4.

1   I   ____ II^6 ____ V   ____ IV^{-6} ____ IV   ____ V   ____ I

2   ____ IV   ____ V   ____ VI^- ____ II^6 ____ V   ____ IV^{-6} ____ IV

3   ____ V   ____ V^{-6} ____ I   ____ III^- ____ IV   ____ I   ____ II^6

4   ____ V   ____ I^{-6} ____ II^6 ____ V   ____ V^{-6} ____ I   ____ IV

5   ____ II^- ____ V   ____ IV^{-6} ____ II^- ____ II^6 ____ V   ____ I^{-6}

6   ____ IV   ____ II^- ____ V   ____ V^{-6} ____ I   ____ VI^- ____ II^6

7   ____ V   ____ VI^- ____ II^- ____ V^{-6} ____ I   ____ III^- ____ IV

8   ____ II^- ____ V^{-6} ____ IV^{-6} ____ II^- ____ V   ____ I^{-6} ____ II^6

9   ____ V   ____ VI^- ____ II^- ____ V^{-6} ____ I   ____ I^{-6} ____ II^6

10   ____ V   ____ VI^- ____ IV   ____ I^{-6} ____ II^6 ____ V   ____ I

Dominant seventh chords and diminished triads in first inversion

This series involves two new types of chords as well as the chords found in previous lessons. The new chords are the dominant seventh chord in first inversion and the diminished triad in first inversion.

The upper tones of the dominant seventh chord in first inversion are at the intervals of a minor sixth, a diminished fifth and a minor third above the bass.

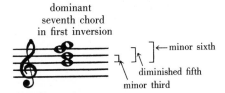

The diminished triad is shown in root position and in first inversion in the following example:

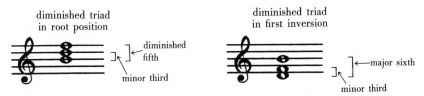

In root position, the upper tones of a diminished triad are at the intervals of a diminished fifth and a minor third above the bass. In first inversion, the upper tones are at the intervals of a major sixth and minor third above the bass. In this volume, the diminished triad will not appear in root position, but only in first inversion, which is the only common form of this chord.

When you have done this series, take Test C5, which includes sections on each of the four kinds of lessons found in this series.

C5-1a
(Copy 1)

Chord dictation

Shield the answers. Listen to the chord and notate the upper tones above the given note; then uncover the answer and compare your response. Circle incorrect responses. Goal: No more than seven errors.

C5-1a
(Copy 2)

Chord dictation

Shield the answers. Listen to the chord and notate the upper tones above the given note; then uncover the answer and compare your response. Circle incorrect responses. Goal: No more than seven errors.

C5-1a

(Copy 3)

Chord dictation

Shield the answers. Listen to the chord and notate the upper tones above the given note; then uncover the answer and compare your response. Circle incorrect responses. Goal: No more than seven errors.

142

C5-1a
(Copy 4)

Chord dictation

Shield the answers. Listen to the chord and notate the upper tones above the given note; then uncover the answer and compare your response. Circle incorrect responses. Goal: No more than seven errors.

143

C5-1a
(Copy 5)

Chord dictation

Shield the answers. Listen to the chord and notate the upper tones above the given note; then uncover the answer and compare your response. Circle incorrect responses. Goal: No more than seven errors.

The intervals between the upper tones and the bass of a dominant seventh chord in first inversion are a minor sixth, a diminished fifth and a minor third. The complete figured bass symbol is $\frac{-6}{d5}$, and the abbreviated symbol is $\frac{-6}{d5}$. The letter d is a qualifying sign that appears in a figured bass symbol for a diminished interval.

The intervals between the upper tones and the bass of a diminished triad in first inversion are a major sixth and a minor third. The complete figured bass symbol is $\frac{-6}{3}$, and the abbreviated symbol is $\underline{6}$.

C5-1b
(Copy 1)

Chord identification

Shield the answer. Listen to the chord and write the figured bass symbol ($^{-7}$, $\frac{-6}{d5}$, or $\underline{6}$); then uncover the answer and compare your response. Circle incorrect responses. Goal: No more than seven errors.

#							
1	-7	-6/d5	6/-	-7	-6/d5	6/-	-7
2	-6/d5	6/-	-7	6/-	-6/d5	-7	-6/d5
3	6/-	-6/d5	-6/d5	6/-	-7	-6/d5	6/-
4	-6/d5	-7	-6/d5	6/-	-6/d5	6/-	-7
5	-6/d5	-6/d5	6/-	-7	-6/d5	6/-	-6/d5
6	-7	6/-	-6/d5	-7	-6/d5	-7	6/-
7	-6/d5	-7	6/-	-6/d5	-7	6/-	-7
8	6/-	-6/d5	6/-	6/-	-6/d5	-7	6/-
9	-6/d5	-7	6/-	-7	-6/d5	6/-	-7
10	-6/d5	6/-	-7	6/-	-6/d5	6/-	-7

Chord identification

Shield the answer. Listen to the chord and write the figured bass symbol ($^{-7}$, $\frac{-6}{d5}$, or $\frac{6}{-}$); then uncover the answer and compare your response. Circle incorrect responses. Goal: No more than seven errors.

#							
1	-7	$\frac{-6}{d5}$	$\frac{6}{-}$	-7	$\frac{-6}{d5}$	$\frac{6}{-}$	-7
2	$\frac{-6}{d5}$	$\frac{6}{-}$	-7	$\frac{6}{-}$	$\frac{-6}{d5}$	-7	$\frac{-6}{d5}$
3	$\frac{6}{-}$	$\frac{-6}{d5}$	$\frac{-6}{d5}$	$\frac{6}{-}$	-7	$\frac{-6}{d5}$	$\frac{6}{-}$
4	$\frac{-6}{d5}$	-7	$\frac{-6}{d5}$	$\frac{6}{-}$	$\frac{-6}{d5}$	$\frac{6}{-}$	-7
5	$\frac{-6}{d5}$	$\frac{-6}{d5}$	$\frac{6}{-}$	-7	$\frac{-6}{d5}$	$\frac{6}{-}$	$\frac{-6}{d5}$
6	-7	$\frac{6}{-}$	$\frac{-6}{d5}$	-7	$\frac{-6}{d5}$	-7	$\frac{6}{-}$
7	$\frac{-6}{d5}$	-7	$\frac{6}{-}$	$\frac{-6}{d5}$	-7	$\frac{6}{-}$	-7
8	$\frac{6}{-}$	$\frac{-6}{d5}$	$\frac{6}{-}$	$\frac{6}{-}$	$\frac{-6}{d5}$	-7	$\frac{6}{-}$
9	$\frac{-6}{d5}$	-7	$\frac{6}{-}$	-7	$\frac{-6}{d5}$	$\frac{6}{-}$	-7
10	$\frac{-6}{d5}$	$\frac{6}{-}$	-7	$\frac{6}{-}$	$\frac{-6}{d5}$	$\frac{6}{-}$	-7

C5–1b
(Copy 3)

Chord identification

Shield the answer. Listen to the chord and write the figured bass symbol ($^{-7}$, $\frac{-6}{d5}$, or $\frac{6}{-}$); then uncover the answer and compare your response. Circle incorrect responses. Goal: No more than seven errors.

#							
1	-7	$\frac{-6}{d5}$	$\frac{6}{-}$	-7	$\frac{-6}{d5}$	$\frac{6}{-}$	-7
2	$\frac{-6}{d5}$	$\frac{6}{-}$	-7	$\frac{6}{-}$	$\frac{-6}{d5}$	-7	$\frac{-6}{d5}$
3	$\frac{6}{-}$	$\frac{-6}{d5}$	$\frac{-6}{d5}$	$\frac{6}{-}$	-7	$\frac{-6}{d5}$	$\frac{6}{-}$
4	$\frac{-6}{d5}$	-7	$\frac{-6}{d5}$	$\frac{6}{-}$	$\frac{-6}{d5}$	$\frac{6}{-}$	-7
5	$\frac{-6}{d5}$	$\frac{-6}{d5}$	$\frac{6}{-}$	-7	$\frac{-6}{d5}$	$\frac{6}{-}$	$\frac{-6}{d5}$
6	-7	$\frac{6}{-}$	$\frac{-6}{d5}$	-7	$\frac{-6}{d5}$	-7	$\frac{6}{-}$
7	$\frac{-6}{d5}$	-7	$\frac{6}{-}$	$\frac{-6}{d5}$	-7	$\frac{6}{-}$	-7
8	$\frac{6}{-}$	$\frac{-6}{d5}$	$\frac{6}{-}$	$\frac{6}{-}$	$\frac{-6}{d5}$	-7	$\frac{6}{-}$
9	$\frac{-6}{d5}$	-7	$\frac{6}{-}$	-7	$\frac{-6}{d5}$	$\frac{6}{-}$	-7
10	$\frac{-6}{d5}$	$\frac{6}{-}$	-7	$\frac{6}{-}$	$\frac{-6}{d5}$	$\frac{6}{-}$	-7

C5-1b
(Copy 4)

Chord identification

Shield the answer. Listen to the chord and write the figured bass symbol (⁻⁷, ⁻⁶/d5, or ⁶/_); then uncover the answer and compare your response. Circle incorrect responses. Goal: No more than seven errors.

#							
1	⁻⁷	⁻⁶ d5	⁶ _	⁻⁷	⁻⁶ d5	⁶ _	⁻⁷
2	⁻⁶ d5	⁶ _	⁻⁷	⁶ _	⁻⁶ d5	⁻⁷	⁻⁶ d5
3	⁶ _	⁻⁶ d5	⁻⁶ d5	⁶ _	⁻⁷	⁻⁶ d5	⁶ _
4	⁻⁶ d5	⁻⁷	⁻⁶ d5	⁶ _	⁻⁶ d5	⁶ _	⁻⁷
5	⁻⁶ d5	⁻⁶ d5	⁶ _	⁻⁷	⁻⁶ d5	⁶ _	⁻⁶ d5
6	⁻⁷	⁶ _	⁻⁶ d5	⁻⁷	⁻⁶ d5	⁻⁷	⁶ _
7	⁻⁶ d5	⁻⁷	⁶ _	⁻⁶ d5	⁻⁷	⁶ _	⁻⁷
8	⁶ _	⁻⁶ d5	⁶ _	⁶ _	⁻⁶ d5	⁻⁷	⁶ _
9	⁻⁶ d5	⁻⁷	⁶ _	⁻⁷	⁻⁶ d5	⁶ _	⁻⁷
10	⁻⁶ d5	⁶ _	⁻⁷	⁶ _	⁻⁶ d5	⁶ _	⁻⁷

C5-1b
(Copy 5)

Chord identification

Shield the answer. Listen to the chord and write the figured bass symbol (⁻⁷, ⁻⁶/d5, or ⁶/_); then uncover the answer and compare your response. Circle incorrect responses. Goal: No more than seven errors.

#							
1	⁻⁷	⁻⁶ d5	⁶ _	⁻⁷	⁻⁶ d5	⁶ _	⁻⁷
2	⁻⁶ d5	⁶ _	⁻⁷	⁶ _	⁻⁶ d5	⁻⁷	⁻⁶ d5
3	⁶ _	⁻⁶ d5	⁻⁶ d5	⁶ _	⁻⁷	⁻⁶ d5	⁶ _
4	⁻⁶ d5	⁻⁷	⁻⁶ d5	⁶ _	⁻⁶ d5	⁶ _	⁻⁷
5	⁻⁶ d5	⁻⁶ d5	⁶ _	⁻⁷	⁻⁶ d5	⁶ _	⁻⁶ d5
6	⁻⁷	⁶ _	⁻⁶ d5	⁻⁷	⁻⁶ d5	⁻⁷	⁶ _
7	⁻⁶ d5	⁻⁷	⁶ _	⁻⁶ d5	⁻⁷	⁶ _	⁻⁷
8	⁶ _	⁻⁶ d5	⁶ _	⁶ _	⁻⁶ d5	⁻⁷	⁶ _
9	⁻⁶ d5	⁻⁷	⁶ _	⁻⁷	⁻⁶ d5	⁶ _	⁻⁷
10	⁻⁶ d5	⁶ _	⁻⁷	⁶ _	⁻⁶ d5	⁶ _	⁻⁷

C5-2
(Copy 1)

Chord identification

Shield the answer. Listen to the chord and write the figured bass symbol (-7, -6/d5, or 6/-); then uncover the answer and compare your response. Circle incorrect responses. Goal: No more than seven errors.

#							
1	-7	-6/d5	6/-	-6/d5	-7	6/-	-6/d5
2	6/-	-7	-6/d5	-7	6/-	-6/d5	6/-
3	-6/d5	-7	-7	6/-	-7	-6/d5	6/-
4	-7	-7	-6/d5	6/-	-7	6/-	-6/d5
5	-7	6/-	-6/d5	-7	-6/d5	6/-	-7
6	-6/d5	6/-	-6/d5	-7	6/-	-7	-6/d5
7	6/-	-7	-6/d5	6/-	-6/d5	-7	-6/d5
8	-7	6/-	-6/d5	-7	6/-	-7	-6/d5
9	-7	-6/d5	6/-	-7	-6/d5	-6/d5	6/-
10	-7	6/-	-6/d5	6/-	-7	-6/d5	-7

C5-2
(Copy 2)

Chord identification

Shield the answer. Listen to the chord and write the figured bass symbol (-7, -6/d5, or 6/-); then uncover the answer and compare your response. Circle incorrect responses. Goal: No more than seven errors.

#							
1	-7	-6/d5	6/-	-6/d5	-7	6/-	-6/d5
2	6/-	-7	-6/d5	-7	6/-	-6/d5	6/-
3	-6/d5	-7	-7	6/-	-7	-6/d5	6/-
4	-7	-7	-6/d5	6/-	-7	6/-	-6/d5
5	-7	6/-	-6/d5	-7	-6/d5	6/-	-7
6	-6/d5	6/-	-6/d5	-7	6/-	-7	-6/d5
7	6/-	-7	-6/d5	6/-	-6/d5	-7	-6/d5
8	-7	6/-	-6/d5	-7	6/-	-7	-6/d5
9	-7	-6/d5	6/-	-7	-6/d5	-6/d5	6/-
10	-7	6/-	-6/d5	6/-	-7	-6/d5	-7

C5-2
(Copy 3)

Chord identification

Shield the answer. Listen to the chord and write the figured bass symbol ($^{-7}$, $^{-6}_{d5}$, or $^6_-$); then uncover the answer and compare your response. Circle incorrect responses. Goal: No more than seven errors.

#							
1	$^{-7}$	$^{-6}_{d5}$	$^6_-$	$^{-6}_{d5}$	$^{-7}$	$^6_-$	$^{-6}_{d5}$
2	$^6_-$	$^{-7}$	$^{-6}_{d5}$	$^{-7}$	$^6_-$	$^{-6}_{d5}$	$^6_-$
3	$^{-6}_{d5}$	$^{-7}$	$^{-7}$	$^6_-$	$^{-7}$	$^{-6}_{d5}$	$^6_-$
4	$^{-7}$	$^{-7}$	$^{-6}_{d5}$	$^6_-$	$^{-7}$	$^6_-$	$^{-6}_{d5}$
5	$^{-7}$	$^6_-$	$^{-6}_{d5}$	$^{-7}$	$^{-6}_{d5}$	$^6_-$	$^{-7}$
6	$^{-6}_{d5}$	$^6_-$	$^{-6}_{d5}$	$^{-7}$	$^6_-$	$^{-7}$	$^{-6}_{d5}$
7	$^6_-$	$^{-7}$	$^{-6}_{d5}$	$^6_-$	$^{-6}_{d5}$	$^{-7}$	$^{-6}_{d5}$
8	$^{-7}$	$^6_-$	$^{-6}_{d5}$	$^{-7}$	$^6_-$	$^{-7}$	$^{-6}_{d5}$
9	$^{-7}$	$^{-6}_{d5}$	$^6_-$	$^{-7}$	$^{-6}_{d5}$	$^{-6}_{d5}$	$^6_-$
10	$^{-7}$	$^6_-$	$^{-6}_{d5}$	$^6_-$	$^{-7}$	$^{-6}_{d5}$	$^{-7}$

C5-2
(Copy 4)

Chord identification

Shield the answer. Listen to the chord and write the figured bass symbol ($^{-7}$, $^{-6}_{d5}$, or $^6_-$); then uncover the answer and compare your response. Circle incorrect responses. Goal: No more than seven errors.

#							
1	$^{-7}$	$^{-6}_{d5}$	$^6_-$	$^{-6}_{d5}$	$^{-7}$	$^6_-$	$^{-6}_{d5}$
2	$^6_-$	$^{-7}$	$^{-6}_{d5}$	$^{-7}$	$^6_-$	$^{-6}_{d5}$	$^6_-$
3	$^{-6}_{d5}$	$^{-7}$	$^{-7}$	$^6_-$	$^{-7}$	$^{-6}_{d5}$	$^6_-$
4	$^{-7}$	$^{-7}$	$^{-6}_{d5}$	$^6_-$	$^{-7}$	$^6_-$	$^{-6}_{d5}$
5	$^{-7}$	$^6_-$	$^{-6}_{d5}$	$^{-7}$	$^{-6}_{d5}$	$^6_-$	$^{-7}$
6	$^{-6}_{d5}$	$^6_-$	$^{-6}_{d5}$	$^{-7}$	$^6_-$	$^{-7}$	$^{-6}_{d5}$
7	$^6_-$	$^{-7}$	$^{-6}_{d5}$	$^6_-$	$^{-6}_{d5}$	$^{-7}$	$^{-6}_{d5}$
8	$^{-7}$	$^6_-$	$^{-6}_{d5}$	$^{-7}$	$^6_-$	$^{-7}$	$^{-6}_{d5}$
9	$^{-7}$	$^{-6}_{d5}$	$^6_-$	$^{-7}$	$^{-6}_{d5}$	$^{-6}_{d5}$	$^6_-$
10	$^{-7}$	$^6_-$	$^{-6}_{d5}$	$^6_-$	$^{-7}$	$^{-6}_{d5}$	$^{-7}$

C5–2

Chord identification

Shield the answer. Listen to the chord and write the figured bass symbol ($^{-7}$, $^{-6}_{d5}$, or $^{6}_{-}$); then uncover the answer and compare your response. Circle incorrect responses. Goal: No more than seven errors.

1 ____ $^{-7}$ ____ $^{-6}_{d5}$ ____ $^{6}_{-}$ ____ $^{-6}_{d5}$ ____ $^{-7}$ ____ $^{6}_{-}$ ____ $^{-6}_{d5}$

2 ____ $^{6}_{-}$ ____ $^{-7}$ ____ $^{-6}_{d5}$ ____ $^{-7}$ ____ $^{6}_{-}$ ____ $^{-6}_{d5}$ ____ $^{6}_{-}$

3 ____ $^{-6}_{d5}$ ____ $^{-7}$ ____ $^{-7}$ ____ $^{6}_{-}$ ____ $^{-7}$ ____ $^{-6}_{d5}$ ____ $^{6}_{-}$

4 ____ $^{-7}$ ____ $^{-7}$ ____ $^{-6}_{d5}$ ____ $^{6}_{-}$ ____ $^{-7}$ ____ $^{6}_{-}$ ____ $^{-6}_{d5}$

5 ____ $^{-7}$ ____ $^{6}_{-}$ ____ $^{-6}_{d5}$ ____ $^{-7}$ ____ $^{-6}_{d5}$ ____ $^{6}_{-}$ ____ $^{-7}$

6 ____ $^{-6}_{d5}$ ____ $^{6}_{-}$ ____ $^{-6}_{d5}$ ____ $^{-7}$ ____ $^{6}_{-}$ ____ $^{-7}$ ____ $^{-6}_{d5}$

7 ____ $^{6}_{-}$ ____ $^{-7}$ ____ $^{-6}_{d5}$ ____ $^{6}_{-}$ ____ $^{-6}_{d5}$ ____ $^{-7}$ ____ $^{-6}_{d5}$

8 ____ $^{-7}$ ____ $^{6}_{-}$ ____ $^{-6}_{d5}$ ____ $^{-7}$ ____ $^{6}_{-}$ ____ $^{-7}$ ____ $^{-6}_{d5}$

9 ____ $^{-7}$ ____ $^{-6}_{d5}$ ____ $^{6}_{-}$ ____ $^{-7}$ ____ $^{-6}_{d5}$ ____ $^{-6}_{d5}$ ____ $^{6}_{-}$

10 ____ $^{-7}$ ____ $^{6}_{-}$ ____ $^{-6}_{d5}$ ____ $^{6}_{-}$ ____ $^{-7}$ ____ $^{-6}_{d5}$ ____ $^{-7}$

C5-3a
(Copy 1)

Figured bass dictation

Shield the answer. Listen to the chord and write the bass note and the figured bass symbol; then uncover the answer and compare your response. Circle incorrect responses. Goal: No more than seven errors. The first frame requires no response.

C5-3a

(Copy 2)

Figured bass dictation

Shield the answer. Listen to the chord and write the bass note and the figured bass symbol; then uncover the answer and compare your response. Circle incorrect responses. Goal: No more than seven errors. The first frame requires no response.

C5-3a

(Copy 3)

Figured bass dictation

Shield the answer. Listen to the chord and write the bass note and the figured bass symbol; then uncover the answer and compare your response. Circle incorrect responses. Goal: No more than seven errors. The first frame requires no response.

C5-3a
(Copy 4)

Figured bass dictation

Shield the answer. Listen to the chord and write the bass note and the figured bass symbol; then uncover the answer and compare your response. Circle incorrect responses. Goal: No more than seven errors. The first frame requires no response.

C5-3a

(Copy 5)

Figured bass dictation

Shield the answer. Listen to the chord and write the bass note and the figured bass symbol; then uncover the answer and compare your response. Circle incorrect responses. Goal: No more than seven errors. The first frame requires no response.

The composite chord symbol for the seventh chord in first inversion on the fifth degree of both major and minor keys is V_{d5}^{-6}. The third of this chord, which appears in the bass, in the *leading tone,* or seventh degree of the key.

The composite chord symbol for the triad in first inversion on the leading tone of both major and minor keys is $VII^{\underline{6}}$. The triad on the leading tone of the key is diminished, so the figured bass portion of the symbol is $\underline{6}$. The third of this chord, which appears in the bass, is the second degree of the key. When the second degree of the key appears in the bass in this lesson, the chord may be either II^- or $VII^{\underline{6}}$.

C5-3b
(Copy 1)

Chord identification in a key

Shield the answer. Listen to the chord and write the composite chord symbol; then uncover the answer and compare your response. Circle incorrect responses. Goal: No more than seven errors. The first frame requires no response.

1	I	___	V_{d5}^{-6}	___	V^{-7}	___	I	___	$VII^{\underline{6}}$	___	I^{-6}	___	$VII^{\underline{6}}$
2	___ I	___	IV	___	$VII^{\underline{6}}$	___	V_{d5}^{-6}	___	I	___	V	___	V_{d5}^{-6}
3	___ I	___	$VII^{\underline{6}}$	___	I^{-6}	___	V^{-7}	___	IV^{-6}	___	V_{d5}^{-6}	___	I
4	___ VI^-	___	$VII^{\underline{6}}$	___	I^{-6}	___	V_{d5}^{-6}	___	I	___	II^6	___	$VII^{\underline{6}}$
5	___ I	___	V_{d5}^{-6}	___	I	___	VI^-	___	V^{-6}	___	V^{-7}	___	I
6	___ I^{-6}	___	$VII^{\underline{6}}$	___	I	___	V_{d5}^{-6}	___	V^{-7}	___	IV^{-6}	___	II^-
7	___ $VII^{\underline{6}}$	___	I	___	VI^-	___	V_{d5}^{-6}	___	I	___	II^6	___	V^{-7}
8	___ V_{d5}^{-6}	___	I	___	$VII^{\underline{6}}$	___	I^{-6}	___	V_{d5}^{-6}	___	I	___	IV^{-6}
9	___ V^{-7}	___	I	___	I^{-6}	___	$VII^{\underline{6}}$	___	I	___	VI^-	___	V_{d5}^{-6}
10	___ I	___	IV	___	$VII^{\underline{6}}$	___	V_{d5}^{-6}	___	I	___	V^{-7}	___	I

C5-3b

Chord identification in a key

Shield the answer. Listen to the chord and write the composite chord symbol; then uncover the answer and compare your response. Circle incorrect responses. Goal: No more than seven errors. The first frame requires no response.

1   I   ____ V_{d5}^{-6} ____ V^{-7} ____ I   ____ VII_{-}^{6} ____ I^{-6} ____ VII_{-}^{6}

2   ____ I   ____ IV   ____ VII_{-}^{6} ____ V_{d5}^{-6} ____ I   ____ V   ____ V_{d5}^{-6}

3   ____ I   ____ VII_{-}^{6} ____ I^{-6} ____ V^{-7} ____ IV^{-6} ____ V_{d5}^{-6} ____ I

4   ____ VI^{-} ____ VII_{-}^{6} ____ I^{-6} ____ V_{d5}^{-6} ____ I   ____ II^{6} ____ VII_{-}^{6}

5   ____ I   ____ V_{d5}^{-6} ____ I   ____ VI^{-} ____ V^{-6} ____ V^{-7} ____ I

6   ____ I^{-6} ____ VII_{-}^{6} ____ I   ____ V_{d5}^{-6} ____ V^{-7} ____ IV^{-6} ____ II^{-}

7   ____ VII_{-}^{6} ____ I   ____ VI^{-} ____ V_{d5}^{-6} ____ I   ____ II^{6} ____ V^{-7}

8   ____ V_{d5}^{-6} ____ I   ____ VII_{-}^{6} ____ I^{-6} ____ V_{d5}^{-6} ____ I   ____ IV^{-6}

9   ____ V^{-7} ____ I   ____ I^{-6} ____ VII_{-}^{6} ____ I   ____ VI^{-} ____ V_{d5}^{-6}

10   ____ I   ____ IV   ____ VII_{-}^{6} ____ V_{d5}^{-6} ____ I   ____ V^{-7} ____ I

C5-3b

Chord identification in a key

Shield the answer. Listen to the chord and write the composite chord symbol; then uncover the answer and compare your response. Circle incorrect responses. Goal: No more than seven errors. The first frame requires no response.

1   I   ____ V_{d5}^{-6} ____ V^{-7} ____ I   ____ VII_{-}^{6} ____ I^{-6} ____ VII_{-}^{6}

2   ____ I   ____ IV   ____ VII_{-}^{6} ____ V_{d5}^{-6} ____ I   ____ V   ____ V_{d5}^{-6}

3   ____ I   ____ VII_{-}^{6} ____ I^{-6} ____ V^{-7} ____ IV^{-6} ____ V_{d5}^{-6} ____ I

4   ____ VI^{-} ____ VII_{-}^{6} ____ I^{-6} ____ V_{d5}^{-6} ____ I   ____ II^{6} ____ VII_{-}^{6}

5   ____ I   ____ V_{d5}^{-6} ____ I   ____ VI^{-} ____ V^{-6} ____ V^{-7} ____ I

6   ____ I^{-6} ____ VII_{-}^{6} ____ I   ____ V_{d5}^{-6} ____ V^{-7} ____ IV^{-6} ____ II^{-}

7   ____ VII_{-}^{6} ____ I   ____ VI^{-} ____ V_{d5}^{-6} ____ I   ____ II^{6} ____ V^{-7}

8   ____ V_{d5}^{-6} ____ I   ____ VII_{-}^{6} ____ I^{-6} ____ V_{d5}^{-6} ____ I   ____ IV^{-6}

9   ____ V^{-7} ____ I   ____ I^{-6} ____ VII_{-}^{6} ____ I   ____ VI^{-} ____ V_{d5}^{-6}

10   ____ I   ____ IV   ____ VII_{-}^{6} ____ V_{d5}^{-6} ____ I   ____ V^{-7} ____ I

C5-3b
(Copy 4)

Chord identification in a key

Shield the answer. Listen to the chord and write the composite chord symbol; then uncover the answer and compare your response. Circle incorrect responses. Goal: No more than seven errors. The first frame requires no response.

1. I ___ V_{d5}^{-6} ___ V^{-7} ___ I ___ $VII_{\_}^{6}$ ___ I^{-6} ___ $VII_{\_}^{6}$

2. ___ I ___ IV ___ $VII_{\_}^{6}$ ___ V_{d5}^{-6} ___ I ___ V ___ V_{d5}^{-6}

3. ___ I ___ $VII_{\_}^{6}$ ___ I^{-6} ___ V^{-7} ___ IV^{-6} ___ V_{d5}^{-6} ___ I

4. ___ VI^- ___ $VII_{\_}^{6}$ ___ I^{-6} ___ V_{d5}^{-6} ___ I ___ II^{6} ___ $VII_{\_}^{6}$

5. ___ I ___ V_{d5}^{-6} ___ I ___ VI^- ___ V^{-6} ___ V^{-7} ___ I

6. ___ I^{-6} ___ $VII_{\_}^{6}$ ___ I ___ V_{d5}^{-6} ___ V^{-7} ___ IV^{-6} ___ II^-

7. ___ $VII_{\_}^{6}$ ___ I ___ VI^- ___ V_{d5}^{-6} ___ I ___ II^{6} ___ V^{-7}

8. ___ V_{d5}^{-6} ___ I ___ $VII_{\_}^{6}$ ___ I^{-6} ___ V_{d5}^{-6} ___ I ___ IV^{-6}

9. ___ V^{-7} ___ I ___ I^{-6} ___ $VII_{\_}^{6}$ ___ I ___ VI^- ___ V_{d5}^{-6}

10. ___ I ___ IV ___ $VII_{\_}^{6}$ ___ V_{d5}^{-6} ___ I ___ V^{-7} ___ I

C5-3b
(Copy 5)

Chord identification in a key

Shield the answer. Listen to the chord and write the composite chord symbol; then uncover the answer and compare your response. Circle incorrect responses. Goal: No more than seven errors. The first frame requires no response.

1. I ___ V_{d5}^{-6} ___ V^{-7} ___ I ___ $VII_{\_}^{6}$ ___ I^{-6} ___ $VII_{\_}^{6}$

2. ___ I ___ IV ___ $VII_{\_}^{6}$ ___ V_{d5}^{-6} ___ I ___ V ___ V_{d5}^{-6}

3. ___ I ___ $VII_{\_}^{6}$ ___ I^{-6} ___ V^{-7} ___ IV^{-6} ___ V_{d5}^{-6} ___ I

4. ___ VI^- ___ $VII_{\_}^{6}$ ___ I^{-6} ___ V_{d5}^{-6} ___ I ___ II^{6} ___ $VII_{\_}^{6}$

5. ___ I ___ V_{d5}^{-6} ___ I ___ VI^- ___ V^{-6} ___ V^{-7} ___ I

6. ___ I^{-6} ___ $VII_{\_}^{6}$ ___ I ___ V_{d5}^{-6} ___ V^{-7} ___ IV^{-6} ___ II^-

7. ___ $VII_{\_}^{6}$ ___ I ___ VI^- ___ V_{d5}^{-6} ___ I ___ II^{6} ___ V^{-7}

8. ___ V_{d5}^{-6} ___ I ___ $VII_{\_}^{6}$ ___ I^{-6} ___ V_{d5}^{-6} ___ I ___ IV^{-6}

9. ___ V^{-7} ___ I ___ I^{-6} ___ $VII_{\_}^{6}$ ___ I ___ VI^- ___ V_{d5}^{-6}

10. ___ I ___ IV ___ $VII_{\_}^{6}$ ___ V_{d5}^{-6} ___ I ___ V^{-7} ___ I

C5-4a

(Copy 1)

Figured bass dictation

Shield the answer. Listen to the chord and write the bass note and the figured bass symbol; then uncover the answer and compare your response. Circle incorrect responses. Goal: No more than seven errors. The first frame requires no response.

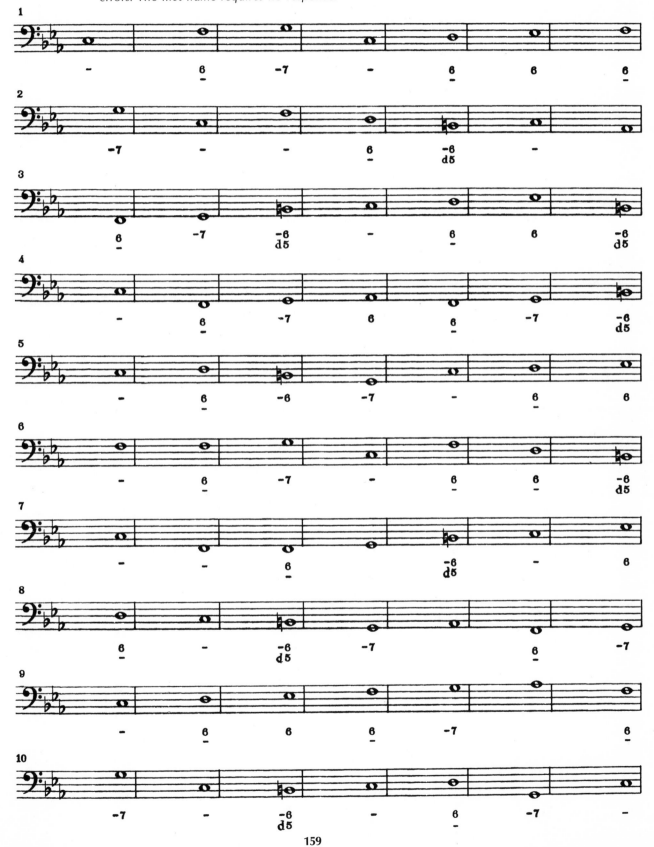

C5-4a

(Copy 2)

Figured bass dictation

Shield the answer. Listen to the chord and write the bass note and the figured bass symbol; then uncover the answer and compare your response. Circle incorrect responses. Goal: No more than seven errors. The first frame requires no response.

160

C5-4a

Figured bass dictation

Shield the answer. Listen to the chord and write the bass note and the figured bass symbol; then uncover the answer and compare your response. Circle incorrect responses. Goal: No more than seven errors. The first frame requires no response.

161

C5-4a
(Copy 4)

Figured bass dictation

Shield the answer. Listen to the chord and write the bass note and the figured bass symbol; then uncover the answer and compare your response. Circle incorrect responses. Goal: No more than seven errors. The first frame requires no response.

162

C5-4a Figured bass dictation

(Copy 5)

Shield the answer. Listen to the chord and write the bass note and the figured bass symbol; then uncover the answer and compare your response. Circle incorrect responses. Goal: No more than seven errors. The first frame requires no response.

This lesson introduces the composite chord symbol for the triad in first inversion on the second degree of a minor key. This triad is diminished, so the figured bass portion of the composite chord symbol is $\underline{6}$, and the composite chord symbol is $\text{II}^{\underline{6}}$. The third of this chord, which appears in the bass, is the fourth degree of the key. When the fourth degree of the key appears in the bass in this lesson, the chord may be either IV^- or $\text{II}^{\underline{6}}$.

C5-4b
(Copy 1)

Chord identification in a key

Shield the answer. Listen to the chord and write the composite chord symbol; then uncover the answer and compare your response. Circle incorrect responses. Goal: No more than seven errors. The first frame requires no response. After you have done this lesson, take Test C5.

1 I^- ___ $\text{II}^{\underline{6}}$ ___ V^{-7} ___ I^- ___ $\text{VII}^{\underline{6}}$ ___ I^6 ___ $\text{II}^{\underline{6}}$

2 ___ V^{-7} ___ I^- ___ IV^- ___ $\text{VII}^{\underline{6}}$ ___ V^{-6}_{d5} ___ I^- ___ ^-VI

3 ___ $\text{II}^{\underline{6}}$ ___ V^{-7} ___ V^{-6}_{d5} ___ I^- ___ $\text{VII}^{\underline{6}}$ ___ I^6 ___ V^{-6}_{d5}

4 ___ I^- ___ $\text{II}^{\underline{6}}$ ___ V^{-7} ___ IV^6 ___ $\text{II}^{\underline{6}}$ ___ V^{-7} ___ V^{-6}_{d5}

5 ___ I^- ___ $\text{VII}^{\underline{6}}$ ___ V^{-6} ___ V^{-7} ___ I^- ___ $\text{VII}^{\underline{6}}$ ___ I^6

6 ___ IV^- ___ $\text{II}^{\underline{6}}$ ___ V^{-7} ___ I^- ___ $\text{II}^{\underline{6}}$ ___ $\text{VII}^{\underline{6}}$ ___ V^{-6}_{d5}

7 ___ I^- ___ IV^- ___ $\text{II}^{\underline{6}}$ ___ V ___ V^{-6}_{d5} ___ I^- ___ I^6

8 ___ $\text{VII}^{\underline{6}}$ ___ I^- ___ V^{-6}_{d5} ___ V^{-7} ___ ^-VI ___ $\text{II}^{\underline{6}}$ ___ V^{-7}

9 ___ I^- ___ $\text{VII}^{\underline{6}}$ ___ I^6 ___ $\text{II}^{\underline{6}}$ ___ V^{-7} ___ ^-VI ___ $\text{II}^{\underline{6}}$

10 ___ V^{-7} ___ I^- ___ V^{-6}_{d5} ___ I^- ___ $\text{VII}^{\underline{6}}$ ___ V^{-7} ___ I^-

C5-4b
(Copy 2)

Chord identification in a key

Shield the answer. Listen to the chord and write the composite chord symbol; then uncover the answer and compare your response. Circle incorrect responses. Goal: No more than seven errors. The first frame requires no response. After you have done this lesson, take Test C5.

1   I^- ___ II^6_- ___ V^{-7} ___ I^- ___ VII^6_- ___ I^6 ___ II^6_-

2   ___ V^{-7} ___ I^- ___ IV^- ___ VII^6_- ___ V^{-6}_{d5} ___ I^- ___ ^-VI

3   ___ II^6_- ___ V^{-7} ___ V^{-6}_{d5} ___ I^- ___ VII^6_- ___ I^6 ___ V^{-6}_{d5}

4   ___ I^- ___ II^6_- ___ V^{-7} ___ IV^6 ___ II^6_- ___ V^{-7} ___ V^{-6}_{d5}

5   ___ I^- ___ VII^6_- ___ V^{-6} ___ V^{-7} ___ I^- ___ VII^6_- ___ I^6

6   ___ IV^- ___ II^6_- ___ V^{-7} ___ I^- ___ II^6_- ___ VII^6_- ___ V^{-6}_{d5}

7   ___ I^- ___ IV^- ___ II^6_- ___ V ___ V^{-6}_{d5} ___ I^- ___ I^6

8   ___ VII^6_- ___ I^- ___ V^{-6}_{d5} ___ V^{-7} ___ ^-VI ___ II^6_- ___ V^{-7}

9   ___ I^- ___ VII^6_- ___ I^6 ___ II^6_- ___ V^{-7} ___ ^-VI ___ II^6_-

10   ___ V^{-7} ___ I^- ___ V^{-6}_{d5} ___ I^- ___ VII^6_- ___ V^{-7} ___ I^-

C5-4b
(Copy 3)

Chord identification in a key

Shield the answer. Listen to the chord and write the composite chord symbol; then uncover the answer and compare your response. Circle incorrect responses. Goal: No more than seven errors. The first frame requires no response. After you have done this lesson, take Test C5.

1   I^- ___ II^6_- ___ V^{-7} ___ I^- ___ VII^6_- ___ I^6 ___ II^6_-

2   ___ V^{-7} ___ I^- ___ IV^- ___ VII^6_- ___ V^{-6}_{d5} ___ I^- ___ ^-VI

3   ___ II^6_- ___ V^{-7} ___ V^{-6}_{d5} ___ I^- ___ VII^6_- ___ I^6 ___ V^{-6}_{d5}

4   ___ I^- ___ II^6_- ___ V^{-7} ___ IV^6 ___ II^6_- ___ V^{-7} ___ V^{-6}_{d5}

5   ___ I^- ___ VII^6_- ___ V^{-6} ___ V^{-7} ___ I^- ___ VII^6_- ___ I^6

6   ___ IV^- ___ II^6_- ___ V^{-7} ___ I^- ___ II^6_- ___ VII^6_- ___ V^{-6}_{d5}

7   ___ I^- ___ IV^- ___ II^6_- ___ V ___ V^{-6}_{d5} ___ I^- ___ I^6

8   ___ VII^6_- ___ I^- ___ V^{-6}_{d5} ___ V^{-7} ___ ^-VI ___ II^6_- ___ V^{-7}

9   ___ I^- ___ VII^6_- ___ I^6 ___ II^6_- ___ V^{-7} ___ ^-VI ___ II^6_-

10   ___ V^{-7} ___ I^- ___ V^{-6}_{d5} ___ I^- ___ VII^6_- ___ V^{-7} ___ I^-

Chord identification in a key

Shield the answer. Listen to the chord and write the composite chord symbol; then uncover the answer and compare your response. Circle incorrect responses. Goal: No more than seven errors. The first frame requires no response. After you have done this lesson, take Test C5.

1 I^- ____ II_-^6 ____ V^{-7} ____ I^- ____ VII_-^6 ____ I^6 ____ II_-^6

2 ____ V^{-7} ____ I^- ____ IV^- ____ VII_-^6 ____ V_{d5}^{-6} ____ I^- ____ ^-VI

3 ____ II_-^6 ____ V^{-7} ____ V_{d5}^{-6} ____ I^- ____ VII_-^6 ____ I^6 ____ V_{d5}^{-6}

4 ____ I^- ____ II_-^6 ____ V^{-7} ____ IV^6 ____ II_-^6 ____ V^{-7} ____ V_{d5}^{-6}

5 ____ I^- ____ VII_-^6 ____ V^{-6} ____ V^{-7} ____ I^- ____ VII_-^6 ____ I^6

6 ____ IV^- ____ II_-^6 ____ V^{-7} ____ I^- ____ II_-^6 ____ VII_-^6 ____ V_{d5}^{-6}

7 ____ I^- ____ IV^- ____ II_-^6 ____ V ____ V_{d5}^{-6} ____ I^- ____ I^6

8 ____ VII_-^6 ____ I^- ____ V_{d5}^{-6} ____ V^{-7} ____ ^-VI ____ II_-^6 ____ V^{-7}

9 ____ I^- ____ VII_-^6 ____ I^6 ____ II_-^6 ____ V^{-7} ____ ^-VI ____ II_-^6

10 ____ V^{-7} ____ I^- ____ V_{d5}^{-6} ____ I^- ____ VII_-^6 ____ V^{-7} ____ I^-

Chord identification in a key

Shield the answer. Listen to the chord and write the composite chord symbol; then uncover the answer and compare your response. Circle incorrect responses. Goal: No more than seven errors. The first frame requires no response. After you have done this lesson, take Test C5.

1 I^- ____ II_-^6 ____ V^{-7} ____ I^- ____ VII_-^6 ____ I^6 ____ II_-^6

2 ____ V^{-7} ____ I^- ____ IV^- ____ VII_-^6 ____ V_{d5}^{-6} ____ I^- ____ ^-VI

3 ____ II_-^6 ____ V^{-7} ____ V_{d5}^{-6} ____ I^- ____ VII_-^6 ____ I^6 ____ V_{d5}^{-6}

4 ____ I^- ____ II_-^6 ____ V^{-7} ____ IV^6 ____ II_-^6 ____ V^{-7} ____ V_{d5}^{-6}

5 ____ I^- ____ VII_-^6 ____ V^{-6} ____ V^{-7} ____ I^- ____ VII_-^6 ____ I^6

6 ____ IV^- ____ II_-^6 ____ V^{-7} ____ I^- ____ II_-^6 ____ VII_-^6 ____ V_{d5}^{-6}

7 ____ I^- ____ IV^- ____ II_-^6 ____ V ____ V_{d5}^{-6} ____ I^- ____ I^6

8 ____ VII_-^6 ____ I^- ____ V_{d5}^{-6} ____ V^{-7} ____ ^-VI ____ II_-^6 ____ V^{-7}

9 ____ I^- ____ VII_-^6 ____ I^6 ____ II_-^6 ____ V^{-7} ____ ^-VI ____ II_-^6

10 ____ V^{-7} ____ I^- ____ V_{d5}^{-6} ____ I^- ____ VII_-^6 ____ V^{-7} ____ I^-

Major and Minor Triads
in Second Inversion

SERIES C6

This series introduces the major and minor triad in second inversion and includes all the chords studied in previous lessons. A triad is said to be in second inversion when the fifth of the chord appears as the lowest note or bass. The upper tones of a major triad in second inversion are at the intervals of a major sixth and perfect fourth above the bass. The upper tones of a minor triad in second inversion are at the intervals of a minor sixth and perfect fourth above the bass.

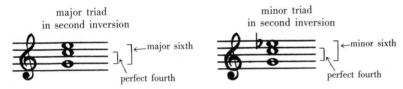

When you have done this series, take Test C6, which includes sections on each of the four kinds of lessons found in this series.

C6-1a

(Copy 1)

Chord dictation

Shield the answer. Listen to the chord and notate the upper tones above the given note; then uncover the answer and compare your response. Circle incorrect responses. Goal: No more than seven errors.

C6-1a

Chord dictation

Shield the answer. Listen to the chord and notate the upper tones above the given note; then uncover the answer and compare your response. Circle incorrect responses. Goal: No more than seven errors.

169

C6-1a
(Copy 3)

Chord dictation

Shield the answer. Listen to the chord and notate the upper tones above the given note; then uncover the answer and compare your response. Circle incorrect responses. Goal: No more than seven errors.

C6-1a

Chord dictation

*Shield the answer. Listen to the chord and notate the upper tones above the given note; then uncover
the answer and compare your response. Circle incorrect responses. Goal: No more than seven errors.*

C6-1a

Chord dictation

Shield the answer. Listen to the chord and notate the upper tones above the given note; then uncover the answer and compare your response. Circle incorrect responses. Goal: No more than seven errors.

172

Lesson **C6-1b**

This lesson introduces the figured bass symbols for the major and minor triads in second inversion. The intervals between upper tones and the bass of a major triad in second inversion are a major sixth and a perfect fourth, and the complete figured bass symbol is $^6_4$. The intervals between the upper tones and the bass of a minor triad in second inversion are a minor sixth and a perfect fourth, and the complete figured bass symbol is $^{-6}_4$. These symbols are not abbreviated; use the complete symbol to identify these chords.

C6-1b
(Copy 1)

Chord identification

Shield the answer. Listen to the chord and write the figured bass symbol (blank, -, $^{-6}$, ^{6}, $^6_4$, or $^{-6}_4$); then uncover the answer and compare your response. Circle incorrect responses. Goal: No more than seven errors.

1. ___ ___ $^6_4$ ___ ___ $^6_4$ ___ ___ $^6_4$ $^{-6}_4$

2. ___ ___ $^{-6}_4$ ___ ^{6} ___ $^{-6}_4$ ___ ___ ^{6} ___ $^6_4$

3. ___ $^6_4$ ___ ___ $^{-6}_4$ $^{-6}_4$ ___ ^{6} ___ $^{-6}_4$ $^6_4$

4. ___ ___ $^{-6}_4$ $^{-6}_4$ ___ $^6_4$ ___ $^{-6}$ ___ $^6_4$ $^6_4$

5. ___ ___ $^{-6}_4$ ___ $^6_4$ ___ ^{6} ___ $^{-6}_4$ ___ $-$ ___ $^{-6}$

6. ___ $^6_4$ $^{-6}_4$ ___ ___ ___ $^6_4$ ___ ___ $^{-6}_4$ ___

7. ___ ^{6} ___ $^6_4$ ___ $^{-6}$ ___ $^{-6}_4$ $^6_4$ ___ ___ $^{-6}$

8. ___ $^{-6}_4$ ___ ___ ^{6} ___ $^{-6}_4$ ___ ___ $^{-6}$ $^6_4$

9. ___ ^{6} ___ $^6_4$ ___ $-$ ___ $^6_4$ ___ $-$ ___ $^6_4$ ___

10. ___ $^{-6}_4$ ___ ^{6} ___ ___ ___ $^{-6}_4$ $^{-6}_4$ ___ ___ ^{6}

C6-1b
(Copy 2)

Chord identification

Shield the answer. Listen to the chord and write the figured bass symbol (blank, ⁻, -6, 6, 6/4, or -6/4); then uncover the answer and compare your response. Circle incorrect responses. Goal: No more than seven errors.

No.	1	2	3	4	5	6	7	8
1	___	___ 6/4	___	___ 6/4	___	___ 6/4	___	___ -6/4
2	___	___ -6/4	___ 6	___ -6/4	___	___	___ 6	___ 6/4
3	___	___ 6/4	___	___ -6/4	___ -6/4	___ 6	___ -6/4	___ 6/4
4	___	___ -6/4	___ -6/4	___ 6/4	___ -6	___	___ 6/4	___ 6/4
5	___	___ -6/4	___ 6/4	___ 6	___ -6/4	___ -	___	___ -6
6	___	___ 6/4	___ -6/4	___	___ 6/4	___	___ -6/4	___
7	___	___ 6	___ 6/4	___ -6	___ -6/4	___ 6/4	___	___ -6
8	___	___ -6/4	___	___ 6	___ -6/4	___	___ -6	___ 6/4
9	___	___ 6	___ 6/4	___ -	___ 6/4	___ -	___ 6/4	___
10	___	___ -6/4	___ 6	___	___ -6/4	___ -6/4	___	___ 6

C6-1b
(Copy 3)

Chord identification

Shield the answer. Listen to the chord and write the figured bass symbol (blank, ⁻, -6, 6, 6/4, or -6/4); then uncover the answer and compare your response. Circle incorrect responses. Goal: No more than seven errors.

No.	1	2	3	4	5	6	7	8
1	___	___ 6/4	___	___ 6/4	___	___ 6/4	___	___ -6/4
2	___	___ -6/4	___ 6	___ -6/4	___	___	___ 6	___ 6/4
3	___	___ 6/4	___	___ -6/4	___ -6/4	___ 6	___ -6/4	___ 6/4
4	___	___ -6/4	___ -6/4	___ 6/4	___ -6	___	___ 6/4	___ 6/4
5	___	___ -6/4	___ 6/4	___ 6	___ -6/4	___ -	___	___ -6
6	___	___ 6/4	___ -6/4	___	___ 6/4	___	___ -6/4	___
7	___	___ 6	___ 6/4	___ -6	___ -6/4	___ 6/4	___	___ -6
8	___	___ -6/4	___	___ 6	___ -6/4	___	___ -6	___ 6/4
9	___	___ 6	___ 6/4	___ -	___ 6/4	___ -	___ 6/4	___
10	___	___ -6/4	___ 6	___	___ -6/4	___ -6/4	___	___ 6

C6-1b
(Copy 4)

Chord identification

Shield the answer. Listen to the chord and write the figured bass symbol (blank, -, -6/4, 6, 6/4, or -6/4); then uncover the answer and compare your response. Circle incorrect responses. Goal: No more than seven errors.

1. ____ ____ 6/4 ____ ____ 6/4 ____ ____ 6/4 ____ -6/4
2. ____ ____ -6/4 6 ____ -6/4 ____ 6 ____ 6/4
3. ____ 6/4 ____ ____ -6/4 ____ -6/4 6 ____ -6/4 ____ 6/4
4. ____ ____ -6/4 ____ -6/4 ____ 6/4 -6 ____ 6/4 ____ 6/4
5. ____ ____ -6/4 ____ 6/4 ____ 6 ____ -6/4 - ____ -6
6. ____ 6/4 ____ -6/4 ____ ____ 6/4 ____ ____ -6/4
7. ____ 6 ____ 6/4 ____ -6 ____ -6/4 6/4 ____ ____ -6
8. ____ -6/4 ____ ____ 6 ____ -6/4 ____ -6 ____ 6/4
9. ____ 6 ____ 6/4 ____ - ____ 6/4 ____ - ____ 6/4 ____
10. ____ -6/4 ____ 6 ____ ____ -6/4 ____ -6/4 ____ 6

C6-1b
(Copy 5)

Chord identification

Shield the answer. Listen to the chord and write the figured bass symbol (blank, -, -6/4, 6, 6/4, or -6/4); then uncover the answer and compare your response. Circle incorrect responses. Goal: No more than seven errors.

1. ____ ____ 6/4 ____ ____ 6/4 ____ ____ 6/4 ____ -6/4
2. ____ ____ -6/4 6 ____ -6/4 ____ ____ 6 ____ 6/4
3. ____ 6/4 ____ ____ -6/4 ____ -6/4 6 ____ -6/4 ____ 6/4
4. ____ ____ -6/4 ____ -6/4 ____ 6/4 -6 ____ 6/4 ____ 6/4
5. ____ ____ -6/4 ____ 6/4 ____ 6 ____ -6/4 - ____ -6
6. ____ 6/4 ____ -6/4 ____ ____ 6/4 ____ ____ -6/4
7. ____ 6 ____ 6/4 ____ -6 ____ -6/4 6/4 ____ ____ -6
8. ____ -6/4 ____ ____ 6 ____ -6/4 ____ -6 ____ 6/4
9. ____ 6 ____ 6/4 ____ - ____ 6/4 ____ - ____ 6/4 ____
10. ____ -6/4 ____ 6 ____ ____ -6/4 ____ -6/4 ____ 6

C6-2
(Copy 1)

Chord identification

Shield the answer. Listen to the chord and write the figured bass symbol (blank, ⁻, ⁻⁶, ⁶, ⁶₄); then uncover the answer and compare your response. Circle incorrect responses. Goal: No more than seven errors.

1 ___ ___ 6/4 ___ -6 ___ 6/4 ___ ___ - ___ -6/4

2 ___ 6 ___ -6/4 ___ -6/4 ___ - ___ -6/4 ___ 6

3 ___ 6/4 ___ - ___ -6/4 ___ -6 ___ 6/4 ___ 6/4

4 ___ ___ -6/4 ___ - ___ -6/4 ___ 6/4 ___ -6

5 ___ 6/4 ___ ___ 6/4 ___ ___ -6/4 ___ -6

6 ___ 6/4 ___ ___ -6/4 ___ -6 ___ 6/4

7 ___ -6/4 ___ ___ 6 ___ 6/4 ___ - ___ 6/4 ___ -6

8 ___ - ___ 6 ___ 6/4 ___ ___ 6/4 ___ ___ 6/4

9 ___ 6/4 ___ ___ 6/4 ___ 6/4 ___ 6 ___ -6/4 ___ -6/4

10 ___ ___ 6 ___ 6/4 ___ - ___ 6/4 ___

C6-2
(Copy 2)

Chord identification

Shield the answer. Listen to the chord and write the figured bass symbol (blank, ⁻, ⁻⁶, ⁶, ⁶₄); then uncover the answer and compare your response. Circle incorrect responses. Goal: No more than seven errors.

1 ___ ___ 6/4 ___ -6 ___ 6/4 ___ ___ - ___ -6/4

2 ___ 6 ___ -6/4 ___ -6/4 ___ - ___ -6/4 ___ 6

3 ___ 6/4 ___ - ___ -6/4 ___ -6 ___ 6/4 ___ 6/4

4 ___ ___ -6/4 ___ - ___ -6/4 ___ 6/4 ___ -6

5 ___ 6/4 ___ ___ 6/4 ___ ___ -6/4 ___ -6

6 ___ 6/4 ___ ___ -6/4 ___ -6 ___ 6/4 ___

7 ___ -6/4 ___ ___ 6 ___ 6/4 ___ - ___ 6/4 ___ -6

8 ___ - ___ 6 ___ 6/4 ___ ___ 6/4 ___ ___ 6/4

9 ___ 6/4 ___ ___ 6/4 ___ 6/4 ___ 6 ___ -6/4 ___ -6/4

10 ___ ___ 6 ___ 6/4 ___ - ___ 6/4 ___

C6-2

Chord identification

Shield the answer. Listen to the chord and write the figured bass symbol (blank, -, -6, 6, 6/4); then uncover the answer and compare your response. Circle incorrect responses. Goal: No more than seven errors.

1   _____   _____ $\frac{6}{4}$ _____ -6   _____ $\frac{6}{4}$ _____   _____ -   _____ $\frac{-6}{4}$

2   _____ 6   _____ $\frac{-6}{4}$ _____ $\frac{-6}{4}$ _____ -   _____ $\frac{-6}{4}$ _____   _____ 6

3   _____ $\frac{6}{4}$ _____ -   _____ $\frac{-6}{4}$ _____   _____ -6   _____ $\frac{6}{4}$ _____ $\frac{6}{4}$

4   _____   _____ $\frac{-6}{4}$ _____ -   _____ $\frac{-6}{4}$ _____   _____ $\frac{6}{4}$ _____ -6

5   _____ $\frac{6}{4}$ _____   _____ $\frac{6}{4}$ _____   _____ $\frac{-6}{4}$ _____ -6

6   _____ $\frac{6}{4}$ _____   _____ $\frac{-6}{4}$ _____   _____ -6   _____ $\frac{6}{4}$

7   _____ $\frac{-6}{4}$ _____   _____ 6   _____ $\frac{6}{4}$ _____ -   _____ $\frac{6}{4}$ _____ -6

8   _____ -   _____ 6   _____ $\frac{6}{4}$ _____   _____ $\frac{6}{4}$ _____   _____ $\frac{6}{4}$

9   _____ $\frac{6}{4}$ _____   _____ $\frac{6}{4}$ _____ $\frac{6}{4}$ _____ 6   _____ $\frac{-6}{4}$ _____ $\frac{-6}{4}$

10 _____   _____ 6   _____ $\frac{6}{4}$ _____ -   _____ $\frac{6}{4}$ _____   _____

C6-2

Chord identification

Shield the answer. Listen to the chord and write the figured bass symbol (blank, -, -6, 6, 6/4); then uncover the answer and compare your response. Circle incorrect responses. Goal: No more than seven errors.

1   _____   _____ $\frac{6}{4}$ _____ -6   _____ $\frac{6}{4}$ _____   _____ -   _____ $\frac{-6}{4}$

2   _____ 6   _____ $\frac{-6}{4}$ _____ $\frac{-6}{4}$ _____ -   _____ $\frac{-6}{4}$ _____   _____ 6

3   _____ $\frac{6}{4}$ _____ -   _____ $\frac{-6}{4}$ _____   _____ -6   _____ $\frac{6}{4}$ _____ $\frac{6}{4}$

4   _____   _____ $\frac{-6}{4}$ _____ -   _____ $\frac{-6}{4}$ _____   _____ $\frac{6}{4}$ _____ -6

5   _____ $\frac{6}{4}$ _____   _____ $\frac{6}{4}$ _____   _____ $\frac{-6}{4}$ _____ -6

6   _____ $\frac{6}{4}$ _____   _____ $\frac{-6}{4}$ _____   _____ -6   _____ $\frac{6}{4}$

7   _____ $\frac{-6}{4}$ _____   _____ 6   _____ $\frac{6}{4}$ _____ -   _____ $\frac{6}{4}$ _____ -6

8   _____ -   _____ 6   _____ $\frac{6}{4}$ _____   _____ $\frac{6}{4}$ _____   _____ $\frac{6}{4}$

9   _____ $\frac{6}{4}$ _____   _____ $\frac{6}{4}$ _____ $\frac{6}{4}$ _____ 6   _____ $\frac{-6}{4}$ _____ $\frac{-6}{4}$

10 _____   _____ 6   _____ $\frac{6}{4}$ _____ -   _____ $\frac{6}{4}$ _____   _____

C6–2

(Copy 5)

Chord identification

Shield the answer. Listen to the chord and write the figured bass symbol (blank, -, -6, 6, $\frac{6}{4}$); then uncover the answer and compare your response. Circle incorrect responses. Goal: No more than seven errors.

1. _____ _____ $\frac{6}{4}$ _____ -6 _____ $\frac{6}{4}$ _____ _____ - _____ $\frac{-6}{4}$

2. _____ 6 _____ $\frac{-6}{4}$ _____ $\frac{-6}{4}$ _____ - _____ $\frac{-6}{4}$ _____ _____ 6

3. _____ $\frac{6}{4}$ _____ - _____ $\frac{-6}{4}$ _____ _____ -6 _____ $\frac{6}{4}$ _____ $\frac{6}{4}$

4. _____ _____ $\frac{-6}{4}$ _____ - _____ $\frac{-6}{4}$ _____ _____ $\frac{6}{4}$ _____ -6

5. _____ $\frac{6}{4}$ _____ _____ $\frac{6}{4}$ _____ _____ $\frac{-6}{4}$ _____ _____ -6

6. _____ $\frac{6}{4}$ _____ _____ $\frac{-6}{4}$ _____ _____ -6 _____ $\frac{6}{4}$ _____

7. _____ $\frac{-6}{4}$ _____ _____ 6 _____ $\frac{6}{4}$ _____ - _____ $\frac{6}{4}$ _____ -6

8. _____ - _____ 6 _____ $\frac{6}{4}$ _____ _____ $\frac{6}{4}$ _____ _____ $\frac{6}{4}$

9. _____ $\frac{6}{4}$ _____ _____ $\frac{6}{4}$ _____ $\frac{6}{4}$ _____ 6 _____ $\frac{-6}{4}$ _____ $\frac{-6}{4}$

10. _____ _____ 6 _____ $\frac{6}{4}$ _____ - _____ $\frac{6}{4}$ _____

178

C6-3a

Figured bass dictation

Shield the answer. Listen to the chord and write the bass note and the figured bass symbol; then uncover the answer and compare your response. Circle incorrect responses. Goal: No more than seven errors.

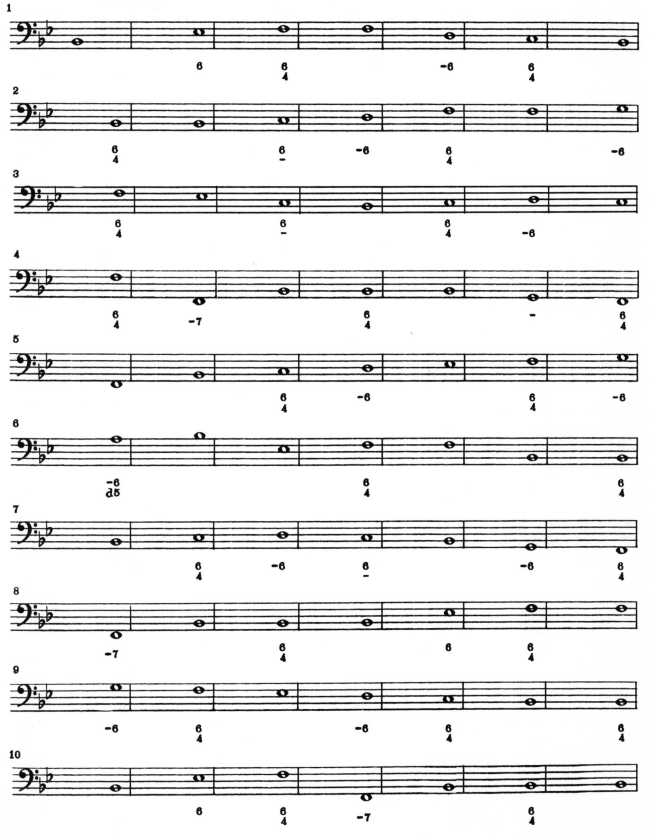

179

C6-3a

Figured bass dictation

Shield the answer. Listen to the chord and write the bass note and the figured bass symbol; then uncover the answer and compare your response. Circle incorrect responses. Goal: No more than seven errors.

C6-3a

Figured bass dictation

Shield the answer. Listen to the chord and write the bass note and the figured bass symbol; then uncover the answer and compare your response. Circle incorrect responses. Goal: No more than seven errors.

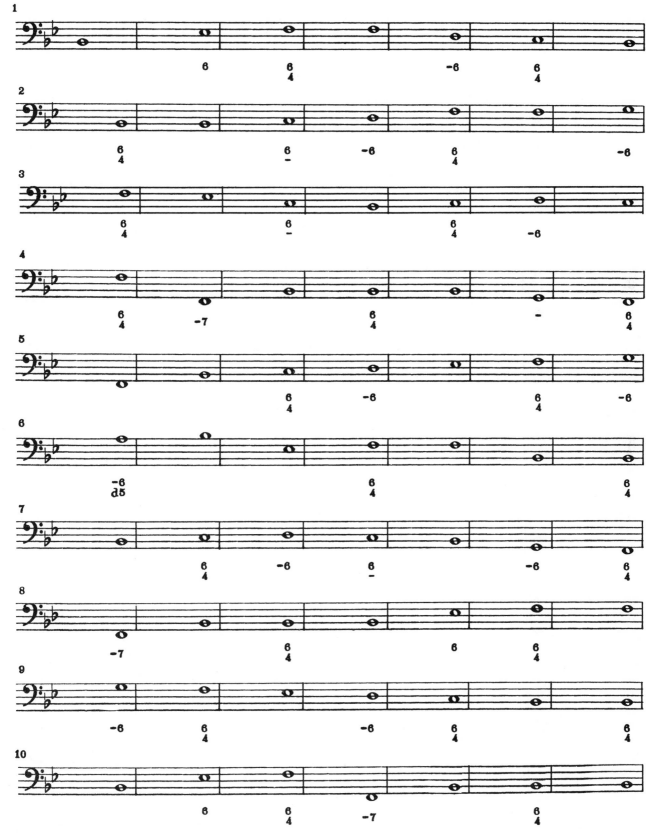

181

C6-3a Figured bass dictation
(Copy 4)

Shield the answer. Listen to the chord and write the bass note and the figured bass symbol; then uncover the answer and compare your response. Circle incorrect responses. Goal: No more than seven errors.

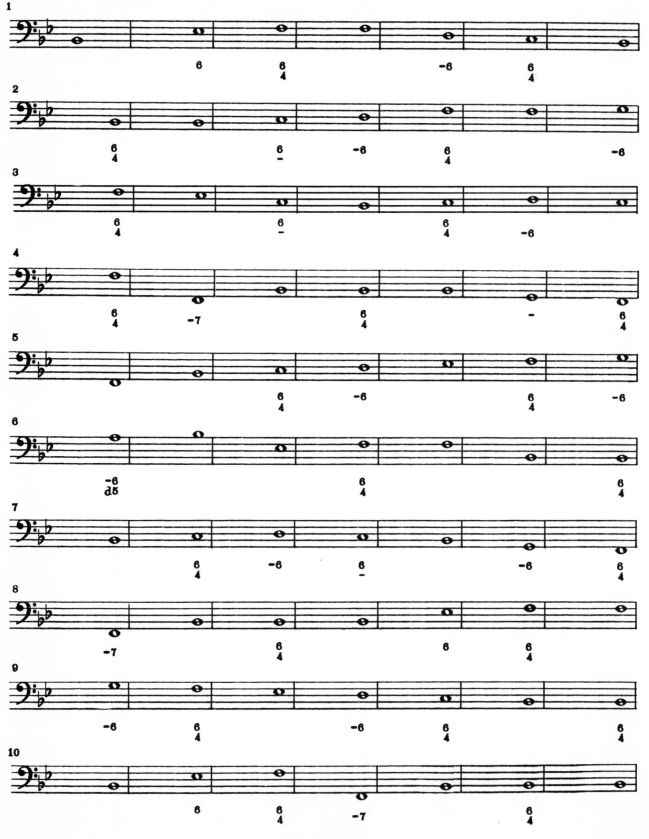

C6-3a Figured bass dictation

(Copy 5)

Shield the answer. Listen to the chord and write the bass note and the figured bass symbol; then uncover the answer and compare your response. Circle incorrect responses. Goal: No more than seven errors.

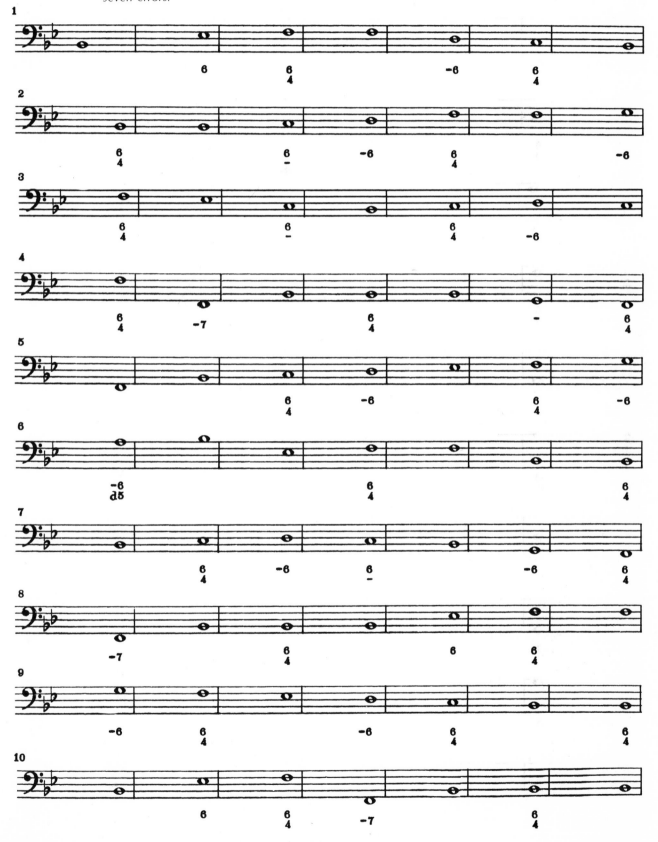

183

This lesson introduces the following composite chord symbols, which appear in a major key: I_4^6, IV_4^6 and V_4^6. The figured bass portion of these symbols is $_4^6$ since the triads on these degrees of a major key are major.

In a six-four chord, the fifth of the chord appears in the bass. Thus, the fifth degree of the key appears in the bass of a I_4^6 chord because that degree is the fifth of the chord. The first degree of the key appears in the bass of a IV_4^6 chord because that is the fifth of the IV chord. The bass of a V_4^6 chord is the second degree of the key.

In this lesson, when the fifth degree of the key is in the bass, the chord may be I_4^6, V or V^{-7}. When the first degree is in the bass, the chord may be IV_4^6 or I. When the second degree is in the bass, the chord may be V_4^6, II^- or VII^6_-.

C6-3b
(Copy 1)

Chord identification in a key

Shield the answer. Listen to the chord and write the composite chord symbol; then uncover the answer and compare your response. Circle incorrect responses. Goal: No more than seven errors. The first frame requires no response.

1   I   ____ II^6 ____ I_4^6 ____ V   ____ I^{-6} ____ V_4^6 ____ I

2   ____ IV_4^6 ____ I   ____ VII^6_- ____ I^{-6} ____ I_4^6 ____ V   ____ IV^{-6}

3   ____ I_4^6 ____ IV   ____ VII^6_- ____ I   ____ V_4^6 ____ I^{-6} ____ II^-

4   ____ I_4^6 ____ V^{-7} ____ I   ____ IV_4^6 ____ I   ____ VI^- ____ I_4^6

5   ____ V   ____ I   ____ V_4^6 ____ I^{-6} ____ IV   ____ I_4^6 ____ IV^{-6}

6   ____ V^{-6}_{d5} ____ I   ____ IV   ____ I_4^6 ____ V   ____ I   ____ IV_4^6

7   ____ I   ____ V_4^6 ____ I^{-6} ____ VII^6_- ____ I   ____ IV^{-6} ____ I_4^6

8   ____ V^{-7} ____ I   ____ IV_4^6 ____ I   ____ II^6 ____ I_4^6 ____ V

9   ____ IV^{-6} ____ I_4^6 ____ IV   ____ I^{-6} ____ V_4^6 ____ I   ____ IV_4^6

10   ____ I   ____ II^6 ____ I_4^6 ____ V^{-7} ____ I   ____ IV_4^6 ____ I

C6-3b
(Copy 2)

Chord identification in a key

Shield the answer. Listen to the chord and write the composite chord symbol; then uncover the answer and compare your response. Circle incorrect responses. Goal: No more than seven errors. The first frame requires no response.

1 I ___ II^6 ___ I^6_4 ___ V ___ I^{-6} ___ V^6_4 ___ I

2 ___ IV^6_4 ___ I ___ VII^6_- ___ I^{-6} ___ I^6_4 ___ V ___ IV^{-6}

3 ___ I^6_4 ___ IV ___ VII^6_- ___ I ___ V^6_4 ___ I^{-6} ___ II^-

4 ___ I^6_4 ___ V^{-7} ___ I ___ IV^6_4 ___ I ___ VI^- ___ I^6_4

5 ___ V ___ I ___ V^6_4 ___ I^{-6} ___ IV ___ I^6_4 ___ IV^{-6}

6 ___ V^{-6}_{d5} ___ I ___ IV ___ I^6_4 ___ V ___ I ___ IV^6_4

7 ___ I ___ V^6_4 ___ I^{-6} ___ VII^6_- ___ I ___ IV^{-6} ___ I^6_4

8 ___ V^{-7} ___ I ___ IV^6_4 ___ I ___ II^6 ___ I^6_4 ___ V

9 ___ IV^{-6} ___ I^6_4 ___ IV ___ I^{-6} ___ V^6_4 ___ I ___ IV^6_4

10 ___ I ___ II^6 ___ I^6_4 ___ V^{-7} ___ I ___ IV^6_4 ___ I

C6-3b
(Copy 3)

Chord identification in a key

Shield the answer. Listen to the chord and write the composite chord symbol; then uncover the answer and compare your response. Circle incorrect responses. Goal: No more than seven errors. The first frame requires no response.

1 I ___ II^6 ___ I^6_4 ___ V ___ I^{-6} ___ V^6_4 ___ I

2 ___ IV^6_4 ___ I ___ VII^6_- ___ I^{-6} ___ I^6_4 ___ V ___ IV^{-6}

3 ___ I^6_4 ___ IV ___ VII^6_- ___ I ___ V^6_4 ___ I^{-6} ___ II^-

4 ___ I^6_4 ___ V^{-7} ___ I ___ IV^6_4 ___ I ___ VI^- ___ I^6_4

5 ___ V ___ I ___ V^6_4 ___ I^{-6} ___ IV ___ I^6_4 ___ IV^{-6}

6 ___ V^{-6}_{d5} ___ I ___ IV ___ I^6_4 ___ V ___ I ___ IV^6_4

7 ___ I ___ V^6_4 ___ I^{-6} ___ VII^6_- ___ I ___ IV^{-6} ___ I^6_4

8 ___ V^{-7} ___ I ___ IV^6_4 ___ I ___ II^6 ___ I^6_4 ___ V

9 ___ IV^{-6} ___ I^6_4 ___ IV ___ I^{-6} ___ V^6_4 ___ I ___ IV^6_4

10 ___ I ___ II^6 ___ I^6_4 ___ V^{-7} ___ I ___ IV^6_4 ___ I

185

C6–3b
(Copy 4)

Chord identification in a key

Shield the answer. Listen to the chord and write the composite chord symbol; then uncover the answer and compare your response. Circle incorrect responses. Goal: No more than seven errors. The first frame requires no response.

1 I   ___ II^6 ___ I^6_4 ___ V   ___ I^{-6} ___ V^6_4 ___ I

2 ___ IV^6_4 ___ I   ___ VII^6_- ___ I^{-6} ___ I^6_4 ___ V   ___ IV^{-6}

3 ___ I^6_4 ___ IV   ___ VII^6_- ___ I   ___ V^6_4 ___ I^{-6} ___ II^{-6}

4 ___ I^6_4 ___ V^{-7} ___ I   ___ IV^6_4 ___ I   ___ VI^- ___ I^6_4

5 ___ V   ___ I   ___ V^6_4 ___ I^{-6} ___ IV   ___ I^6_4 ___ IV^{-6}

6 ___ V^{-6}_{d5} ___ I   ___ IV   ___ I^6_4 ___ V   ___ I   ___ IV^6_4

7 ___ I   ___ V^6_4 ___ I^{-6} ___ VII^6_- ___ I   ___ IV^{-6} ___ I^6_4

8 ___ V^{-7} ___ I   ___ IV^6_4 ___ I   ___ II^6 ___ I^6_4 ___ V

9 ___ IV^{-6} ___ I^6_4 ___ IV   ___ I^{-6} ___ V^6_4 ___ I   ___ IV^6_4

10 ___ I   ___ II^6 ___ I^6_4 ___ V^{-7} ___ I   ___ IV^6_4 ___ I

C6–3b
(Copy 5)

Chord identification in a key

Shield the answer. Listen to the chord and write the composite chord symbol; then uncover the answer and compare your response. Circle incorrect responses. Goal: No more than seven errors. The first frame requires no response.

1 I   ___ II^6 ___ I^6_4 ___ V   ___ I^{-6} ___ V^6_4 ___ I

2 ___ IV^6_4 ___ I   ___ VII^6_- ___ I^{-6} ___ I^6_4 ___ V   ___ IV^{-6}

3 ___ I^6_4 ___ IV   ___ VII^6_- ___ I   ___ V^6_4 ___ I^{-6} ___ II^-

4 ___ I^6_4 ___ V^{-7} ___ I   ___ IV^6_4 ___ I   ___ VI^- ___ I^6_4

5 ___ V   ___ I   ___ V^6_4 ___ I^{-6} ___ IV   ___ I^6_4 ___ IV^{-6}

6 ___ V^{-6}_{d5} ___ I   ___ IV   ___ I^6_4 ___ V   ___ I   ___ IV^6_4

7 ___ I   ___ V^6_4 ___ I^{-6} ___ VII^6_- ___ I   ___ IV^{-6} ___ I^6_4

8 ___ V^{-7} ___ I   ___ IV^6_4 ___ I   ___ II^6 ___ I^6_4 ___ V

9 ___ IV^{-6} ___ I^6_4 ___ IV   ___ I^{-6} ___ V^6_4 ___ I   ___ IV^6_4

10 ___ I   ___ II^6 ___ I^6_4 ___ V^{-7} ___ I   ___ IV^6_4 ___ I

C6-4a

(Copy 1)

Figured bass dictation

Shield the answer. Listen to the chord and write the bass note and the figured bass symbol; then uncover the answer and compare your response. Circle incorrect responses. Goal: No more than seven errors.

C6-4a
(Copy 2)

Figured bass dictation

Shield the answer. Listen to the chord and write the bass note and the figured bass symbol; then uncover the answer and compare your response. Circle incorrect responses. Goal: No more than seven errors.

C6-4a

Figured bass dictation

(Copy 3)

Shield the answer. Listen to the chord and write the bass note and the figured bass symbol; then uncover the answer and compare your response. Circle incorrect responses. Goal: No more than seven errors.

C6-4a

(Copy 4)

Figured bass dictation

Shield the answer. Listen to the chord and write the bass note and the figured bass symbol; then uncover the answer and compare your response. Circle incorrect responses. Goal: No more than seven errors.

C6-4a

Figured bass dictation

(Copy 5)

Shield the answer. Listen to the chord and write the bass note and the figured bass symbol; then uncover the answer and compare your response. Circle incorrect responses. Goal: No more than seven errors.

This lesson introduces the triads in second inversion on the first, fourth, and fifth degree of a minor key. The composite chord symbols for these chords are $I^{-6}_{\ 4}$, $IV^{-6}_{\ 4}$, and V^6_4. Note that the figured bass portions of these symbols in a minor key are $^{-6}_{\ 4}$ for the triads on the first and fourth degree and $^6_4$ for the triad on the fifth degree. Thus the composite chord symbol V^6_4 occurs in both major and minor keys. The symbols $I^{-6}_{\ 4}$ and $IV^{-6}_{\ 4}$ occur in minor keys, and I^6_4 and IV^6_4 in major keys.

C6-4b
(Copy 1)

Chord identification in a key

Shield the answer. Listen to the chord and write the composite chord symbol; then uncover the answer and compare your response. Circle incorrect responses. Goal: No more than seven errors. The first frame requires no response. After you have done this lesson, take Test C6.

1 I^- ___ $IV^{-6}_{\ 4}$ ___ I^- ___ $I^{-6}_{\ 4}$ ___ V ___ I^6 ___ V^6_4

2 ___ I^- ___ II^6_- ___ $I^{-6}_{\ 4}$ ___ V^{-7} ___ I^- ___ VII^6_- ___ I^6

3 ___ V^6_4 ___ I^- ___ $IV^{-6}_{\ 4}$ ___ I^- ___ IV^- ___ $I^{-6}_{\ 4}$ ___ IV^6

4 ___ $I^{-6}_{\ 4}$ ___ V^{-7} ___ I^- ___ V^6_4 ___ I^6 ___ IV^- ___ IV^6

5 ___ $I^{-6}_{\ 4}$ ___ V ___ I^6 ___ VII^6_- ___ I^- ___ $IV^{-6}_{\ 4}$ ___ I^-

6 ___ IV^- ___ I^6 ___ V^6_4 ___ I^- ___ II^6_- ___ $I^{-6}_{\ 4}$ ___ V^{-7}

7 ___ ^-VI ___ IV^- ___ $I^{-6}_{\ 4}$ ___ V ___ I^6 ___ V^6_4 ___ I^-

8 ___ $IV^{-6}_{\ 4}$ ___ I^- ___ ^-III ___ IV^- ___ $I^{-6}_{\ 4}$ ___ IV^6 ___ I^-

9 ___ $IV^{-6}_{\ 4}$ ___ I^- ___ ^-VI ___ $I^{-6}_{\ 4}$ ___ V^{-7} ___ I^- ___ V^6_4

10 ___ I^6 ___ $I^{-6}_{\ 4}$ ___ V ___ V^{-6}_{d5} ___ I^- ___ $IV^{-6}_{\ 4}$ ___ I^-

C6-4b
(Copy 2)

Chord identification in a key

Shield the answer. Listen to the chord and write the composite chord symbol; then uncover the answer and compare your response. Circle incorrect responses. Goal: No more than seven errors. The first frame requires no response. After you have done this lesson, take Test C6.

1 I^- ___ IV^{-6}_4 ___ I^- ___ I^{-6}_4 ___ V ___ I^6 ___ V^6_4

2 ___ I^- ___ $II^6_{\underline{-}}$ ___ I^{-6}_4 ___ V^{-7} ___ I^- ___ $VII^6_{\underline{-}}$ ___ I^6

3 ___ V^6_4 ___ I^- ___ IV^{-6}_4 ___ I^- ___ IV^- ___ I^{-6}_4 ___ IV^6

4 ___ I^{-6}_4 ___ V^{-7} ___ I^- ___ V^6_4 ___ I^6 ___ IV^- ___ IV^6

5 ___ I^{-6}_4 ___ V ___ I^6 ___ $VII^6_{\underline{-}}$ ___ I^- ___ IV^{-6}_4 ___ I^-

6 ___ IV^- ___ I^6 ___ V^6_4 ___ I^- ___ $II^6_{\underline{-}}$ ___ I^{-6}_4 ___ V^{-7}

7 ___ ^-VI ___ IV^- ___ I^{-6}_4 ___ V ___ I^6 ___ V^6_4 ___ I^-

8 ___ IV^{-6}_4 ___ I^- ___ ^-III ___ IV^- ___ I^{-6}_4 ___ IV^6 ___ I^-

9 ___ IV^{-6}_4 ___ I^- ___ ^-VI ___ I^{-6}_4 ___ V^{-7} ___ I^- ___ V^6_4

10 ___ I^6 ___ I^{-6}_4 ___ V ___ V^{-6}_{d5} ___ I^- ___ IV^{-6}_4 ___ I^-

C6-4b
(Copy 3)

Chord identification in a key

Shield the answer. Listen to the chord and write the composite chord symbol; then uncover the answer and compare your response. Circle incorrect responses. Goal: No more than seven errors. The first frame requires no response. After you have done this lesson, take Test C6.

1 I^- ___ IV^{-6}_4 ___ I^- ___ I^{-6}_4 ___ V ___ I^6 ___ V^6_4

2 ___ I^- ___ $II^6_{\underline{-}}$ ___ I^{-6}_4 ___ V^{-7} ___ I^- ___ $VII^6_{\underline{-}}$ ___ I^6

3 ___ V^6_4 ___ I^- ___ IV^{-6}_4 ___ I^- ___ IV^- ___ I^{-6}_4 ___ IV^6

4 ___ I^{-6}_4 ___ V^{-7} ___ I^- ___ V^6_4 ___ I^6 ___ IV^- ___ IV^6

5 ___ I^{-6}_4 ___ V ___ I^6 ___ $VII^6_{\underline{-}}$ ___ I^- ___ IV^{-6}_4 ___ I^-

6 ___ IV^- ___ I^6 ___ V^6_4 ___ I^- ___ $II^6_{\underline{-}}$ ___ I^{-6}_4 ___ V^{-7}

7 ___ ^-VI ___ IV^- ___ I^{-6}_4 ___ V ___ I^6 ___ V^6_4 ___ I^-

8 ___ IV^{-6}_4 ___ I^- ___ ^-III ___ IV^- ___ I^{-6}_4 ___ IV^6 ___ I^-

9 ___ IV^{-6}_4 ___ I^- ___ ^-VI ___ I^{-6}_4 ___ V^{-7} ___ I^- ___ V^6_4

10 ___ I^6 ___ I^{-6}_4 ___ V ___ V^{-6}_{d5} ___ I^- ___ IV^{-6}_4 ___ I^-

C6-4b
(Copy 4)

Chord identification in a key

Shield the answer. Listen to the chord and write the composite chord symbol; then uncover the answer and compare your response. Circle incorrect responses. Goal: No more than seven errors. The first frame requires no response. After you have done this lesson, take Test C6.

1 I^- _____ IV^{-6}_4 _____ I^- _____ I^{-6}_4 _____ V _____ I^6 _____ V^6_4

2 _____ I^- _____ II^6_- _____ I^{-6}_4 _____ V^{-7} _____ I^- _____ VII^6_- _____ I^6

3 _____ V^6_4 _____ I^- _____ IV^{-6}_4 _____ I^- _____ IV^- _____ I^{-6}_4 _____ IV^6

4 _____ I^{-6}_4 _____ V^{-7} _____ I^- _____ V^6_4 _____ I^6 _____ IV^- _____ IV^6

5 _____ I^{-6}_4 _____ V _____ I^6 _____ VII^6_- _____ I^- _____ IV^{-6}_4 _____ I^-

6 _____ IV^- _____ I^6 _____ V^6_4 _____ I^- _____ II^6_- _____ I^{-6}_4 _____ V^{-7}

7 _____ ^-VI _____ IV^- _____ I^{-6}_4 _____ V _____ I^6 _____ V^6_4 _____ I^-

8 _____ IV^{-6}_4 _____ I^- _____ ^-III _____ IV^- _____ I^{-6}_4 _____ IV^6 _____ I^-

9 _____ IV^{-6}_4 _____ I^- _____ ^-VI _____ I^{-6}_4 _____ V^{-7} _____ I^- _____ V^6_4

10 _____ I^6 _____ I^{-6}_4 _____ V _____ V^{-6}_{d5} _____ I^- _____ IV^{-6}_4 _____ I^-

C6-4b
(Copy 5)

Chord identification in a key

Shield the answer. Listen to the chord and write the composite chord symbol; then uncover the answer and compare your response. Circle incorrect responses. Goal: No more than seven errors. The first frame requires no response. After you have done this lesson, take Test C6.

1 I^- _____ IV^{-6}_4 _____ I^- _____ I^{-6}_4 _____ V _____ I^6 _____ V^6_4

2 _____ I^- _____ II^6_- _____ I^{-6}_4 _____ V^{-7} _____ I^- _____ VII^6_- _____ I^6

3 _____ V^6_4 _____ I^- _____ IV^{-6}_4 _____ I^- _____ IV^- _____ I^{-6}_4 _____ IV^6

4 _____ I^{-6}_4 _____ V^{-7} _____ I^- _____ V^6_4 _____ I^6 _____ IV^- _____ IV^6

5 _____ I^{-6}_4 _____ V _____ I^6 _____ VII^6_- _____ I^- _____ IV^{-6}_4 _____ I^-

6 _____ IV^- _____ I^6 _____ V^6_4 _____ I^- _____ II^6_- _____ I^{-6}_4 _____ V^{-7}

7 _____ ^-VI _____ IV^- _____ I^{-6}_4 _____ V _____ I^6 _____ V^6_4 _____ I^-

8 _____ IV^{-6}_4 _____ I^- _____ ^-III _____ IV^- _____ I^{-6}_4 _____ IV^6 _____ I^-

9 _____ IV^{-6}_4 _____ I^- _____ ^-VI _____ I^{-6}_4 _____ V^{-7} _____ I^- _____ V^6_4

10 _____ I^6 _____ I^{-6}_4 _____ V _____ V^{-6}_{d5} _____ I^- _____ IV^{-6}_4 _____ I^-

194

All Chords Previously Studied   SERIES C7

This series is designed as a summary, in which each of the skills that have been developed in the preceding six series is applied to all chords studied so far. In the tests for this series, the four skills of chord dictation, chord identification, figured bass dictation, and chord identification in a key are tested separately, rather than together as in the earlier series. If you wish to improve your score on any of these tests, you may find it helpful to review earlier lessons on that particular skill.

Test C7a is a test in chord dictation and should be taken after you have done lesson C7-1. The lessons that may be reviewed for this test are C1-1a, C1-2a, C2-1a, C3-1a, C4-1a, C5-1a, and C6-1a.

Test C7b is a test in chord identification and should be taken after you have done lesson C7-2. The lessons that may be reviewed for this test are C1-3, C2-2, C3-2, C4-2, C5-2, and C6-2.

Test C7c is a test in figured bass dictation and should be taken after you have done lessons C7-3a and C7-4a. The lessons that may be reviewed for this test are C1-4a, C1-5a, C1-6a, C1-7a, C2-3a, C2-4a, C3-3a, C3-4a, C4-3a, C5-3a, C5-4a, C6-3a, and C6-4a.

Test C7d is a test in chord identification in a key and should be taken after you have done lessons C7-3b and C7-4b. The lessons that may be reviewed for this test are C1-4b, C1-5b, C1-6b, C1-7b, C2-3b, C2-4b, C3-3b, C3-4b, C4-3b, C5-3b, C5-4b, C6-3b, and C6-4b.

C7-1

(Copy 1)

Chord dictation

Shield the answer. Listen to the chord and notate the upper tones above the given note; then uncover the answer and compare your response. Circle incorrect responses. Goal: No more than seven errors. After you have done this lesson, take Test C7a.

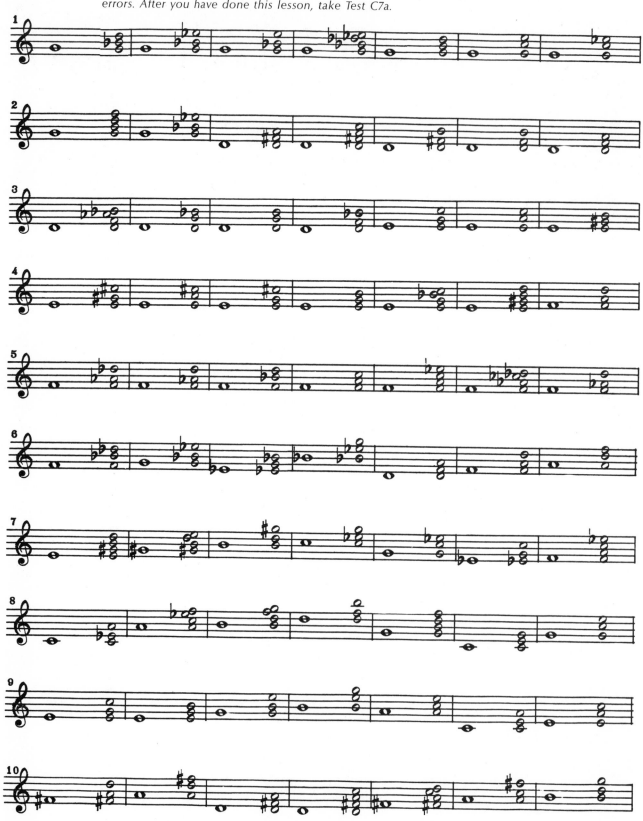

196

C7-1

Chord dictation

Shield the answer. Listen to the chord and notate the upper tones above the given note; then un-cover the answer and compare your response. Circle incorrect responses. Goal: No more than seven errors. After you have done this lesson, take Test C7a.

C7-1

(Copy 3)

Chord dictation

Shield the answer. Listen to the chord and notate the upper tones above the given note; then uncover the answer and compare your response. Circle incorrect responses. Goal: No more than seven errors. After you have done this lesson, take Test C7a.

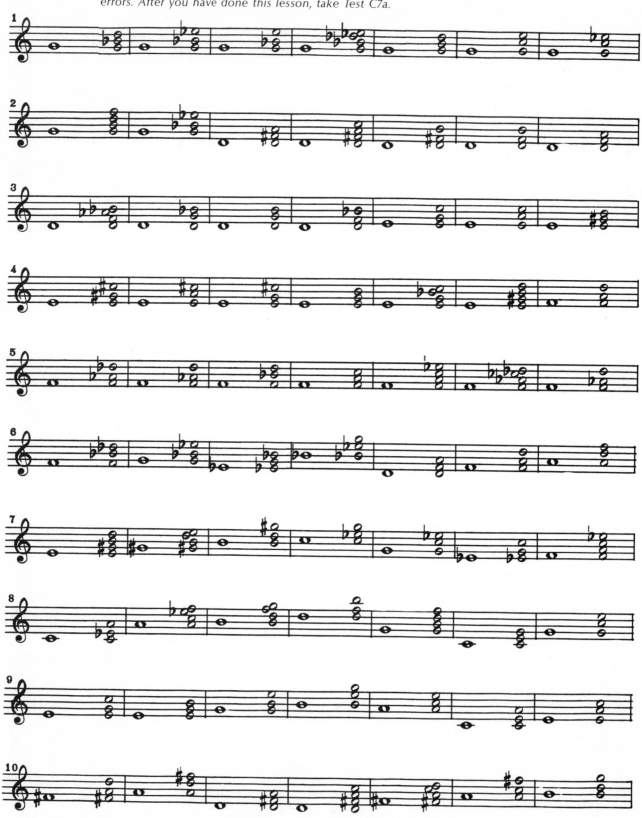

C7-1
(Copy 4)

Chord dictation

Shield the answer. Listen to the chord and notate the upper tones above the given note; then uncover the answer and compare your response. Circle incorrect responses. Goal: No more than seven errors. After you have done this lesson, take Test C7a.

C7-1

(Copy 5)

Chord dictation

Shield the answer. Listen to the chord and notate the upper tones above the given note; then un-cover the answer and compare your response. Circle incorrect responses. Goal: No more than seven errors. After you have done this lesson, take Test C7a.

00

C7-2
(Copy 1)

Chord identification

Shield the answer. Listen to the chord and write the figured bass symbol; then uncover the answer and compare your response. Circle incorrect responses. Goal: No more than seven errors. After you have done this lesson, take Test C7b.

#							
1	___	___ -6	___ 6/4	___ -6/4	___ 6	___ -	___ -6/d5
2	___ 6/-	___ -7	___	___ 6/4	___ -6	___ -	___ -6/4
3	___ 6	___ -7	___ -6/d5	___ 6/-	___ 6	___ -	___ -6/4
4	___ -7	___ -6/d5	___ -	___ 6/-	___ 6	___ 6/4	___ -
5	___	___ -6	___ 6/4	___	___ 6/-	___ -7	___ -6/d5
6	___ -	___ 6	___ -	___ -6/4	___ 6	___ 6/-	___ -7
7	___ -6/d5	___ -	___	___ 6/4	___ -6	___ 6	___ -
8	___ -6/4	___ -7	___ -	___ 6/-	___ -6/d5	___ -	___ 6
9	___	___ -6	___ -	___ 6/4	___ 6	___ 6/-	___ -6/4
10	___ -7	___	___ -6	___ -	___ 6/-	___ -7	___

C7-2
(Copy 2)

Chord identification

Shield the answer. Listen to the chord and write the figured bass symbol; then uncover the answer and compare your response. Circle incorrect responses. Goal: No more than seven errors. After you have done this lesson, take Test C7b.

#							
1	___	___ -6	___ 6/4	___ -6/4	___ 6	___ -	___ -6/d5
2	___ 6/-	___ -7	___	___ 6/4	___ -6	___ -	___ -6/4
3	___ 6	___ -7	___ -6/d5	___ 6/-	___ 6	___ -	___ -6/4
4	___ -7	___ -6/d5	___ -	___ 6/-	___ 6	___ 6/4	___ -
5	___	___ -6	___ 6/4	___	___ 6/-	___ -7	___ -6/d5
6	___ -	___ 6	___ -	___ -6/4	___ 6	___ 6/-	___ -7
7	___ -6/d5	___ -	___	___ 6/4	___ -6	___ 6	___ -
8	___ -6/4	___ -7	___ -	___ 6/-	___ -6/d5	___ -	___ 6
9	___	___ -6	___ -	___ 6/4	___ 6	___ 6/-	___ -6/4
10	___ -7	___	___ -6	___ -	___ 6/-	___ -7	___

C7-2

Chord identification

Shield the answer. Listen to the chord and write the figured bass symbol; then uncover the answer and compare your response. Circle incorrect responses. Goal: No more than seven errors. After you have done this lesson, take Test C7b.

#							
1	___	___ -6	___ 6/4	___ -6/4	___ 6	___ -	___ -6/d5
2	___ 6/-	___ -7	___	___ 6/4	___ -6	___ -	___ -6/4
3	___ 6	___ -7	___ -6/d5	___ 6/-	___ 6	___ -	___ -6/4
4	___ -7	___ -6/d5	___ -	___ 6/-	___ 6	___ 6/4	___ -
5	___	___ -6	___ 6/4	___	___ 6/-	___ -7	___ -6/d5
6	___ -	___ 6	___ -	___ -6/4	___ 6	___ 6/-	___ -7
7	___ -6/d5	___ -	___	___ 6/4	___ -6	___ 6	___ -
8	___ -6/4	___ -7	___ -	___ 6/-	___ -6/d5	___ -	___ 6
9	___	___ -6	___	___ 6/4	___ 6	___ 6/-	___ -6/4
10	___ -7	___	___ -6	___ -	___ 6/-	___ -7	___

C7-2

Chord identification

Shield the answer. Listen to the chord and write the figured bass symbol; then uncover the answer and compare your response. Circle incorrect responses. Goal: No more than seven errors. After you have done this lesson, take Test C7b.

#							
1	___	___ -6	___ 6/4	___ -6/4	___ 6	___ -	___ -6/d5
2	___ 6/-	___ -7	___	___ 6/4	___ -6	___ -	___ -6/4
3	___ 6	___ -7	___ -6/d5	___ 6/-	___ 6	___ -	___ -6/4
4	___ -7	___ -6/d5	___ -	___ 6/-	___ 6	___ 6/4	___ -
5	___	___ -6	___ 6/4	___	___ 6/-	___ -7	___ -6/d5
6	___ -	___ 6	___ -	___ -6/4	___ 6	___ 6/-	___ -7
7	___ -6/d5	___ -	___	___ 6/4	___ -6	___ 6	___ -
8	___ -6/4	___ -7	___ -	___ 6/-	___ -6/d5	___ -	___ 6
9	___	___ -6	___	___ 6/4	___ 6	___ 6/-	___ -6/4
10	___ -7	___	___ -6	___ -	___ 6/-	___ -7	___

C7-2

Chord identification

Shield the answer. Listen to the chord and write the figured bass symbol; then uncover the answer and compare your response. Circle incorrect responses. Goal: No more than seven errors. After you have done this lesson, take Test C7b.

#							
1	___	___ -6	___ $\frac{6}{4}$	___ $\frac{-6}{4}$	___ 6	___ -	___ $\frac{-6}{d5}$
2	___ $\frac{6}{-}$	___ -7	___	___ $\frac{6}{4}$	___ -6	___ -	___ $\frac{-6}{4}$
3	___ 6	___ -7	___ $\frac{-6}{d5}$	___ $\frac{6}{-}$	___ 6	___ -	___ $\frac{-6}{4}$
4	___ -7	___ $\frac{-6}{d5}$	___ -	___ $\frac{6}{-}$	___ 6	___ $\frac{6}{4}$	___ -
5	___	___ -6	___ $\frac{6}{4}$	___	___ $\frac{6}{-}$	___ -7	___ $\frac{-6}{d5}$
6	___ -	___ 6	___ -	___ $\frac{-6}{4}$	___ 6	___ $\frac{6}{-}$	___ -7
7	___ $\frac{-6}{d5}$	___ -	___	___ $\frac{6}{4}$	___ -6	___ 6	___ -
8	___ $\frac{-6}{4}$	___ -7	___ -	___ $\frac{6}{-}$	___ $\frac{-6}{d5}$	___ -	___ 6
9	___	___ -6	___ -	___ $\frac{6}{4}$	___ 6	___ $\frac{6}{-}$	___ $\frac{-6}{4}$
10	___ -7	___	___ -6	___ -	___ $\frac{6}{-}$	___ -7	___

C7-3a
(Copy 1)

Figured bass dictation

Shield the answer. Listen to the chord and write the bass note and the figured bass symbol; then uncover the answer and compare your response. Circle incorrect responses. Goal: No more than seven errors. The first frame requires no response. After you have done this lesson, skip to lesson C7-4a in preparation for Test C7c.

C7-3a

Figured bass dictation

Shield the answer. Listen to the chord and write the bass note and the figured bass symbol; then uncover the answer and compare your response. Circle incorrect responses. Goal: No more than seven errors. The first frame requires no response. After you have done this lesson, skip to lesson C7-4a in preparation for Test C7c.

C7-3a
(Copy 3)

Figured bass dictation

Shield the answer. Listen to the chord and write the bass note and the figured bass symbol; then uncover the answer and compare your response. Circle incorrect responses. Goal: No more than seven errors. The first frame requires no response. After you have done this lesson, skip to lesson C7-4a in preparation for Test C7c.

C7-3a
(Copy 4)

Figured bass dictation

Shield the answer. Listen to the chord and write the bass note and the figured bass symbol; then uncover the answer and compare your response. Circle incorrect responses. Goal: No more than seven errors. The first frame requires no response. After you have done this lesson, skip to lesson C7-4a in preparation for Test C7c.

C7-3a
(Copy 5)

Figured bass dictation

Shield the answer. Listen to the chord and write the bass note and the figured bass symbol; then uncover the answer and compare your response. Circle incorrect responses. Goal: No more than seven errors. The first frame requires no response. After you have done this lesson, skip to lesson C7-4a in preparation for Test C7c.

C7–3b
(Copy 1)

Chord identification in a key

Shield the answers. Listen to the chord and write the composite chord symbol; then uncover the answer and compare your response. Circle incorrect responses. Goal: No more than seven errors. The first frame requires no response.

1 I   ___ V^{-7} ___ I   ___ I^{-6} ___ V^6_4 ___ I   ___ V^{-6}_{d5}

2   ___ I   ___ VI^- ___ IV   ___ V   ___ VI^- ___ II^6 ___ V

3   ___ IV^{-6} ___ II^- ___ V   ___ I   ___ IV^{-6} ___ IV   ___ I^6_4

4   ___ V^{-7} ___ I   ___ III^- ___ IV   ___ II^- ___ VII^6_- ___ V^{-6}_{d5}

5   ___ V^{-7} ___ VI^- ___ II^- ___ V   ___ I   ___ IV^6_4 ___ I

6   ___ II^6 ___ V   ___ I   ___ IV   ___ II^- ___ V^{-6}_{d5} ___ I

7   ___ IV^{-6} ___ V   ___ VI^- ___ II^6 ___ V^{-7} ___ I   ___ V^{-6}_{d5}

8   ___ I   ___ III^- ___ VI^- ___ II^6 ___ I^6_4 ___ V^{-7} ___ I

9   ___ IV^6_4 ___ I   ___ I^{-6} ___ V^6_4 ___ I   ___ III^- ___ IV^{-6}

10   ___ IV   ___ V^{-7} ___ IV^{-6} ___ II^6 ___ I^6_4 ___ V^{-7} ___ I

C7–3b
(Copy 2)

Chord identification in a key

Shield the answers. Listen to the chord and write the composite chord symbol; then uncover the answer and compare your response. Circle incorrect responses. Goal: No more than seven errors. The first frame requires no response.

1 I   ___ V^{-7} ___ I   ___ I^{-6} ___ V^6_4 ___ I   ___ V^{-6}_{d5}

2   ___ I   ___ VI^- ___ IV   ___ V   ___ VI^- ___ II^6 ___ V

3   ___ IV^{-6} ___ II^- ___ V   ___ I   ___ IV^{-6} ___ IV   ___ I^6_4

4   ___ V^{-7} ___ I   ___ III^- ___ IV   ___ II^- ___ VII^6_- ___ V^{-6}_{d5}

5   ___ V^{-7} ___ VI^- ___ II^- ___ V   ___ I   ___ IV^6_4 ___ I

6   ___ II^6 ___ V   ___ I   ___ IV   ___ II^- ___ V^{-6}_{d5} ___ I

7   ___ IV^{-6} ___ V   ___ VI^- ___ II^6 ___ V^{-7} ___ I   ___ V^{-6}_{d5}

8   ___ I   ___ III^- ___ VI^- ___ II^6 ___ I^6_4 ___ V^{-7} ___ I

9   ___ IV^6_4 ___ I   ___ I^{-6} ___ V^6_4 ___ I   ___ III^- ___ IV^{-6}

10   ___ IV   ___ V^{-7} ___ IV^{-6} ___ II^6 ___ I^6_4 ___ V^{-7} ___ I

C7–3b
(Copy 3)

Chord identification in a key

Shield the answers. Listen to the chord and write the composite chord symbol; then uncover the answer and compare your response. Circle incorrect responses. Goal: No more than seven errors. The first frame requires no response.

1   I   ___ V^{-7} ___ I   ___ I^{-6} ___ V^6_4 ___ I   ___ V^{-6}_{d5}

2   ___ I   ___ VI^- ___ IV   ___ V   ___ VI^- ___ II^6 ___ V

3   ___ IV^{-6} ___ II^- ___ V   ___ I   ___ IV^{-6} ___ IV   ___ I^6_4

4   ___ V^{-7} ___ I   ___ III^- ___ IV   ___ II^- ___ VII^6_- ___ V^{-6}_{d5}

5   ___ V^{-7} ___ VI^- ___ II^- ___ V   ___ I   ___ IV^6_4 ___ I

6   ___ II^6 ___ V   ___ I   ___ IV   ___ II^- ___ V^{-6}_{d5} ___ I

7   ___ IV^{-6} ___ V   ___ VI^- ___ II^6 ___ V^{-7} ___ I   ___ V^{-6}_{d5}

8   ___ I   ___ III^- ___ VI^- ___ II^6 ___ I^6_4 ___ V^{-7} ___ I

9   ___ IV^6_4 ___ I   ___ I^{-6} ___ V^6_4 ___ I   ___ III^- ___ IV^{-6}

10   ___ IV   ___ V^{-7} ___ IV^{-6} ___ II^6 ___ I^6_4 ___ V^{-7} ___ I

C7–3b
(Copy 4)

Chord identification in a key

Shield the answers. Listen to the chord and write the composite chord symbol; then uncover the answer and compare your response. Circle incorrect responses. Goal: No more than seven errors. The first frame requires no response.

1   I   ___ V^{-7} ___ I   ___ I^{-6} ___ V^6_4 ___ I   ___ V^{-6}_{d5}

2   ___ I   ___ VI^- ___ IV   ___ V   ___ VI^- ___ II^6 ___ V

3   ___ IV^{-6} ___ II^- ___ V   ___ I   ___ IV^{-6} ___ IV   ___ I^6_4

4   ___ V^{-7} ___ I   ___ III^- ___ IV   ___ II^- ___ VII^6_- ___ V^{-6}_{d5}

5   ___ V^{-7} ___ VI^- ___ II^- ___ V   ___ I   ___ IV^6_4 ___ I

6   ___ II^6 ___ V   ___ I   ___ IV   ___ II^- ___ V^{-6}_{d5} ___ I

7   ___ IV^{-6} ___ V   ___ VI^- ___ II^6 ___ V^{-7} ___ I   ___ V^{-6}_{d5}

8   ___ I   ___ III^- ___ VI^- ___ II^6 ___ I^6_4 ___ V^{-7} ___ I

9   ___ IV^6_4 ___ I   ___ I^{-6} ___ V^6_4 ___ I   ___ III^- ___ IV^{-6}

10   ___ IV   ___ V^{-7} ___ IV^{-6} ___ II^6 ___ I^6_4 ___ V^{-7} ___ I

C7-3b

Chord identification in a key

Shield the answers. Listen to the chord and write the composite chord symbol; then uncover the answer and compare your response. Circle incorrect responses. Goal: No more than seven errors. The first frame requires no response.

1   I   ____ V^{-7} ____ I   ____ I^{-6} ____ V^6_4 ____ I   ____ V^{-6}_{d5}

2   ____ I   ____ VI^- ____ IV   ____ V   ____ VI^- ____ II^6 ____ V

3   ____ IV^{-6} ____ II^- ____ V   ____ I   ____ IV^{-6} ____ IV I^6_4

4   ____ V^{-7} ____ I   ____ III^- ____ IV   ____ II^- ____ VII^6_- ____ V^{-6}_{d5}

5   ____ V^{-7} ____ VI^- ____ II^- ____ V   ____ I   ____ IV^6_4 ____ I

6   ____ II^6 ____ V   ____ I   ____ IV   ____ II^- ____ V^{-6}_{d5} ____ I

7   ____ IV^{-6} ____ V   ____ VI^- ____ II^6 ____ V^{-7} ____ I   ____ V^{-6}_{d5}

8   ____ I   ____ III^- ____ VI^- ____ II^6 ____ I^6_4 ____ V^{-7} ____ I

9   ____ IV^6_4 ____ I   ____ I^{-6} ____ V^6_4 ____ I   ____ III^- ____ IV^{-6}

10 ____ IV   ____ V^{-7} ____ IV^{-6} ____ II^6 ____ I^6_4 ____ V^{-7} ____ I

C7-4a
(Copy 1)

Figured bass dictation

Shield the answer. Listen to the chord and write the bass note and the figured bass symbol; then uncover the answer and compare your response. Circle incorrect responses. Goal: No more than seven errors. The first frame requires no response. After you have done this lesson, take Test C7c.

C7-4a

Figured bass dictation

Shield the answer. Listen to the chord and write the bass note and the figured bass symbol; then uncover the answer and compare your response. Circle incorrect responses. Goal: No more than seven errors. The first frame requires no response. After you have done this lesson, take Test C7c.

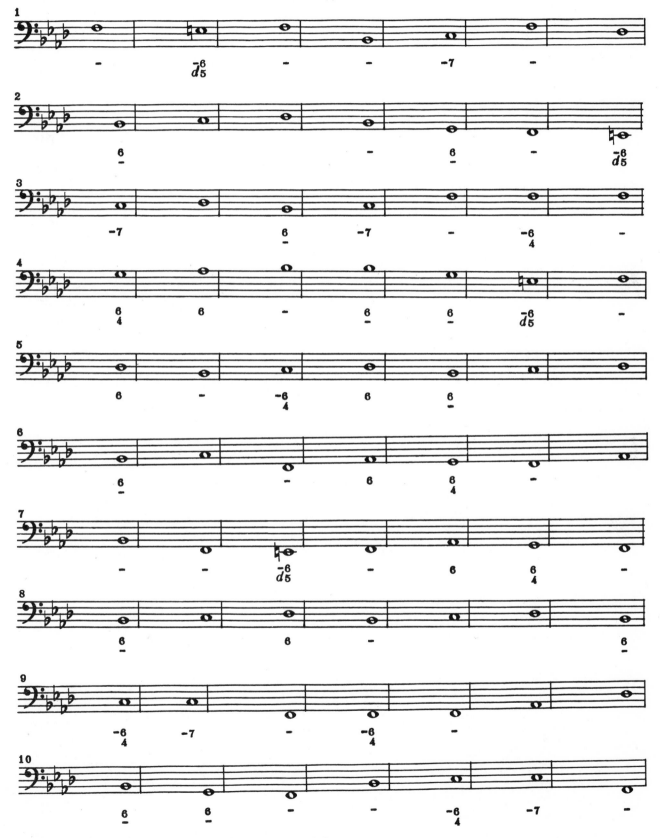

C7-4a
(Copy 3)

Figured bass dictation

Shield the answer. Listen to the chord and write the bass note and the figured bass symbol; then uncover the answer and compare your response. Circle incorrect responses. Goal: No more than seven errors. The first frame requires no response. After you have done this lesson, take Test C7c.

C7-4a

Figured bass dictation

Shield the answer. Listen to the chord and write the bass note and the figured bass symbol; then uncover the answer and compare your response. Circle incorrect responses. Goal: No more than seven errors. The first frame requires no response. After you have done this lesson, take Test C7c.

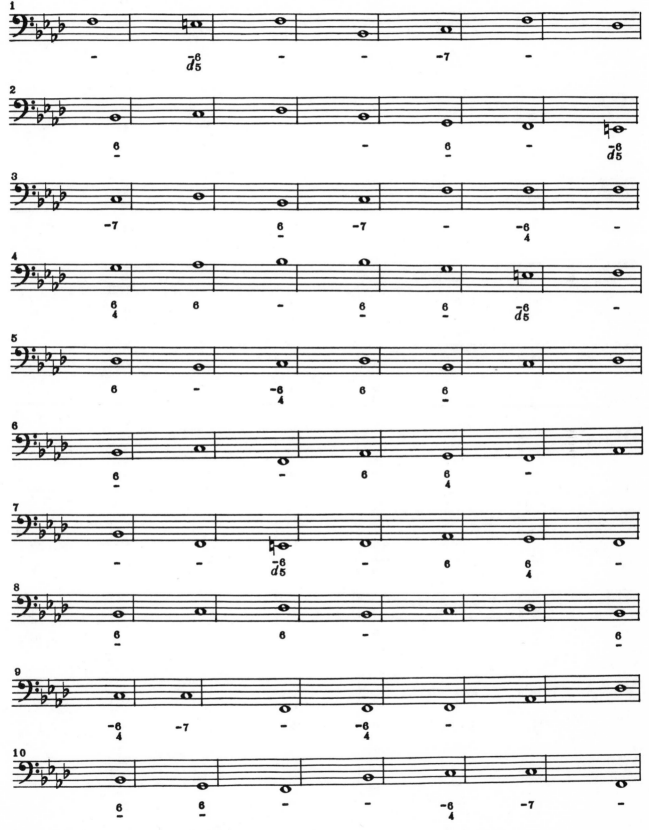

215

C7-4a

(Copy 5)

Figured bass dictation

Shield the answer. Listen to the chord and write the bass note and the figured bass symbol; then uncover the answer and compare your response. Circle incorrect responses. Goal: No more than seven errors. The first frame requires no response. After you have done this lesson, take Test C7c.

C7-4b
(Copy 1)

Chord identification in a key

Shield the answer. Listen to the chord and write the composite chord symbol; then uncover the answer and compare your response. Circle incorrect responses. Goal: No more than seven errors. After you have done this lesson, take Test C7d.

1   I^- ___ V^{-6}_{d5} ___ I^- ___ IV^- ___ V^{-7} ___ I^- ___ ^-VI

2   ___ II^6_- ___ V ___ ^-VI ___ IV^- ___ VII^6_- ___ I^- ___ V^{-6}_{d5}

3   ___ V^{-7} ___ ^-VI ___ II^6_- ___ V^{-7} ___ I^- ___ IV^{-6}_4 ___ I^-

4   ___ V^6_4 ___ I^6 ___ IV^- ___ II^6_- ___ VII^6_- ___ V^{-6}_{d5} ___ I^-

5   ___ IV^6 ___ IV^- ___ I^{-6}_4 ___ IV^6 ___ II^6_- ___ V ___ ^-VI

6   ___ II^6_- ___ V ___ I^- ___ I^6 ___ V^6_4 ___ I^- ___ ^-III

7   ___ IV^- ___ I^- ___ V^{-6}_{d5} ___ I^- ___ I^6 ___ V^6_4 ___ I^-

8   ___ II^6_- ___ V ___ IV^6 ___ IV^- ___ V ___ ^-VI ___ II^6_-

9   ___ I^{-6}_4 ___ V^{-7} ___ I^- ___ IV^{-6}_4 ___ I^- ___ ^-III ___ ^-VI

10   ___ II^6_- ___ VII^6_- ___ I^- ___ IV^- ___ I^{-6}_4 ___ V^{-7} ___ I^-

C7-4b
(Copy 2)

Chord identification in a key

Shield the answer. Listen to the chord and write the composite chord symbol; then uncover the answer and compare your response. Circle incorrect responses. Goal: No more than seven errors. After you have done this lesson, take Test C7d.

1   I^- ___ V^{-6}_{d5} ___ I^- ___ IV^- ___ V^{-7} ___ I^- ___ ^-VI

2   ___ II^6_- ___ V ___ ^-VI ___ IV^- ___ VII^6_- ___ I^- ___ V^{-6}_{d5}

3   ___ V^{-7} ___ ^-VI ___ II^6_- ___ V^{-7} ___ I^- ___ IV^{-6}_4 ___ I^-

4   ___ V^6_4 ___ I^6 ___ IV^- ___ II^6_- ___ VII^6_- ___ V^{-6}_{d5} ___ I^-

5   ___ IV^6 ___ IV^- ___ I^{-6}_4 ___ IV^6 ___ II^6_- ___ V ___ ^-VI

6   ___ II^6_- ___ V ___ I^- ___ I^6 ___ V^6_4 ___ I^- ___ ^-III

7   ___ IV^- ___ I^- ___ V^{-6}_{d5} ___ I^- ___ I^6 ___ V^6_4 ___ I^-

8   ___ II^6_- ___ V ___ IV^6 ___ IV^- ___ V ___ ^-VI ___ II^6_-

9   ___ I^{-6}_4 ___ V^{-7} ___ I^- ___ IV^{-6}_4 ___ I^- ___ ^-III ___ ^-VI

10   ___ II^6_- ___ VII^6_- ___ I^- ___ IV^- ___ I^{-6}_4 ___ V^{-7} ___ I^-

C7-4b
(Copy 3)

Chord identification in a key

Shield the answer. Listen to the chord and write the composite chord symbol; then uncover the answer and compare your response. Circle incorrect responses. Goal: No more than seven errors. After you have done this lesson, take Test C7d.

1 I^- ___ V_{d5}^{-6} ___ I^- ___ IV^- ___ V^{-7} ___ I^- ___ ^-VI

2 ___ II_-^6 ___ V ___ ^-VI ___ IV^- ___ VII_-^6 ___ I^- ___ V_{d5}^{-6}

3 ___ V^{-7} ___ ^-VI ___ II_-^6 ___ V^{-7} ___ I^- ___ IV_4^{-6} ___ I^-

4 ___ V_4^6 ___ I^6 ___ IV^- ___ II_-^6 ___ VII_-^6 ___ V_{d5}^{-6} ___ I^-

5 ___ IV^6 ___ IV^- ___ I_4^{-6} ___ IV^6 ___ II_-^6 ___ V ___ ^-VI

6 ___ II_-^6 ___ V ___ I^- ___ I^6 ___ V_4^6 ___ I^- ___ ^-III

7 ___ IV^- ___ I^- ___ V_{d5}^{-6} ___ I^- ___ I^6 ___ V_4^6 ___ I^-

8 ___ II_-^6 ___ V ___ IV^6 ___ IV^- ___ V ___ ^-VI ___ II_-^6

9 ___ I_4^{-6} ___ V^{-7} ___ I^- ___ IV_4^{-6} ___ I^- ___ ^-III ___ ^-VI

10 ___ II_-^6 ___ VII_-^6 ___ I^- ___ IV^- ___ I_4^{-6} ___ V^{-7} ___ I^-

C7-4b
(Copy 4)

Chord identification in a key

Shield the answer. Listen to the chord and write the composite chord symbol; then uncover the answer and compare your response. Circle incorrect responses. Goal: No more than seven errors. After you have done this lesson, take Test C7d.

1 I^- ___ V_{d5}^{-6} ___ I^- ___ IV^- ___ V^{-7} ___ I^- ___ ^-VI

2 ___ II_-^6 ___ V ___ ^-VI ___ IV^- ___ VII_-^6 ___ I^- ___ V_{d5}^{-6}

3 ___ V^{-7} ___ ^-VI ___ II_-^6 ___ V^{-7} ___ I^- ___ IV_4^{-6} ___ I^-

4 ___ V_4^6 ___ I^6 ___ IV^- ___ II_-^6 ___ VII_-^6 ___ V_{d5}^{-6} ___ I^-

5 ___ IV^6 ___ IV^- ___ I_4^{-6} ___ IV^6 ___ II_-^6 ___ V ___ ^-VI

6 ___ II_-^6 ___ V ___ I^- ___ I^6 ___ V_4^6 ___ I^- ___ ^-III

7 ___ IV^- ___ I^- ___ V_{d5}^{-6} ___ I^- ___ I^6 ___ V_4^6 ___ I^-

8 ___ II_-^6 ___ V ___ IV^6 ___ IV^- ___ V ___ ^-VI ___ II_-^6

9 ___ I_4^{-6} ___ V^{-7} ___ I^- ___ IV_4^{-6} ___ I^- ___ ^-III ___ ^-VI

10 ___ II_-^6 ___ VII_-^6 ___ I^- ___ IV^- ___ I_4^{-6} ___ V^{-7} ___ I^-

C7-4b

Chord identification in a key

Shield the answer. Listen to the chord and write the composite chord symbol; then uncover the answer and compare your response. Circle incorrect responses. Goal: No more than seven errors. After you have done this lesson, take Test C7d.

1 I^- ____ V^{-6}_{d5} ____ I^- ____ IV^- ____ V^{-7} ____ I^- ____ ^-VI

2 ____ II^6_- ____ V ____ ^-VI ____ IV^- ____ VII^6_- ____ I^- ____ V^{-6}_{d5}

3 ____ V^{-7} ____ ^-VI ____ II^6_- ____ V^{-7} ____ I^- ____ IV^{-6}_4 ____ I^-

4 ____ V^6_4 ____ I^6 ____ IV^- ____ II^6_- ____ VII^6_- ____ V^{-6}_{d5} ____ I^-

5 ____ IV^6 ____ IV^- ____ I^{-6}_4 ____ IV^6 ____ II^6_- ____ V ____ ^-VI

6 ____ II^6_- ____ V ____ I^- ____ I^6 ____ V^6_4 ____ I^- ____ ^-III

7 ____ IV^- ____ I^- ____ V^{-6}_{d5} ____ I^- ____ I^6 ____ V^6_4 ____ I^-

8 ____ II^6_- ____ V ____ IV^6 ____ IV^- ____ V ____ ^-VI ____ II^6_-

9 ____ I^{-6}_4 ____ V^{-7} ____ I^- ____ IV^{-6}_4 ____ I^- ____ ^-III ____ ^-VI

10 ____ II^6_- ____ VII^6_- ____ I^- ____ IV^- ____ I^{-6}_4 ____ V^{-7} ____ I^-

Arpeggio Singing   SERIES C8

This series involves all types of chords previously studied. There are two kinds of lessons: arpeggio singing from figured bass symbols and arpeggio singing from composite chord symbols. When you have done this series, take Test C8. The test does not include arpeggio singing from figured bass symbols. While your achievement in this skill is not tested, it will help you with arpeggio singing from composite chord symbols, which is tested.

Lessons **C8-1, C8-2** and **C8-3**

These are lessons in arpeggio singing from figured bass symbols. The purpose of these lessons is to develop your ability to hear mentally various types of chords and to sing the pitches in arpeggio fashion. The frames are separated by bar lines. Each frame contains a figured bass symbol. If a frame is empty, the figured bass symbol is a blank representing a major triad in root position. The format for each frame on the tape is as follows: you will hear a tone giving the pitch of the starting tone, followed by four clicks on the metronome. Sing the arpeggio in time with the clicks. Immediately after the clicks you will hear an arpeggio giving the pitches you should have sung. You can then judge if you sang the arpeggio correctly.

Sing the triads in the following fashion:

Sing the seventh chords in the following fashion:

Depending on the range of your voice, you may find it necessary to sing in a different octave from that of the tones you hear on the tape recording. You may also find it necessary to change octaves in the course of a lesson. Sing in the most comfortable part of your vocal range at all times.

Whenever you have sung a frame incorrectly, make a tally mark on a piece of paper. Your goal is to complete each lesson with no more than eight incorrect frames. When you have done so, go on to the next lesson. If you have more than eight incorrect frames, repeat the lesson until you reach the goal or until you have done the lesson five times, at which point you should go on to the next lesson regardless of the number of incorrect frames.

C8-1

Arpeggio singing from figured bass symbols

Listen to the tone, then sing the arpeggio in time with the metronome. Compare your response with the arpeggio you then hear and tally errors separately. Goal: No more than eight incorrect frames.

1		-			6/4			-	-6/4	6/4		-7	
2	-	-6/4	-			6/4		-7	-	-6/4	-7		
3		-7		6/4			-	-6/4	-	-6/4	-7		
4		6/4		-7	-	-7	-			-			
5	6/4	-7			-	-6/4	-7	-		6/4			

C8-2

Arpeggio singing from figured bass symbols

Listen to the tone, then sing the arpeggio in time with the metronome. Compare your response with the arpeggio you then hear and tally errors separately. Goal: No more than eight incorrect frames.

1		-6		-6		-6	-	6	-	6	
2	6		-	-6	-6/d5		-7	-6/d5		-6	
3	-6/d5		6	-6	-6	-7	-6/d5	-	6	-	
4	6	-7	-6/d5		-6		-6/d5	-7	-6	-6/d5	
5	-	6		-6/d5		-6	6		-6/d5		

C8-3

Arpeggio singing from figured bass symbols

Listen to the tone, then sing the arpeggio in time with the metronome. Compare your response with the arpeggio you then hear and tally errors separately. Goal: No more than eight incorrect frames.

1	-	-6	-6/d5	6/-	6	-	6/-	-6/4	-7		
2	6/4	-6	6/-		-7	-6	6/-		6/4	-7	
3	-	6/-	6	6/-		6	6/-	6	6	6/4	
4	-	-6/d5		6	6/4	-7	-	6	6/-	-	
5	-7	-6/d5	6/-	-	6	6/-	-6/4		-6/d5	-	

223

Lessons **C8-4, C8-5, C8-6** and **C8-7**

These are lessons in arpeggio singing from composite chord symbols. The purpose of these lessons is to develop your ability to hear chord progressions mentally, and to sing the pitches involved in arpeggio fashion. Each frame on the worksheet contains one composite chord symbol. Work across the page from left to right. You will be given the starting pitch for the first frame only. In subsequent frames, you must sing each new arpeggio using the preceding arpeggio as a frame of reference. In each frame you will hear four clicks along with which you should sing the arpeggio as you did in the lessons in arpeggio singing from figured bass symbols. Immediately after the clicks, you will hear an arpeggio that will tell you the pitches you should have sung. Then sing the next arpeggio with the following clicks.

The first tone you sing should be the bass that is appropriate for the given chord symbol. For example, if the chord symbol is V, the first tone you sing should be the fifth degree of the key, because the chord is in root position. If the given chord symbol is V^{-6}, you should start with the seventh degree of the scale because this degree is the third of the chord and the chord is in first inversion.

The goal for these lessons is the same as in the previous lessons in arpeggio singing from figured bass symbols.

C8-4   Arpeggio singing from composite chord symbols

Sing the arpeggio in time with the metronome. Compare your response with the arpeggio you then hear and tally your errors. The starting tone is given for the first frame only. Goal: No more than eight incorrect frames.

1	I	V^{-7}	I	VI⁻	IV	I	IV	II⁻	V^{-7}	I	IV	V
2	VI⁻	IV	V	I	VI⁻	II⁻	V	I	III⁻	IV	I	V^{-7}
3	VI⁻	IV	II⁻	V	VI⁻	II⁻	V	I	III⁻	IV	I	VI⁻
4	II⁻	V	I	III⁻	VI⁻	II⁻	V	VI⁻	IV	I	III⁻	VI⁻
5	IV	V	I	IV	II⁻	V	VI⁻	II⁻	V	VI⁻	V^{-7}	I

C8-5

Arpeggio singing from composite chord symbols

Sing the arpeggio in time with the metronome. Compare your response with the arpeggio you then hear and tally your errors. The starting tone is given for the first frame only. Goal: No more than eight incorrect frames.

1	I^-	V^{-7}	I^-	IV^-	V^{-7}	I^-	^-VI	IV^-	V	I^-	IV^-	V^{-7}
2	I^-	^-III	IV^-	I^-	^-III	^-VI	IV^-	V	I^-	IV^-	V^{-7}	I^-
3	^-III	^-VI	V	I^-	^-III	^-VI	IV^-	V^{-7}	I^-	IV^-	V	^-VI
4	IV^-	I^-	^-III	^-VI	IV^-	I^-	^-III	IV^-	I^-	^-VI	IV^-	V^{-7}
5	^-VI	IV^-	I^-	^-III	IV^-	I^-	IV^-	V	^-VI	IV^-	V^{-7}	I^-

C8-6

Arpeggio singing from composite chord symbols

Sing the arpeggio in time with the metronome. Compare your response with the arpeggio you then hear and tally your errors. The starting tone is given for the first frame only. Goal: No more than eight incorrect frames.

1	I	V^{-6}	I	I^{-6}	IV	IV^{-6}	V^{-7}	V^{-6}_{d5}	I	IV^{-6}	V^{-6}_{d5}	I
2	IV	II^6	V	I^{-6}	IV	V	IV^{-6}	V^{-7}	VI^-	II^6	V^{-7}	I
3	V^{-6}_{d5}	I	VII^6_-	I^{-6}	I	IV	I^{-6}	II^-	V	I^{-6}	I	IV
4	I^{-6}	VII^6_-	I	II^6	V	I	IV^6_4	I	I^6_4	V^{-7}	I	IV
5	I^{-6}	V^6_4	I	I^{-6}	VII^6_-	I	II^6	I^6_4	V^{-7}	I	IV^6_4	I

C8-7

Arpeggio singing from composite chord symbols

Sing the arpeggio in time with the metronome. Compare your response with the arpeggio you then hear and tally your errors. The starting tone is given for the first frame only. Goal: No more than eight incorrect frames. After you have done this lesson, take Test C8.

1	I^-	V^{-6}_{d5}	I^-	^-VI	IV^-	II^6_-	V^{-7}	I^-	II^6_-	I^{-6}_4	V	V^{-6}_{d5}
2	I^-	IV^6	IV^-	I^6	VII^6_-	I^-	V^6_4	I^6	II^6_-	VII^6_-	I^-	IV^{-6}_4
3	I^-	VII^6_-	I^6	V	V^{-6}	I^-	IV^6	I^{-6}_4	IV^-	VII^6_-	I^6	II^6_-
4	I^{-6}_4	V^{-7}	I^-	^-III	IV^-	I^6	IV^6	V	I^6	II^6_-	I^{-6}_4	V^{-7}
5	V^{-6}_{d5}	I^-	^-VI	II^6_-	V	I^6	V^6_4	I^-	IV^-	I^6	V^6_4	I^-

Soprano and Bass Dictation with Composite Chord Symbols

This series involves all types of chords that appear in previous lessons. There are three kinds of lessons: two-part dictation; soprano and bass dictation with composite chord symbols, done one chord at a time; and soprano and bass dictation with composite chord symbols, done in phrases. The instructions for these lessons appear with each lesson. When you have done this series take Test C9, which is a test in soprano and bass dictation with composite chord symbols done in phrases. The test does not include sections on two-voice dictation or on soprano and bass dictation with composite chord symbols done one chord at a time. While your achievement in these lessons is not tested, these skills will help you with the lessons that follow.

Lessons **C9-1** and **C9-2**

These are lessons in two-part dictation. The purpose is to develop your ability to write intervals by following two melodic lines. The frames on the worksheet are separated by bar lines. The first interval on the tape and answer sheet is given as a starting reference and requires no response. All subsequent frames require a response. To do each frame, start by shielding the answer. When you hear the interval, write both notes. In lesson C9-1 the interval is written on the treble staff and in lesson C9-2 it is written on the great staff. To determine the notes of the interval, listen to the movement of each part from the previous frame to the frame in question. When you have responded, slide the shield to the right and compare your response with the printed answer. Circle each frame in which your response is incorrect. Your goal is to complete the lesson with no more than eight errors. When you have done so, go on to the next lesson. If you have made more than eight errors, repeat the lesson until you reach the goal or until you have done the lesson five times, at which point you should go on to the next lesson regardless of the number of errors.

C9-1
(Copy 1)

Two-part dictation

Shield the answer. Listen to the interval and write both tones; then uncover the answer and compare your response. Circle incorrect responses. Goal: No more than eight errors. The first frame requires no response.

Two-part dictation

Shield the answer. Listen to the interval and write both tones; then uncover the answer and compare your response. Circle incorrect responses. Goal: No more than eight errors. The first frame requires no response.

C9-1
(Copy 3)

Two-part dictation

Shield the answer. Listen to the interval and write both tones; then uncover the answer and compare your response. Circle incorrect responses. Goal: No more than eight errors. The first frame requires no response.

C9-1
(Copy 4)

Two-part dictation

Shield the answer. Listen to the interval and write both tones; then uncover the answer and compare your response. Circle incorrect responses. Goal: No more than eight errors. The first frame requires no response.

232

C9-1
(Copy 5)

Two-part dictation

Shield the answer. Listen to the interval and write both tones; then uncover the answer and compare your response. Circle incorrect responses. Goal: No more than eight errors. The first frame requires no response.

C9-2
(Copy 1)

Two-part dictation

Shield the answer. Listen to the interval and write both tones; then uncover the answer and compare your response. Circle incorrect responses. Goal: No more than eight errors. The first frame requires no response.

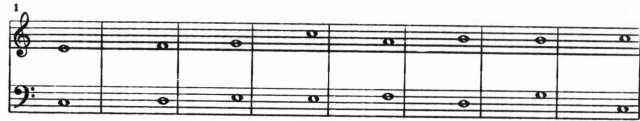

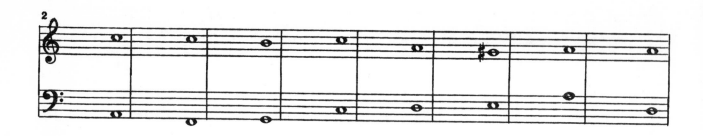

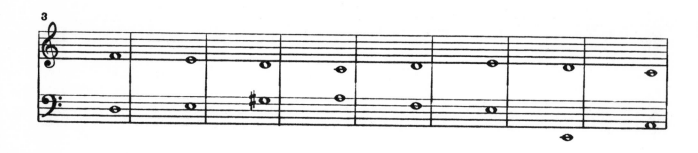

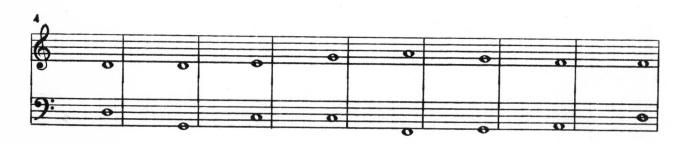

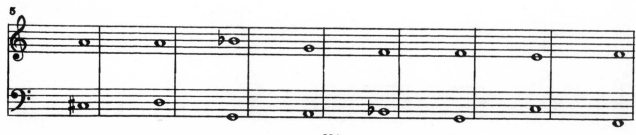

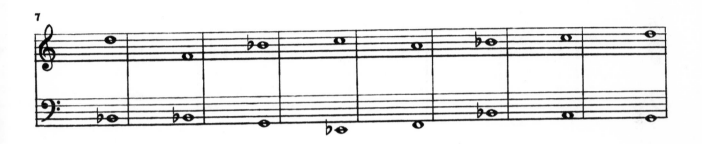

C9-2
(Copy 2)

Two-part dictation

Shield the answer. Listen to the interval and write both tones; then uncover the answer and compare your response. Circle incorrect responses. Goal: No more than eight errors. The first frame requires no response.

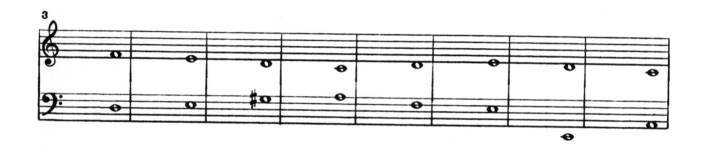

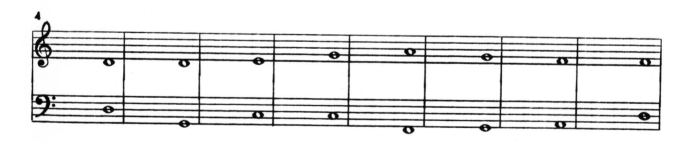

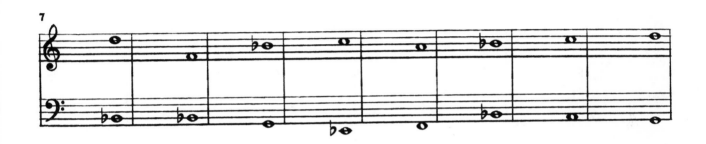

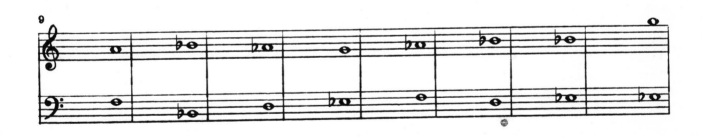

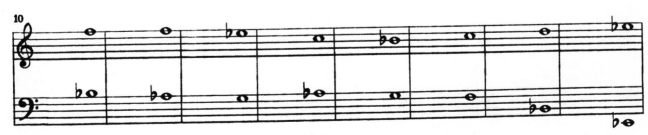

C9–2

(Copy 3)

Two-part dictation

Shield the answer. Listen to the interval and write both tones; then uncover the answer and compare your response. Circle incorrect responses. Goal: No more than eight errors. The first frame requires no response.

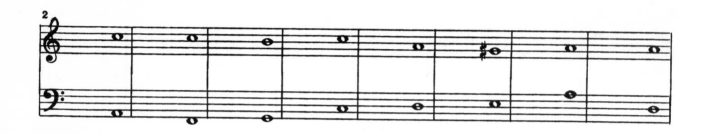

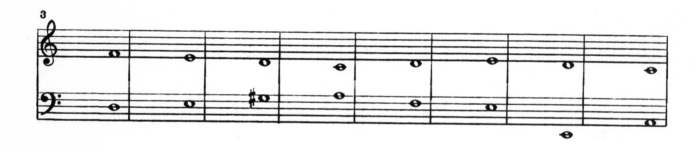

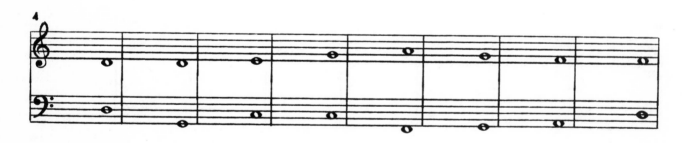

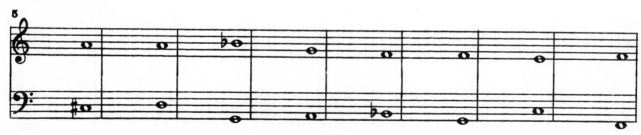

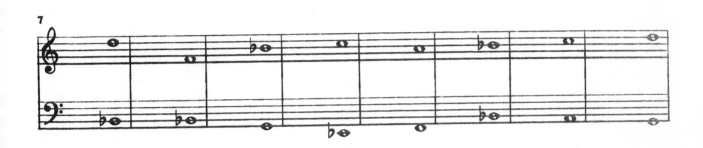

C9-2

Two-part dictation

Shield the answer. Listen to the interval and write both tones; then uncover the answer and compare your response. Circle incorrect responses. Goal: No more than eight errors. The first frame requires no response.

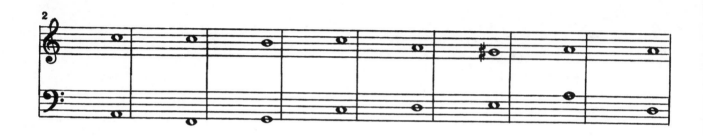

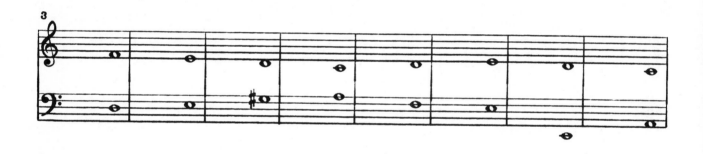

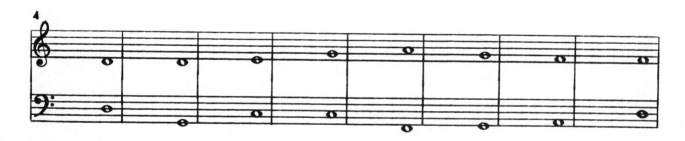

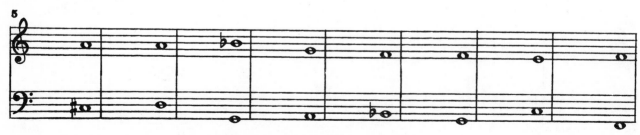

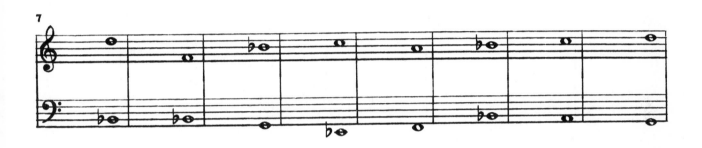

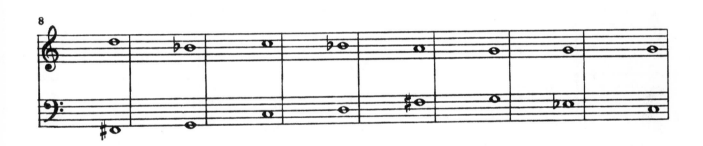

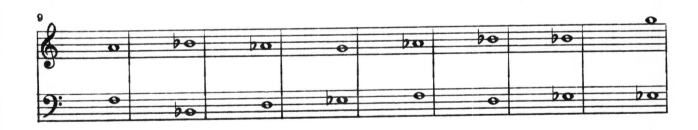

C9-2
(Copy 5)

Two-part dictation

Shield the answer. Listen to the interval and write both tones; then uncover the answer and compare your response. Circle incorrect responses. Goal: No more than eight errors. The first frame requires no response.

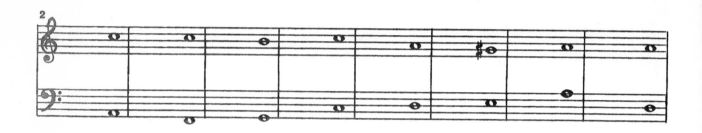

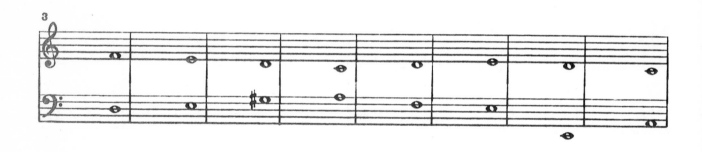

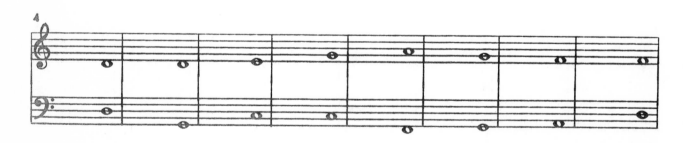

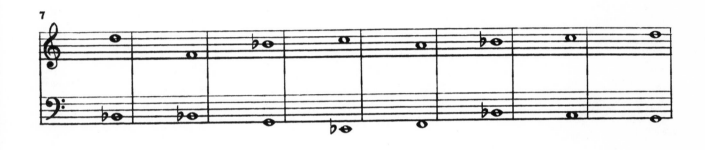

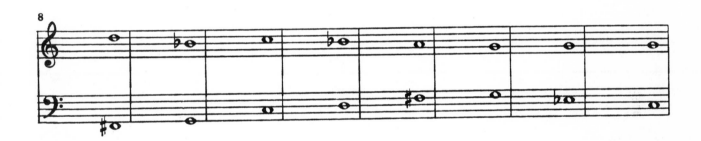

Lessons **C9–3** and **C9–4**

These are lessons in soprano and bass dictation with composite chord symbols. The procedure is the same as for C9–1, with the addition of composite chord symbols. You will hear a chord in these lessons instead of an interval. Write the soprano and bass notes of the chord and the composite chord symbol. The key is given with a capital letter for a major key and a lower-case letter for a minor key. The goal for these lessons is no more than eight errors per lesson.

C9-3
(Copy 1)

Soprano and bass dictation with composite chord symbols

Shield the answer. Listen to the chord and write the soprano and bass notes and the composite chord symbol; then uncover the answer and compare your response. Circle incorrect responses. Goal: No more than eight errors. The first frame requires no response.

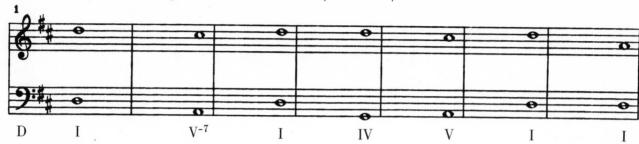

| D | I | | V⁻⁷ | I | IV | V | I | I |

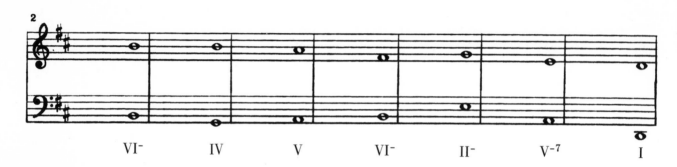

| VI⁻ | IV | V | VI⁻ | II⁻ | V⁻⁷ | I |

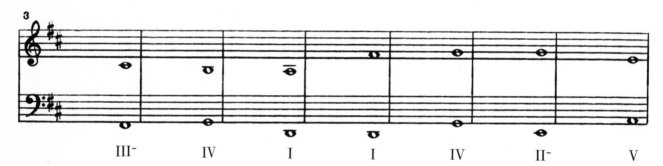

| III⁻ | IV | I | I | IV | II⁻ | V |

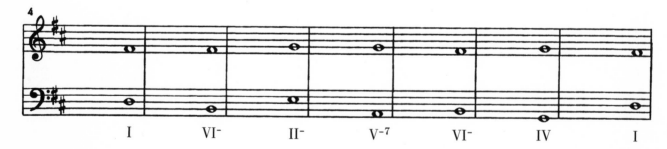

| I | VI⁻ | II⁻ | V⁻⁷ | VI⁻ | IV | I |

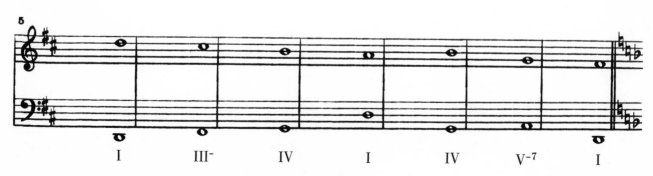

| I | III⁻ | IV | I | IV | V⁻⁷ | I |

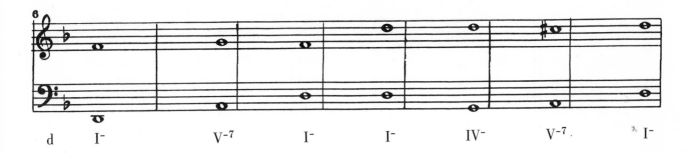

d   I⁻   V⁻⁷   I⁻   I⁻   IV⁻   V⁻⁷   I⁻

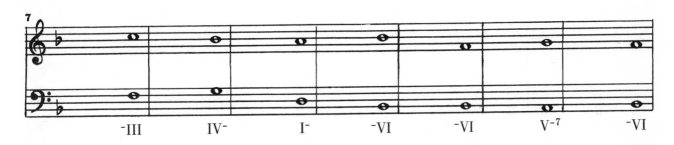

⁻III   IV⁻   I⁻   ⁻VI   ⁻VI   V⁻⁷   ⁻VI

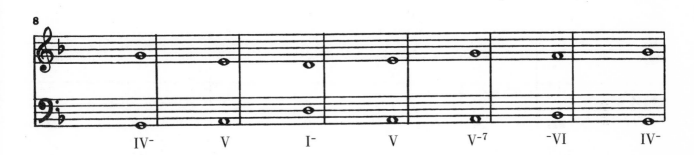

IV⁻   V   I⁻   V   V⁻⁷   ⁻VI   IV⁻

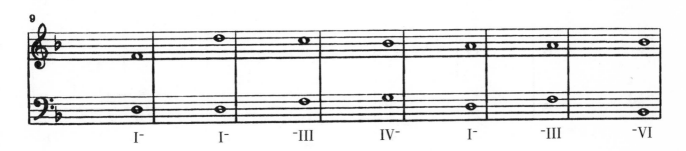

I⁻   I⁻   ⁻III   IV⁻   I⁻   ⁻III   ⁻VI

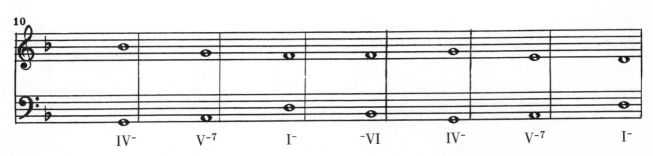

IV⁻   V⁻⁷   I⁻   ⁻VI   IV⁻   V⁻⁷   I⁻

C9-3
(Copy 2)

Soprano and bass dictation with composite chord symbols

Shield the answer. Listen to the chord and write the soprano and bass notes and the composite chord symbol; then uncover the answer and compare your response. Circle incorrect responses. Goal: No more than eight errors. The first frame requires no response.

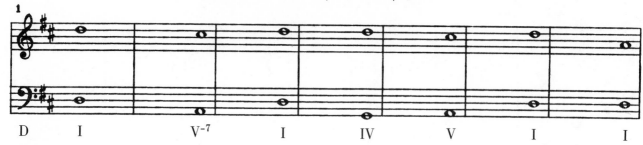

1.
D   I   V⁻⁷   I   IV   V   I   I

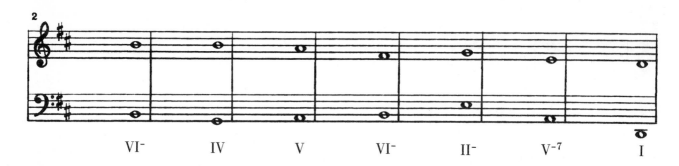

2.
     VI⁻   IV   V   VI⁻   II⁻   V⁻⁷   I

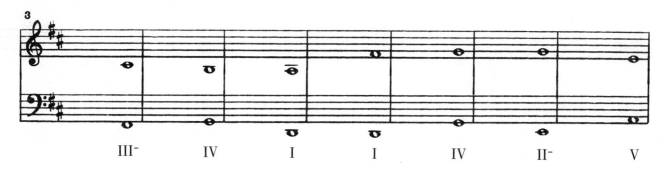

3.
     III⁻   IV   I   I   IV   II⁻   V

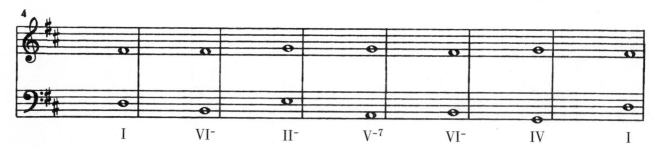

4.
     I   VI⁻   II⁻   V⁻⁷   VI⁻   IV   I

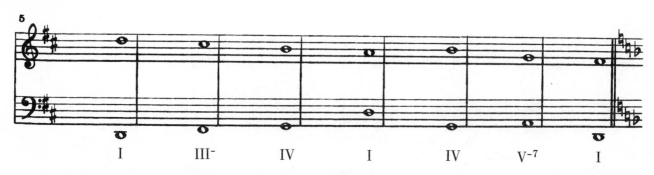

5.
     I   III⁻   IV   I   IV   V⁻⁷   I

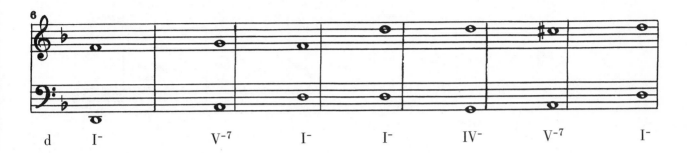

d   I⁻   V⁻⁷   I⁻   I⁻   IV⁻   V⁻⁷   I⁻

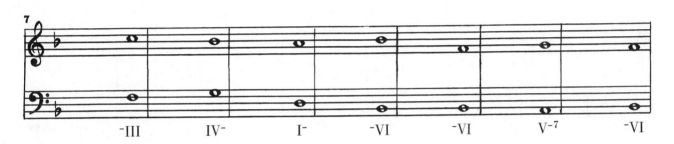

⁻III   IV⁻   I⁻   ⁻VI   ⁻VI   V⁻⁷   ⁻VI

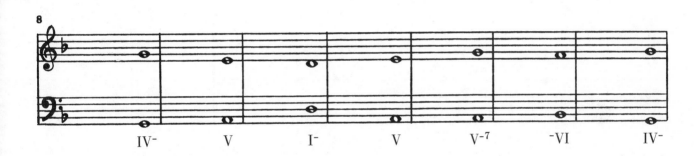

IV⁻   V   I⁻   V   V⁻⁷   ⁻VI   IV⁻

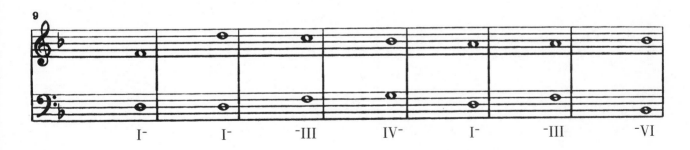

I⁻   I⁻   ⁻III   IV⁻   I⁻   ⁻III   ⁻VI

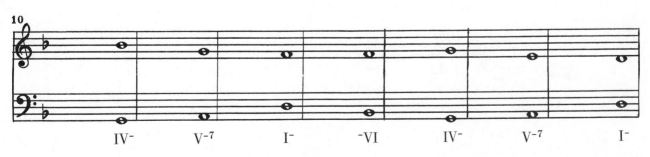

IV⁻   V⁻⁷   I⁻   ⁻VI   IV⁻   V⁻⁷   I⁻

C9-3
(Copy 3)

Soprano and bass dictation with composite chord symbols

Shield the answer. Listen to the chord and write the soprano and bass notes and the composite chord symbol; then uncover the answer and compare your response. Circle incorrect responses. Goal: No more than eight errors. The first frame requires no response.

D   I   V⁻⁷   I   IV   V   I   I

VI⁻   IV   V   VI⁻   II⁻   V⁻⁷   I

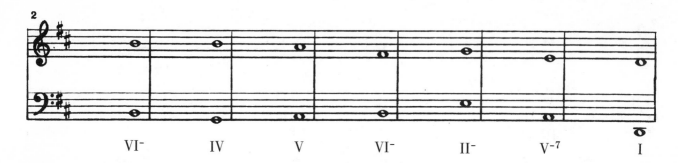

III⁻   IV   I   I   IV   II⁻   V

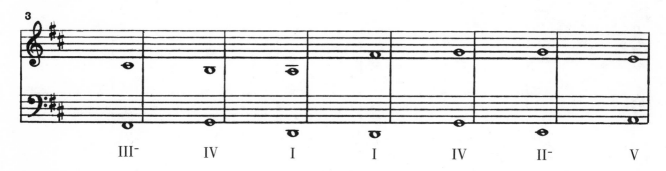

I   VI⁻   II⁻   V⁻⁷   VI⁻   IV   I

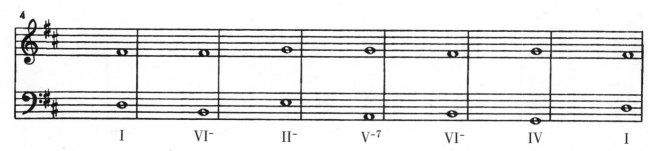

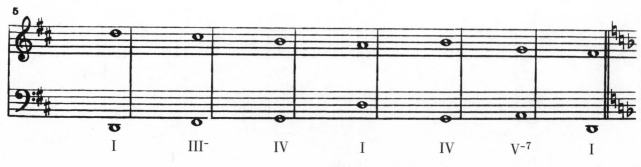

I   III⁻   IV   I   IV   V⁻⁷   I

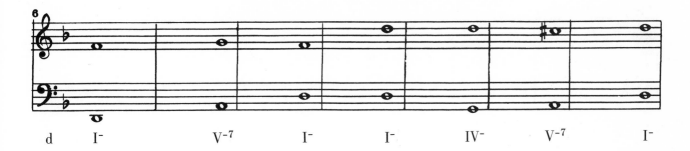

d I⁻   V⁻⁷   I⁻   I⁻   IV⁻   V⁻⁷   I⁻

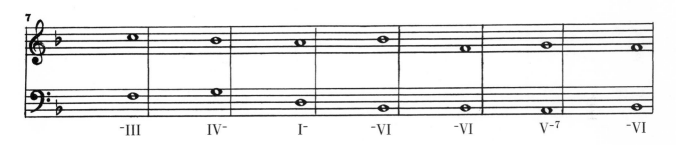

-III   IV⁻   I⁻   -VI   -VI   V⁻⁷   -VI

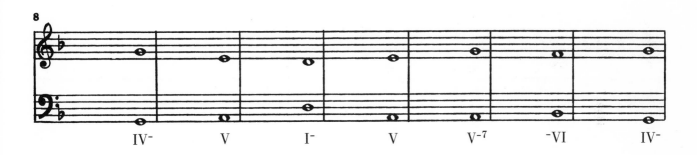

IV⁻   V   I⁻   V   V⁻⁷   -VI   IV⁻

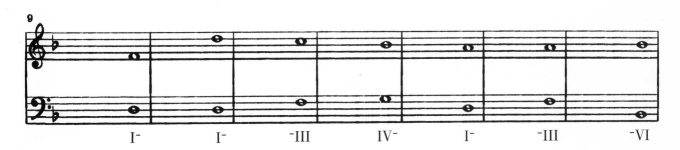

I⁻   I⁻   -III   IV⁻   I⁻   -III   -VI

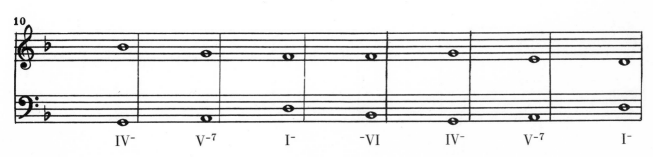

IV⁻   V⁻⁷   I⁻   -VI   IV⁻   V⁻⁷   I⁻

C9-3
(Copy 4)

Soprano and bass dictation with composite chord symbols

Shield the answer. Listen to the chord and write the soprano and bass notes and the composite chord symbol; then uncover the answer and compare your response. Circle incorrect responses. Goal: No more than eight errors. The first frame requires no response.

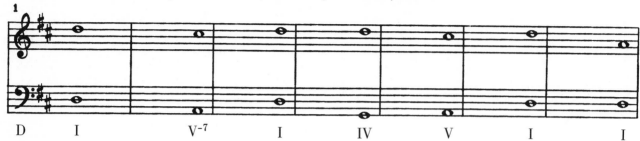

D I   V⁻⁷   I   IV   V   I   I

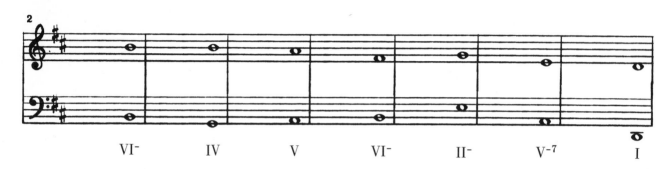

VI⁻   IV   V   VI⁻   II⁻   V⁻⁷   I

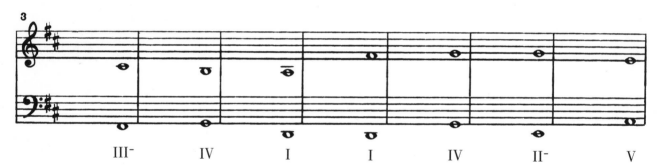

III⁻   IV   I   I   IV   II⁻   V

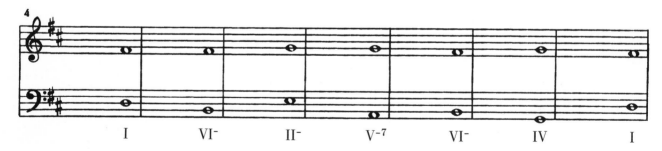

I   VI⁻   II⁻   V⁻⁷   VI⁻   IV   I

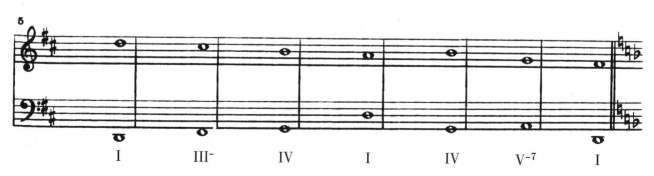

I   III⁻   IV   I   IV   V⁻⁷   I

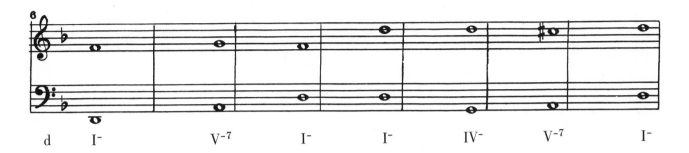

d   I⁻   V⁻⁷   I⁻   I⁻   IV⁻   V⁻⁷   I⁻

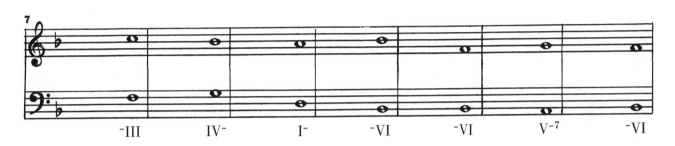

⁻III   IV⁻   I⁻   ⁻VI   ⁻VI   V⁻⁷   ⁻VI

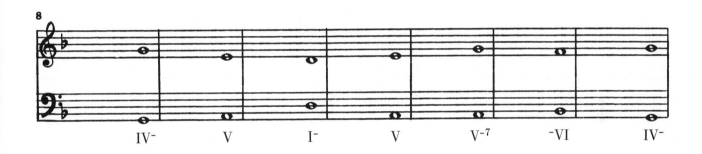

IV⁻   V   I⁻   V   V⁻⁷   ⁻VI   IV⁻

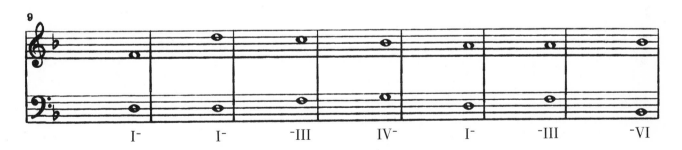

I⁻   I⁻   ⁻III   IV⁻   I⁻   ⁻III   ⁻VI

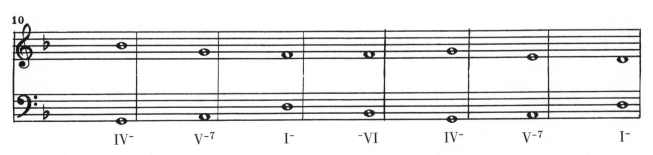

IV⁻   V⁻⁷   I⁻   ⁻VI   IV⁻   V⁻⁷   I⁻

C9-3
(Copy 5)

Soprano and bass dictation with composite chord symbols

Shield the answer. Listen to the chord and write the soprano and bass notes and the composite chord symbol; then uncover the answer and compare your response. Circle incorrect responses. Goal: No more than eight errors. The first frame requires no response.

1

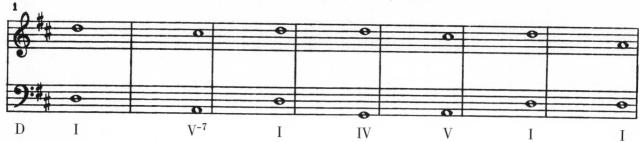

D   I   V⁻⁷   I   IV   V   I   I

2

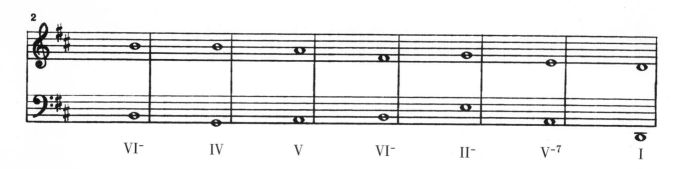

VI⁻   IV   V   VI⁻   II⁻   V⁻⁷   I

3

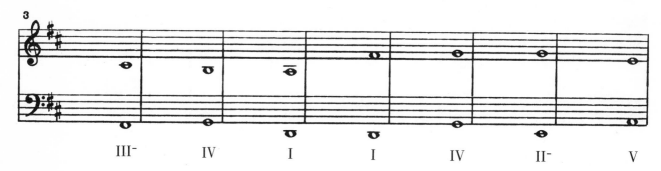

III⁻   IV   I   I   IV   II⁻   V

4

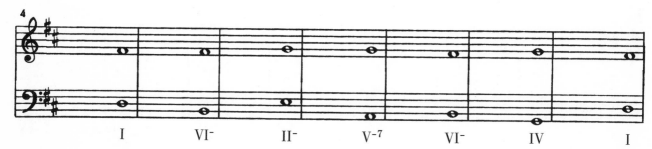

I   VI⁻   II⁻   V⁻⁷   VI⁻   IV   I

5

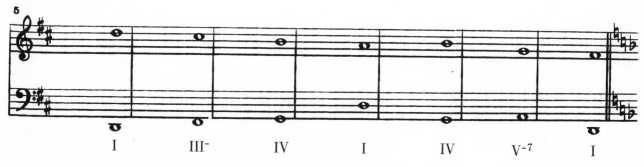

I   III⁻   IV   I   IV   V⁻⁷   I

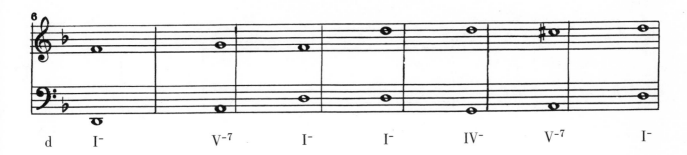

d   I⁻   V⁻⁷   I⁻   I⁻   IV⁻   V⁻⁷   I⁻

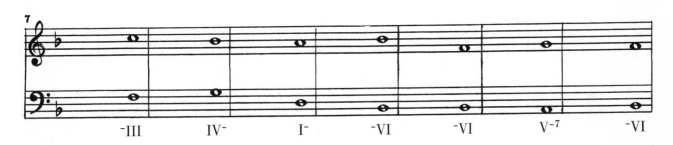

⁻III   IV⁻   I⁻   ⁻VI   ⁻VI   V⁻⁷   ⁻VI

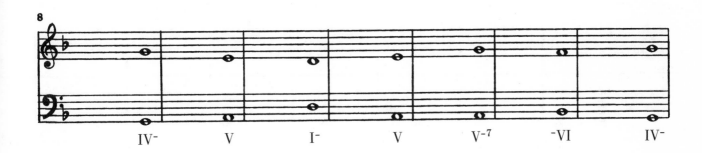

IV⁻   V   I⁻   V   V⁻⁷   ⁻VI   IV⁻

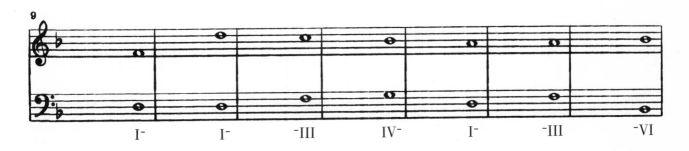

I⁻   I⁻   ⁻III   IV⁻   I⁻   ⁻III   ⁻VI

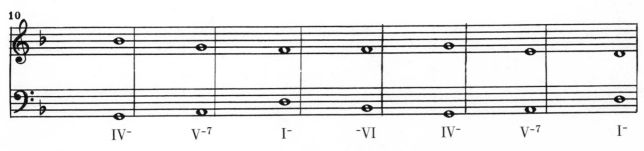

IV⁻   V⁻⁷   I⁻   ⁻VI   IV⁻   V⁻⁷   I⁻

C9-4
(Copy 1)

Soprano and bass dictation with composite chord symbols

Shield the answer. Listen to the chord and write the soprano and bass notes and the composite chord symbol; then uncover the answer and compare your response. Circle incorrect responses. Goal: No more than eight errors. The first frame requires no response.

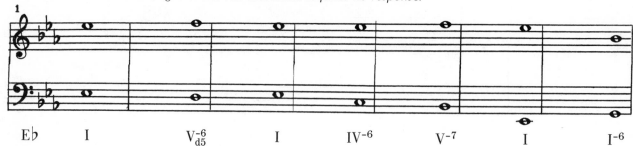

Eb   I   V$_{d5}^{-6}$ I   IV^{-6} V^{-7} I   I^{-6}

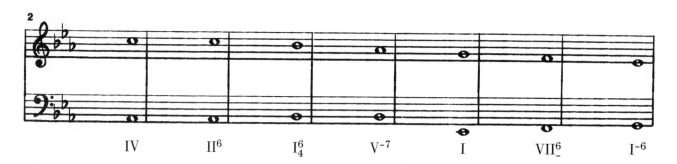

IV   II^6 I$_4^6$ V^{-7} I   VII$_-^6$ I^{-6}

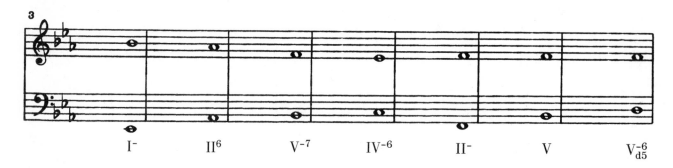

I$^-$ II^6 V^{-7} IV^{-6} II$^-$ V   V$_{d5}^{-6}$

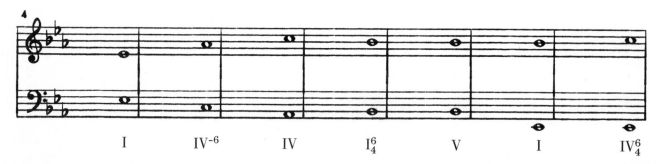

I   IV^{-6} IV   I$_4^6$ V   I   IV$_4^6$

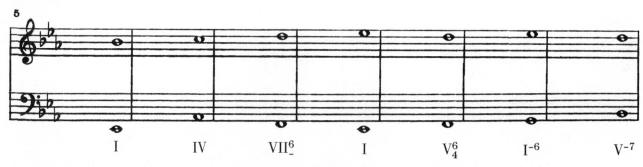

I   IV   VII$_-^6$ I   V$_4^6$ I^{-6} V^{-7}

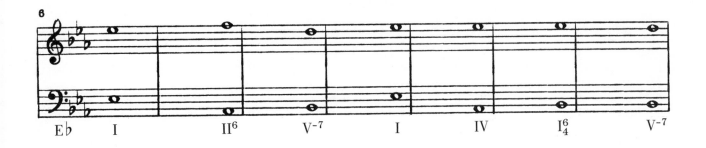

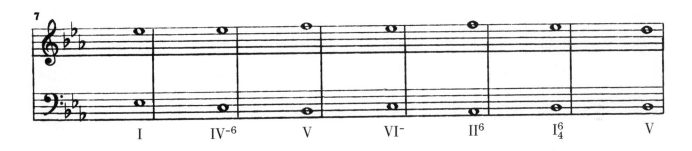

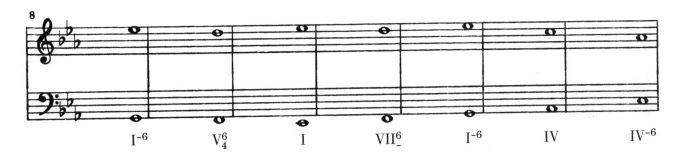

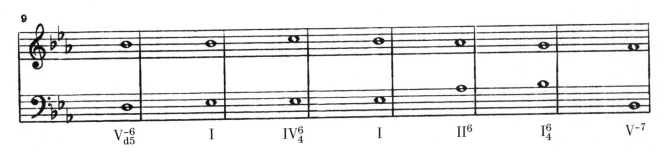

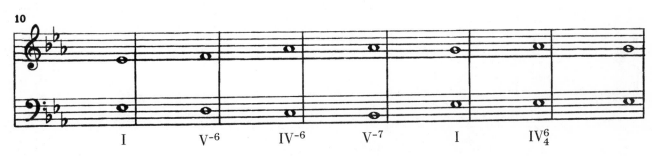

C9-4
(Copy 2)

Soprano and bass dictation with composite chord symbols

Shield the answer. Listen to the chord and write the soprano and bass notes and the composite chord symbol; then uncover the answer and compare your response. Circle incorrect responses. Goal: No more than eight errors. The first frame requires no response.

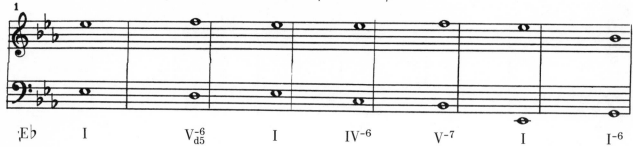

1

Eb   I   V$_{d5}^{-6}$ I   IV^{-6} V^{-7} I   I^{-6}

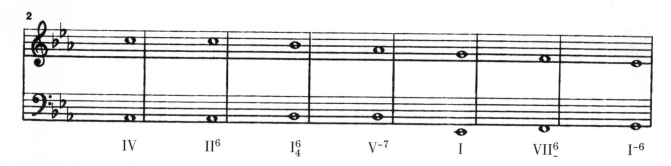

2

IV   II^6 I$_4^6$ V^{-7} I   VII$_-^6$ I^{-6}

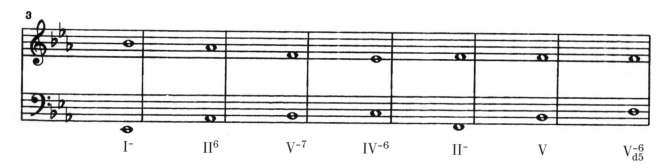

3

I$^-$ II^6 V^{-7} IV^{-6} II$^-$ V   V$_{d5}^{-6}$

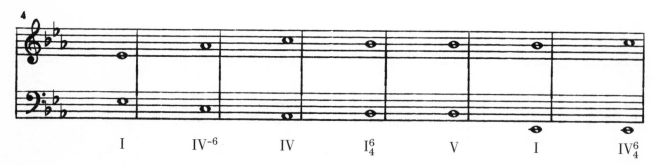

4

I   IV^{-6} IV   I$_4^6$ V   I   IV$_4^6$

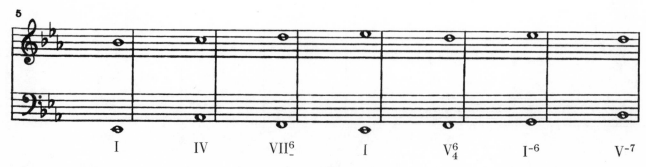

5

I   IV   VII$_-^6$ I   V$_4^6$ I^{-6} V^{-7}

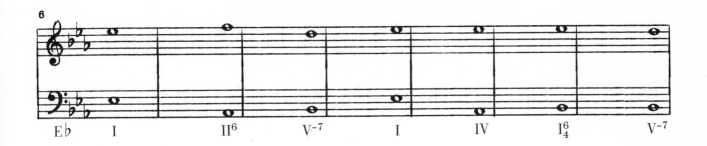

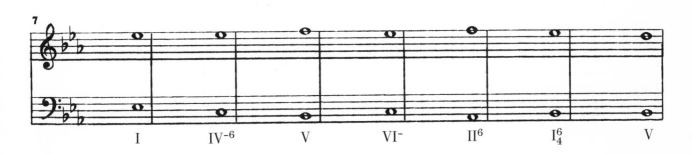

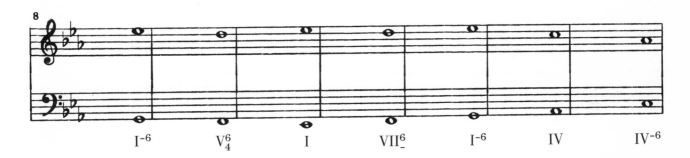

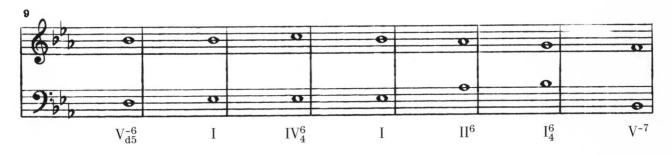

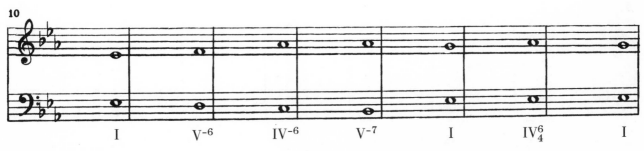

C9-4
(Copy 3)

Soprano and bass dictation with composite chord symbols

Shield the answer. Listen to the chord and write the soprano and bass notes and the composite chord symbol; then uncover the answer and compare your response. Circle incorrect responses. Goal: No more than eight errors. The first frame requires no response.

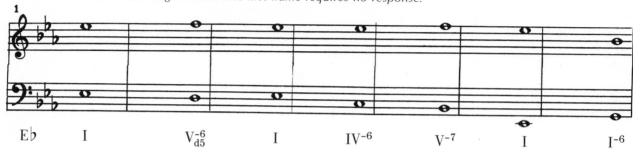

$$E\flat \qquad I \qquad V^{-6}_{d5} \qquad I \qquad IV^{-6} \qquad V^{-7} \qquad I \qquad I^{-6}$$

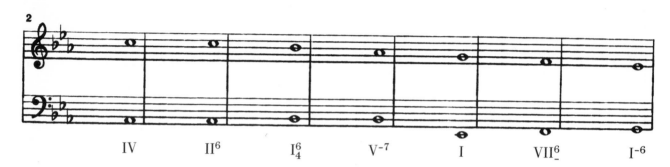

$$IV \qquad II^6 \qquad I^6_4 \qquad V^{-7} \qquad I \qquad VII^6_{\_} \qquad I^{-6}$$

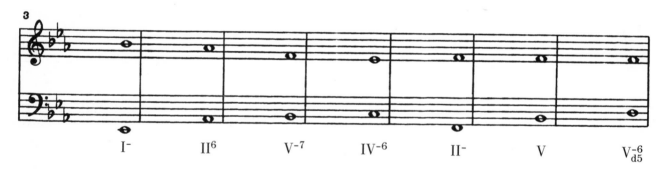

$$I^- \qquad II^6 \qquad V^{-7} \qquad IV^{-6} \qquad II^- \qquad V \qquad V^{-6}_{d5}$$

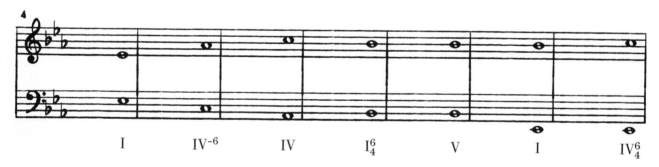

$$I \qquad IV^{-6} \qquad IV \qquad I^6_4 \qquad V \qquad I \qquad IV^6_4$$

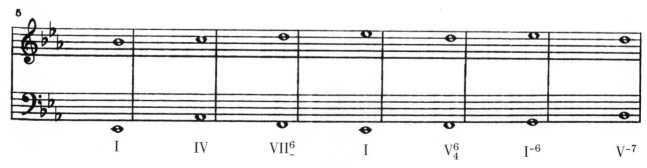

$$I \qquad IV \qquad VII^6_{\_} \qquad I \qquad V^6_4 \qquad I^{-6} \qquad V^{-7}$$

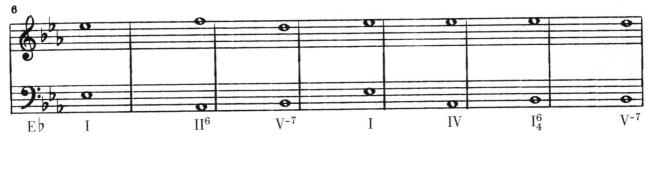

6

Eb I   II⁶   V⁻⁷   I   IV   I⁶₄   V⁻⁷

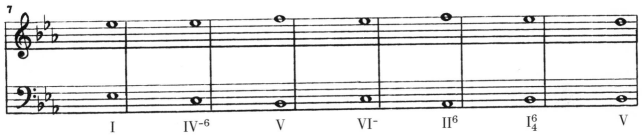

7

I   IV⁻⁶   V   VI⁻   II⁶   I⁶₄   V

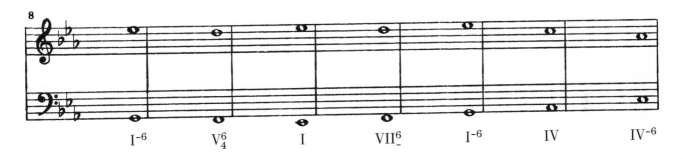

8

I⁻⁶   V⁶₄   I   VII⁶₋   I⁻⁶   IV   IV⁻⁶

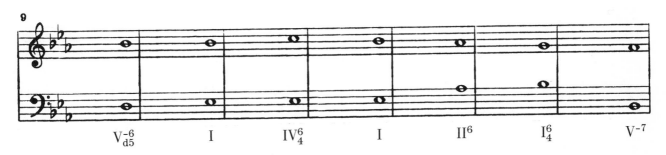

9

V⁻⁶_{d5}   I   IV⁶₄   I   II⁶   I⁶₄   V⁻⁷

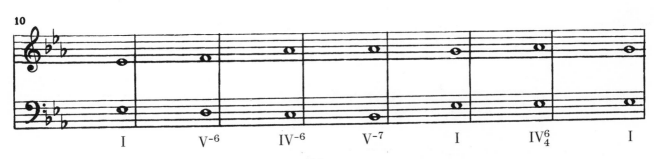

10

I   V⁻⁶   IV⁻⁶   V⁻⁷   I   IV⁶₄   I

C9-4
(Copy 4)

Soprano and bass dictation with composite chord symbols

Shield the answer. Listen to the chord and write the soprano and bass notes and the composite chord symbol; then uncover the answer and compare your response. Circle incorrect responses. Goal: No more than eight errors. The first frame requires no response.

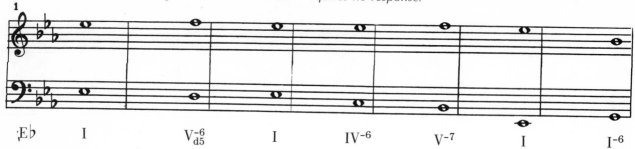

$E\flat$ I V^{-6}_{d5} I IV^{-6} V^{-7} I I^{-6}

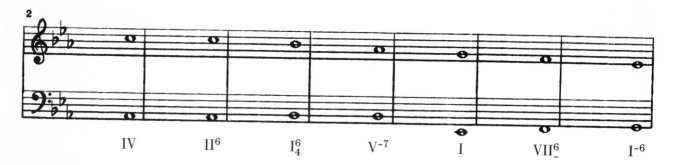

IV II^{6} I^{6}_{4} V^{-7} I VII^{6}_{-} I^{-6}

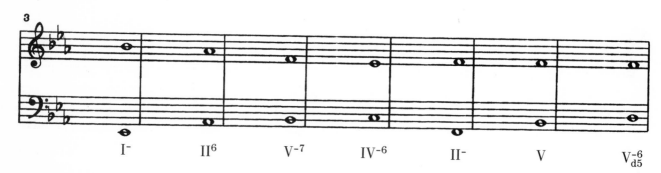

I^{-} II^{6} V^{-7} IV^{-6} II^{-} V V^{-6}_{d5}

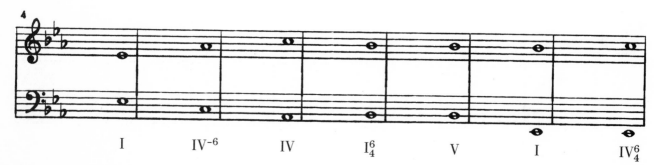

I IV^{-6} IV I^{6}_{4} V   I IV^{6}_{4}

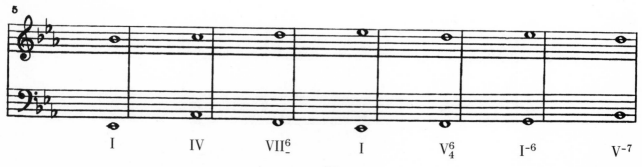

I   IV VII^{6}_{-} I V^{6}_{4} I^{-6} V^{-7}

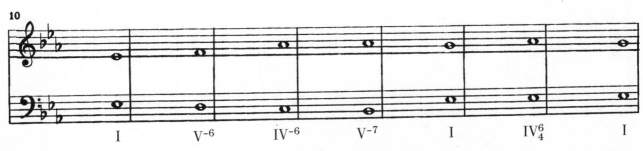

C9-4
(Copy 5)

Soprano and bass dictation with composite chord symbols

Shield the answer. Listen to the chord and write the soprano and bass notes and the composite chord symbol; then uncover the answer and compare your response. Circle incorrect responses. Goal: No more than eight errors. The first frame requires no response.

1

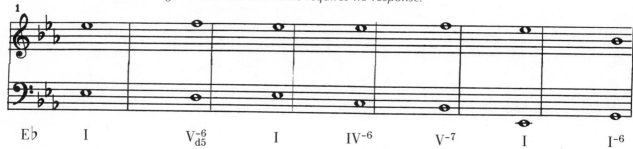

$E\flat$ I V_{d5}^{-6} I IV^{-6} V^{-7} I I^{-6}

2

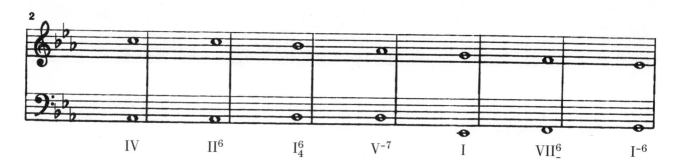

IV II^{6} I_{4}^{6} V^{-7} I VII_{-}^{6} I^{-6}

3

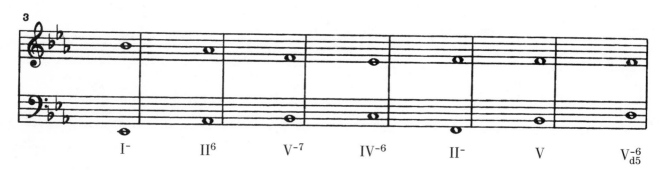

I^{-} II^{6} V^{-7} IV^{-6} II^{-} V V_{d5}^{-6}

4

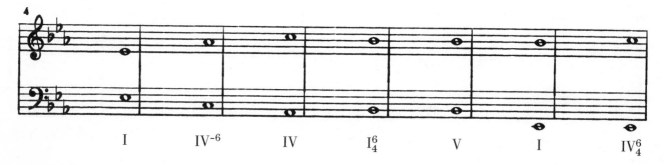

I IV^{-6} IV I_{4}^{6} V   I IV_{4}^{6}

5

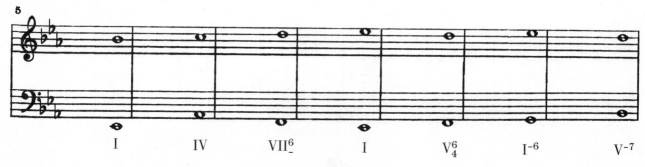

I   IV VII_{-}^{6} I V_{4}^{6} I^{-6} V^{-7}

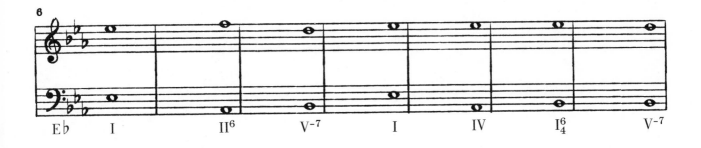

Eb I   II⁶   V⁻⁷   I   IV   I⁶₄   V⁻⁷

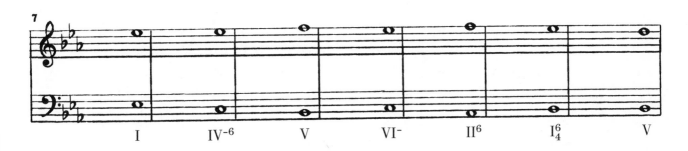

I   IV⁻⁶   V   VI⁻   II⁶   I⁶₄   V

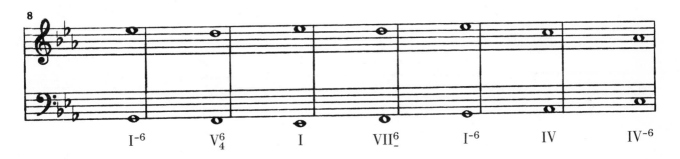

I⁻⁶   V⁶₄   I   VII⁶₋   I⁻⁶   IV   IV⁻⁶

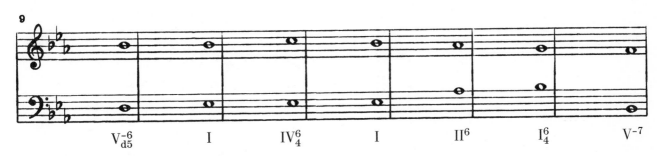

V⁻⁶ d5   I   IV⁶₄   I   II⁶   I⁶₄   V⁻⁷

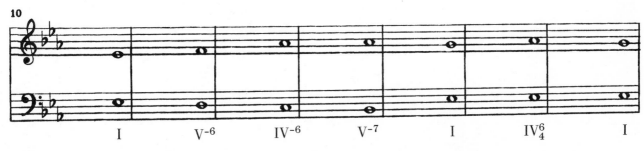

I   V⁻⁶   IV⁻⁶   V⁻⁷   I   IV⁶₄   I

Lessons **C9-5** and **C9-6**

In these lessons in soprano and bass dictation with composite chord symbols, the chords are grouped into phrases. Each phrase occurs only once on the tape recording, but you may rewind the tape for additional hearings. On the test for this series you will hear each phrase six times so you should attempt to complete each phrase in no more than six hearings. For each lesson, you will find a page of initial material followed by answer pages. You will need your own manuscript paper.

To do each frame, start by copying the initial material on your manuscript paper. Then listen to the phrase as many times as you need to in order to write the soprano line, the bass line, and the composite chord symbols. You may find it useful to concentrate in successive hearings on the soprano alone, the bass alone, and the composite chord symbols alone. When you have completed your response, compare it to the phrase found on the answer page. Circle each incorrect chord. Count one error for each chord in which part or all of your response is incorrect. Your goal is to complete five consecutive phrases with no more than five errors in a maximum of six hearings of each phrase. If you have done all the phrases in the lesson without reaching the goal, repeat the lesson. If you have done the lesson three times without achieving the goal, go on to the next lesson regardless of the number of errors. If you reach the goal before doing all the phrases in the lesson the first time through, do the remaining phrases so that you have an opportunity to work in all the keys in the lesson. In repeating the lesson, you may stop as soon as you have reached your goal.

C9-5

Soprano and bass dictation with composite chord symbols

Initial
Material

For each phrase copy the initial material on manuscript paper. Listen to the phrase several times. Write the soprano and bass notes and composite chord symbols; then compare your answers with the answer page. Circle each chord that contains an error. Goal: No more than five errors in five consecutive phrases.

C9-5

C9-6

Soprano and bass dictation with composite chord symbols

Initial
Material

For each phrase copy the initial material on manuscript paper. Listen to the phrase several times. Write the soprano and bass notes and composite chord symbols; then compare your answers with the answer page. Circle each chord that contains an error. Goal: No more than five errors in five consecutive phrases. After you have done this lesson, take Test C8.

C9-6

Answer
Page

1 b · I⁻ · I⁻ · V · V⁻⁶ · I⁻ · IV⁻ · V

2 b · I⁻ · IV⁶ · V · V · I⁻ · IV⁻ · I⁻

3 b · I⁻ · VII⁶ · I⁶ · II⁶ · I⁻⁶₄ · V · I⁻

4 E · I · V⁻⁶ · IV⁻⁶ · I · I⁶₄ · V⁻⁷ · VI⁻

5 E · V⁻⁷ · V⁻⁶_d5 · I · VII⁶ · I⁻⁶ · V · I

6 c♯ · I⁻ · V · IV⁶ · IV⁻ · I⁻ · IV⁶ · V

7 c♯ · I⁻ · ⁻VI · II⁶ · V · IV⁶ · V⁻⁷ · I⁻

8 c♯ · I⁻ · V⁶₄ · I⁶ · II⁶ · V · V⁻⁶_d5 · I⁻

274

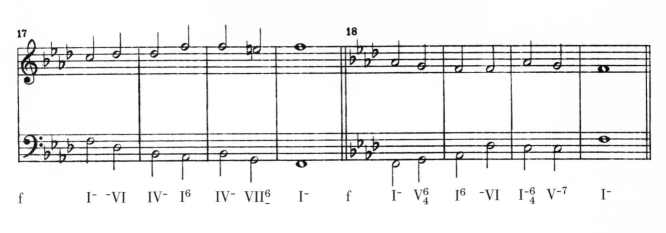

f   I⁻ ⁻VI   IV⁻ I⁶   IV⁻ VII⁶_   I⁻   f   I⁻ V⁶₄   I⁶ ⁻VI   I⁻⁶₄ V⁻⁷   I⁻

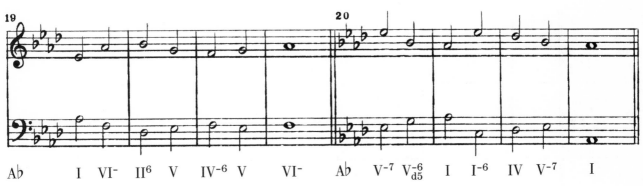

A♭   I VI⁻   II⁶ V   IV⁻⁶ V   VI⁻   A♭   V⁻⁷ V⁻⁶d5   I I⁻⁶   IV V⁻⁷   I

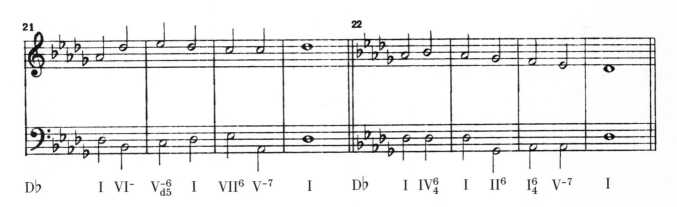

D♭   I VI⁻   V⁻⁶d5 I   VII⁶ V⁻⁷   I   D♭   I IV⁶₄   I II⁶   I⁶₄ V⁻⁷   I

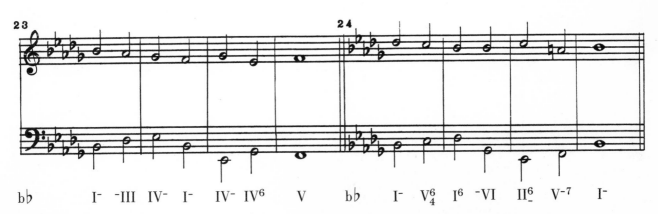

b♭   I⁻ ⁻III   IV⁻ I⁻   IV⁻ IV⁶   V   b♭   I⁻ V⁶₄   I⁶ ⁻VI   II⁶_ V⁻⁷   I⁻

Test Record Sheet

TEST	MAXIMUM	LEVEL			SCORE AND DATE
		1	2	3	
C1	300	249	208	167	
C2	250	207	173	139	
C3	250	207	173	139	
C4	300	249	208	167	
C5	350	290	243	195	
C6	350	290	243	195	
C7a	300	250	208	166	
C7b	300	250	208	166	
C7c	300	250	212	175	
C7d	300	250	212	175	
C8	300	260	220	180	
C9	700	505	427	350	

All test scores are weighted to compensate for the varying length, difficulty, and importance of the series. The maximum score is the highest attainable score on a test. Level 1 represents high achievement. Level 2 represents moderate or average achievement. Level 3 represents low but significant achievement.

B C D E F G H I J
0 1 2 3 4 5 6 7 8 9

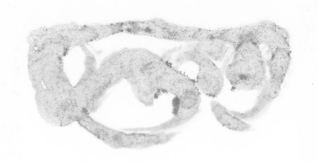

DATE DUE

DEMCO 38-297